Rethinking Welfare: A Critical Perspective

Iain Ferguson
Michael Lavalette
Gerry Mooney

SAGE Publications
London • Thousand Oaks • New Delhi

First published 2002

 SAGE Publications Ltd
6 Bonhill Street
London EC2A 4PU

SAGE Publications Inc.
2455 Teller Road
Thousand Oaks, California 91320

SAGE Publications India Pvt Ltd
32, M-Block Market
Greater Kailash - I
New Delhi 110 048

British Library Cataloguing in Publication data

A catalogue record for this book is available from the British Library

ISBN 0 7619 6417 7
ISBN 0 7619 6418 5 (pbk)

Library of Congress Control Number: 2001135895

Typeset by SIVA Math Setters, Chennai, India
Printed in Great Britain by Athenaeum Press, Gateshead

Rethinking Welfare

Contents

Acknowledgements

We would like to thank a number of people who have helped us during the writing of this book. At Sage both Karen Phillips and Louise Wise have been very supportive of the project from its earliest days. Gill Hubbard, Neil Davidson, Chris Jones, Alan Pratt and a number of anonymous referees read the manuscript and offered useful suggestions as to how the manuscript could be improved; their constructive criticisms were very welcome – although we did not always act upon their advice in ways that they would recognise. Thanks also to Methuen and to Suhrkamp Verlag Frankfurt am Main for permission to use a poem by Brecht. Finally, Dorte, Laura and Ann read various parts of the manuscript and their advice and patience sustained us during the book writing process.

A Bed For The Night

I hear that in New York
At the corner of 26th Street and Broadway
A man stands every evening during the winter months
And gets beds for the homeless there
By appealing to passers-by

It won't change the world
It won't improve relations among men
It will not shorten the age of exploitation
But a few men have a bed for the night
For a night the wind is kept from them
The snow meant for them falls on the roadway

Don't put down the book on reading this, man

A few people have a bed for the night
For a night the wind is kept from them
The snow meant for them falls on the roadway
But it won't change the world
It won't improve relations among men
It will not shorten the age of exploitation

Bertolt Brecht
Poems 1913–1956 (London, Minerva)

Introduction

At the start of the twenty-first century, state welfare remains in crisis. In Britain this crisis is palpable. The state's long-term commitment to pensions for the elderly is under threat, existing pensions are miserly and the government refuses to restore the link with earnings. The National Health Service faces a continuing crisis of underfunding, while New Labour has made it clear that it intends to introduce substantial privatisation into the NHS by allowing commercial companies, supported and underwritten by government, to provide health care for the NHS for profit. Educational provision is becoming more fragmented, less comprehensive and more selective; again the private sector is being encouraged to take a greater role in the provision of educational services. In the Higher Education sector New Labour has brought in student fees, which, alongside maintenance loans, leave the vast majority of students with massive debts on graduation and exclude children from working-class families from universities in the first instance. Benefits are becoming increasingly stigmatised and miserly and are often tied in to a form of 'workfare' where recipients have to work for their benefits. Council housing is in traumatic decline, there is a massive problem of homelessness and in the private sector mortgage arrears and house repossessions are at historically high levels. Finally, social work is becoming more punitive, and social workers more stretched and stressed as they try to deal with their clients' needs in an atmosphere of stringent austerity. In every major area of service delivery private, for-profit companies are playing a greater role in the provision of welfare. For each of these companies the interests of shareholders are paramount. The shift in the mix of welfare providers has had a deleterious effect on the services provided for the working class, for the poor and for those in need.

Britain is not unique. In the US a similar neo-liberal agenda is behind cuts in various state welfare programmes, leaving increasing numbers of the poor working-class population to fend for themselves in the most heartless manner. Neo-liberal agendas operate throughout much of the 'Third World' where the International Monetary Fund, the World Bank and various governments and banks within the advanced economies have enforced structural adjustment programmes (now termed 'poverty reduction programmes') on indebted countries. This forced implementation of neo-liberalism has had a devastating impact on the provision of food, health, education and other welfare services within these countries.

Furthermore, within the US (and increasingly within Britain) the other side of free market policies are visible in the form of a strident authoritarianism. 'Workfare', curfews, stigma and imprisonment are all evidence of the fact that state social policy is becoming increasingly disciplinary, brutal and controlling. The conclusion is that in those countries following the *Anglo–American* or neo-liberal model of social and economic policy, the poor are both criminalized and abandoned by the state.

At the same time neo-liberalism increases inequalities and allows the rich to get richer. In the US, Britain and vast swathes of the world (including the Third World), the 1980s and 1990s witnessed the obscene spectacle of the already fabulously wealthy enriching themselves still further at the expense of the already desperately poor.

In these circumstances one of the concerns of this book is to produce a defence of state welfare and argue against neo-liberal market madness. *Against market madness* because it continually places the pursuit of profit above that of human need – indeed it is incompatible with the pursuit of human need. This is a madness most visible, for example, in the legal case brought by 39 of the world's richest pharmaceutical companies (including the British multi-national GlaxoSmithKline whose first quarter profits for the year 2001 were over £1.5 billion) who tried to stop the South African government buying cheap drugs to treat HIV and AIDS patients. The companies claimed this practice was a breach of patent law and that the South African government should only buy the brand-named drugs covered by patent license. It they had been successful – which thanks to an international campaign they were not – thousands of people would have been condemned to a painful death. For these companies protecting profit was far more important than treating poor people with AIDS (*The Guardian*, 19 April 2001; *The Observer*, 22 April 2001).

We are *for state welfare* because properly funded, universal state services free at the point of use, combined with a commitment to full employment, can provide the minimum needed for people – young and old – to exist and actively take part in social and political life. Of course state welfare is often exploitative and oppressive and we neither ignore nor underestimate this. But the fundamental point is that we live in a world of immense wealth with vast productive capacity, and these mean that we could easily provide welfare services to all across the globe and hence allow the world's population to lead their lives with a degree of dignity.

But while we are *for state welfare* this is not enough. State welfare is not a distinct or separate area of social life but exists, and is intimately tied to, the central drives and social relations of capitalism. State welfare may help alleviate, to some small degree, the worst manifestations of poverty, for example, but poverty itself is created by capitalism.

The contradictions associated with welfare are highlighted in Bertolt Brecht's poem *A Bed For The Night*, reproduced at the start of the book. In the poem Brecht reports the tale of a philanthropist who spends hours each night searching for accommodation for the homeless. This is a never-ending labour of Sisyphus: each night the homeless come back, each night the need for accommodation becomes extreme, each night there is an immense effort in finding 'a bed for the night'. The root cause of such suffering is capitalism, and the immense effort of the philanthropist does nothing to end the exploitation inherent in the system. Yet it does protect people – at least for one night – from the harshness of being homeless. Brecht's poem is a wonderful *leitmotif*, it encapsulates perfectly our attitude to state welfare: state welfare is absolutely vital if we are to ease the worst examples of suffering in capitalist society but it does not alter the fundamental exploitative relations of society which cause so much harm in the first place.

To put the argument another way, revolutionary socialists – those who wish to replace capitalism and its ruthless pursuit of profit at all costs, with a democratically controlled and planned social system geared to meeting human need – are also amongst the most committed supporters of immediate reforms and improvements to people's lives within capitalism. As Rosa Luxemburg put it at the beginning of the twentieth century:

> [Are revolutionary socialists] against reforms? Can we counterpose the social revolution, the transformation of the existing order, our final goal, to social reforms? Certainly not. The daily struggle for reforms, for the amelioration of the condition of the workers within the framework of the existing social order, and for democratic institutions, offers ... the only means of engaging in the proletarian class war and working in the direction of the final goal – the conquest of political power and the suppression of wage labor. Between social reforms and revolution there exists ... an indissoluble tie. The struggle for reforms is its means; the social revolution, its aim. (1900/1970: 8)

In this book we argue that classical Marxism – a tradition which is often ignored or misrepresented within academic social policy and social work – can provide an analysis of social welfare that is nuanced and attuned to the contradictions of welfare in capitalist society – that is committed both to the expansion of state welfare in the present and the abolition of capitalism and its exploitative social relations in the future. It is an approach that contains concepts which aid analysis of welfare regimes and their priorities, of welfare clients and of welfare workers – but at the same time is committed to the fullest emancipatory project: that contains a realisable vision of a more equal, more free and more democratic future.

Ten years ago such a project would have seemed fanciful. Marxism, in both theory and practice we were told, had been consigned to the 'dustbin of history'. In Britain 'Thatcherism' was rampant and opposition apparently stifled. Within the academy the 'detached irony' – and often incomprehensible language – of postmodernism was in vogue. Within welfare theorising there was a growing (if perhaps reluctant) acceptance of the role of markets (internal or otherwise) in service provision.

Yet the start of the twenty-first century has created an opening to re-assert the value of Marx, of commitment and of opposition. During the period when we have been writing this book there have been a number of exciting developments in the world of socialist and oppositional politics. The central turning point occurred in Seattle in November 1999 when the anti-capitalist movement was born. The protest in Seattle was important because it drew together various different single-issue campaigns – for labour rights, for environmental protection, against Third World debt, and so on – and forged them into a single movement against neo-liberalism, against capitalism. The movement has continued to grow and prosper through large demonstrations in Washington, Melbourne, Millau, Prague, Nice, Quebec, Gothenburg and Genoa. Wherever the representatives of governments or international agencies committed to furthering the neo-liberal agenda come together they are met by noisy protest – leading John Pilger (*The Guardian*, 14 July 2001) to claim that the anti-capitalist movement represents the largest international protest wave since the late 1960s.

There are, of course, many varied ideas and perspectives within the anti-capitalist movement – Marxism is only one strand. Yet Marxism can only benefit from a sustained engagement with anti-capitalists. It certainly has something powerful to say about the drives and priorities of capitalism, its consequences on our lives and, importantly, our prospects for a better future. Welfare themes have been part of the concerns of anti-capitalists – concern at child labour, poverty, marketisation, privatisation – and we believe that the classical Marxist tradition has something useful to say to those who are against capitalism but perhaps unsure what the alternative may be.

A second important development is the trend towards the realignment of the left. In Britain the Scottish Socialist Party and the Socialist Alliance (in both England and Wales) have grown as a significant and sustained opposition to Labour from the left. Each of these organisations combine a mixture of traditional left commitments to state welfare and nationalisation, with environmental politics, clear anti-racist and anti-sexist strategies, progressive taxation policies, a commitment to unilateral disarmament and cancellation of Third World debt. They have drawn activists together from various far left organisations, disillusioned Labour party members and various left independents around a 'united front' of basic socialist demands. This trend towards realignment is not unique to Britain. A Socialist Alliance network has been established in Australia, for example, and in the US these tendencies crystallised around the presidential election campaign of veteran environmental campaigner Ralph Nader.

In this context we feel the time is prescient to re-evaluate the relevance of Marxism to the theory and practice of social welfare. The book is divided into three broad sections. In Part One, Chapter 1 we look at the relevance of Marx. Within academia there have been tentative steps towards a re-engagement with aspects of Marx's work. We look at the background to this, in particular by focusing on the growth of inequality, the crisis of the market and the return of working-class opposition to the neo-liberal agenda. However, if there is to be a return to Marx, we suggest, it needs to be one that engages with the classical Marxist tradition – as opposed to the various academic Marxisms that dominated in the late

1960s and 1970s. Having outlined the classical tradition, Chapter 2 proceeds to outline the key concerns of a Marxist approach to the study of social welfare and the welfare state.

In Part Two we move on to outline a range of concepts central to a Marxist approach and argue that they can usefully be developed to offer an insightful account of human welfare, welfare regimes and welfare problems. Chapter 3 looks at the question of class and argues, *contra* dominant sociological and social policy accounts, that the working class today, though different to that of the past, contains the vast majority of the population of the 'advanced' economies. We discuss and reject notions of post-industrialism, post-Fordism and the notion of the expanding white-collar middle class or service-based middle class. Following the earlier work of American Marxist Eric Olin Wright we develop a strongly relational model of class and class location.

Chapter 4 looks at the concept of class struggle. If class analysis has become unpopular in recent years, the notion of class struggle has almost disappeared from academic discourse – except as a notion to be ridiculed. In an earlier work we provided a series of case-studies which emphasised the salience of class struggle to welfare provision (Lavalette and Mooney, 2000a). Here we offer an account which locates class struggle within the very dynamic of capitalism's exploitative social relations, and which involves conflict and confrontation over both paid work and welfare. Yet there is nothing inevitable about such conflicts, and certainly not about their outcome.

Chapter 5 looks at the concept of alienation – perhaps one of the richest concepts in Marx that is directly applicable to the study of welfare. Yet previous Marxist accounts of welfare have avoided the concept – in no small part because the dominant academic Marxism was one influenced by French philosopher and Communist Party member Lois Althusser. Althusser, the philosophical apologist for Stalinism, dismissed Marx's concept of alienation claiming it was 'unscientiffic'. We argue it is a vital and central element within Marxism which emphasises Marx's humanism.

Chapter 6 looks at oppression. In recent years, Marxism has often been accused of ignoring oppression. Rather than being seen as the product of class society, the roots of racism, sexism and disablism are usually located by current theorists of oppression (insofar as they continue to use the term and do not speak simply about 'identity' and 'difference') within particular groups of people – men, whites, straights – who are often seen as having a material interest in perpetuating that oppression. This is a claim that we reject. In this chapter we argue that the fight against oppression is central to Marxism, but needs to be firmly embedded within dominant social relations of production, part of the totality of class society.

Chapter 7 looks at capitalism and the family. Family policy is a central part of state social policy, but such policies contain assumptions about what families look like and what they do. The family is often portrayed as a haven, yet all the evidence points to the fact that it is the site of violence, oppression, abuse and even murder. But given this, why does the family remain so popular? Here we trace the growth and development of the family under capitalism to explain its contradictory nature within class divided societies.

In Part Three we move on to look at the neo-liberal assault on welfare. Chapter 8 looks at effects of neo-liberalism on welfare across the globe, including the impact of structural adjustment programmes on indebted nations. The goals of the neo-liberal agenda are brutal. Yet we argue that there is nothing inevitable about neo-liberal globalisation. Indeed we suggest that the dominant theories of globalisation within academia exaggerate the extent to which states are restricted from protecting and enhancing welfarism: they are overly pessimistic about people's ability to resist the global multinationals.

Chapter 9 traces the evolution of the welfare state in Britain from Beveridge to Blair. It analyses the reasons behind the post-war expansion of welfare and locates it within the post-war boom, fuelled by what we term 'the permanent arms economy'. With the end of the boom there has been increasing restrictions on welfare – first during the Labour government of 1974–79, then during the 18 years of Conservative rule and most recently in the Third Way – neo-liberalism by another name – of Tony Blair's New Labour governments.

Finally, by way of a conclusion, Chapter 10 explores some possible welfare futures. It does this by assessing the possibilities of radical social transformation and by reflecting on what welfare settlements may be like in a society moving beyond the priorities of capitalism. It is important to dream dreams and have visions of what a different kind of society might look like. At the same time, without some notion of how we can get from where we are now to where we would like to be, such visions can seem like empty and futile manifestos that bear no relation to real life. For that reason, the book ends by looking at what is usually referred to as the question of 'agency' through a consideration of the powerful forces that are now beginning to challenge the neo-liberal agenda on a world scale and which point to the end of what has been a long and often frustrating period for those seeking to challenge social inequality and injustice in Britain and elsewhere.

Part 1

The Relevance of Marx

1 'Was he right all along?': Classical Marxism and Social Policy

Following a decade and a half in which Marxist ideas were regarded as at best obsolete, at worst the most pernicious of all the 'grand narratives' decried by postmodern philosophers, Marxism has begun to re-appear on the intellectual and political agenda. The revival of interest has taken a number of different forms. At its most surprising and most populist was the successful nomination of Marx as 'Greatest Thinker of the Millennium' in a BBC Internet poll in 1999. The same year saw the publication of a well-received sympathetic biography of Marx by a leading British journalist (Wheen, 1999). The coincidence of the collapse of the 'Asian Tiger' economies of Thailand, Indonesia and South Korea with the 150th anniversary of the publication of the *Communist Manifesto* in 1998 led to a rediscovery of Marx by the 'quality' press. Typical of the adulatory articles appearing at this time was a *Financial Times* feature that concluded that 'Marx was not only the harbinger of revolutionary hatred but a shrewd, subtle analyst of capitalist society' (*Financial Times*, 25 March 1998). The *Independent on Sunday* similarly carried a three-page article in late 1997 titled 'Was He Right All Along?' describing Marx as the 'the next big thinker' (7 December 1997). The fact that a pocket edition of the Manifesto remained in Waterstone's bestseller lists for several weeks in 1998 suggests that such interest was not confined to a few journalists.

What is perhaps more surprising is that support, albeit heavily qualified, for Marx's ideas also began to emerge within an academic milieu which has poured scorn on these ideas for close to two decades. Thus in 1994 the leading French postmodernist Jacques Derrida argued in his *Specters of Marx* that:

> ... the Marxist inheritance was – and still remains, and so it will remain – absolutely and thoroughly determinate. One need not be a Marxist or a communist to accept this obvious fact. We all live in a world, some would say a culture, that still bears, at an incalculable depth, the mark of this inheritance. (1994: 14)

In a review of Derrida's book, another postmodern thinker, Richard Rorty, while disagreeing with Derrida's assessment of Marx, nevertheless paid Marx a back-handed compliment by arguing for the need to challenge class inequalities in the US and recognise class as the central divide in contemporary capitalist societies (Rorty, 1999).

It would be wrong to exaggerate the extent or depth of this return to Marx. As Rees has observed in a review of the phenomenon, it is a very partial and selective reading of Marx which is now being celebrated: the theorist of capitalist crisis but not of working-class revolution; the man himself but not the revolutionary tradition of Engels, Lenin, Luxemburg, Trotsky and Gramsci to which he gave rise (Rees, 1998b). Furthermore in some notable cases the movement is in the opposite direction. The unexpected embrace of the market by the recently 'relaunched ' *New Left Review* under its original editor Perry Anderson shows that the trend is not all one way. Nevertheless, given the degree of calumny heaped upon Marx in previous years, even the small revival of interest that is taking place is significant and, in our view, welcome. A major aim of this book is to encourage and contribute to that process by demonstrating the relevance of the 'classical Marxist tradition' (see below) to an understanding of social welfare in contemporary capitalist societies. Before then, however, it is necessary to consider why such a revival of interest in Marx's ideas should be taking place at this time. Four factors seem of particular significance.

New World disorder

First, there are the failures of market economies, East and West, during the 1990s. The fall of the Berlin Wall and the collapse of communism in the late 1980s were widely perceived by Western commentators as signifying the triumph of the market as the only rational way of organising society. Politically, the fall of the East European regimes was seen, most explicitly by US State Department official Francis Fukuyama, as ushering in 'the end of history' and a 'New World Order' in which the ideological basis for the conflicts which had plagued the world throughout history no longer existed and in which future conflicts would, unlike the wars of the past, be purely local affairs (Fukuyama, 1992).

At the same time, the rapid growth of the 'Tiger' economies of Southeast Asia during the 1980s and the first half of the 1990s was widely seen as heralding a new era of capitalist expansion, with countries such as South Korea, Singapore and Thailand held up by conservative and 'Third Way' politicians alike as a model for Western economies to follow. The market, once identified as the major source of inequality in social-democratic thought, was now positively embraced by politicians such as former US President Bill Clinton and British Prime Minister Tony Blair who argued that there was no contradiction between support for the market and a commitment to social justice (Blair, 1998).

A decade after the fall of the Berlin Wall, these economic and political hopes lay in tatters. A few statistics illustrate the extent to which the market has failed to deliver prosperity to the peoples of Eastern Europe. By the end of the 1990s, the Ukrainian economy was as third as big as it had been in 1989. The Russian economy had shrunk by half, as had the Bulgarian economy. In East Germany, living standards were only 70 per cent of those in the West. A UNICEF Report from 1999 spelled out the full extent of the impact of introducing market forces. It noted 'significant drops in life expectancy' in several European states and concluded:

> What we are arguing is that the transition to market economies in the region is the biggest killer we have seen in the twentieth century, if you take out famine and wars. The sudden shock and what it did to the system has effectively meant that five million Russian men's lives have been lost in the 1990s. (UNICEF, 1999 cited in *Socialist Worker*, 6/11/99).

As well as the woes of the Russian economy, 1998 witnessed the re-emergence of crisis in other parts of the world economy – particularly in economies previously seen as the most dynamic and path-breaking. Japan and the 'Tiger' economies of Southeast Asia, for example, entered what looks suspiciously like a classical capitalist crisis of overproduction of the sort described by Marx in *Capital* (Sparks, 1998).

Nor, as predicted by Fukuyama, did the end of the Cold War lead to a more stable, less conflict-ridden world. In fact, the decade between 1990 and 2000 saw two wars waged on Iraq by the Western powers; Western intervention in the former Yugoslavia also on two occasions; up to 250,000 killed in East Timor by Indonesian troops; over a million killed in Rwanda as a result of a civil war whose roots lie in Rwanda's colonial past; 30,000 killed and as many as 3 million displaced as a result of the Turkish government's war on the Kurds in Eastern Turkey; two wars conducted in Chechnya by an increasingly desperate Russian ruling class; and a host of local and regional conflicts too numerous to mention. Alongside the general misery and suffering which these wars and economic crises have produced for millions of ordinary people throughout the world, a further major consequence of this new world *disorder* has been the creation of mass movements of refugees on a scale not seen since the Second World War.

The human cost of these wars – both in the immediate and in the long-term – has been immense. As well as the vast numbers killed, injured and maimed by these conflicts the increasing use of radioactive materials, such as depleted uranium to coat shells and bombs, has led to environmental devastation and a horrendous legacy of children born with a variety of deformities, most notably in Iraq. This specific example of environmental ruin is part of a wider trend of ecological destruction. There is a growing recognition that the unbridled expansion of market capitalism is literally destroying the planet. Climate change, depletion of the ozone layer, the greenhouse effect and the development of Genetically Modified Organisms (GMOs), for example, have all been unleashed on the planet by corporations chasing bigger profits at all costs – each of these brings a substantial threat to the future of humanity (McGarr, 2000).

To take climate change, for example, there is now a growing recognition – even by governments – that such developments threaten our existence. In Britain, the Royal Commission on Environmental Pollution has noted:

> Human-induced climate change is threatening to impose very significant shifts in temperature, rainfall, and extremes of weather and sea levels ... The environmental and social consequences of such changes are potentially catastrophic ... [the world] is confronted with a radical challenge of a totally new kind. Strong and effective action has to start immediately. (quoted in McGarr, 2000: 63)

While the Union of Concerned Scientists have argued that:

> There is a serious risk that the climate will change in ways that will seriously disrupt our lives. Amongst the severest impacts: a rise in sea level, more heat waves and droughts, more extreme weather events, producing floods and pro- perty destruction; and tropical diseases spreading to areas where they've never been known before. If we don't take action, global warming will threaten our health, our cities, our farms, and our forests, wetlands and other natural habitats. (UCS, 2000)

Concern over environmental destruction brought the world's govern- ments together at the Earth Summit in Rio de Janeiro, Brazil in 1992 and in 1997 at the climate conference in Kyoto, Japan. Yet these conferences did not produce the required action. As we discuss in Chapter 2, it may be in the interests of capitalism in general to control the greenhouse effect and the more astute state officials, politicians and corporations may recognise the long-term problems they face from environmental destruction, but capitalism in general is an abstraction. The real world is made up of many competing capitals, each pursuing their own selfish interests, their own unquenchable thirst for greater profits. The oil, coal, and gas corporations, and the car and road-construction companies are at the heart of the problem of the 'fossil fuel economy' – they are also amongst the most powerful companies in the world, fêted and protected by their governments. Although the technology to reduce dramatically carbon dioxide production in fossil burning power plants exists and is relatively efficient, its costs would eat into the profits of these powerful companies. Free and integrated transport systems would immediately undermine the 'car culture' and the car's damaging exhaust emissions – but this would threaten the profits of the gigantic car multinationals. The pursuit of profit at all costs is bringing with it environmental destruction which threatens the welfare of all humanity in the course of the twenty-first century.

The reality of the New World Order, then, is one of economic crisis, the threat of environmental catastrophe, and war. It is this *disorder* that has led to interest in various 'anti-capitalist' social theories, including those of the most pronounced anti-capitalist – Karl Marx.

The growth of inequality

Alongside this sense of disorder is a second factor which has underlined the relevance of Marx's ideas, namely the existence of levels of inequality which are quite unprecedented in world history.

Since the late 1980s the United Nations has produced a series of annual *Human Development Reports*. These graphically depict not only the rising levels of inequality both at a global and national level, but also highlight the consequences of this trend for billions of people around the world. In its report for 1998 the UN estimated that the 225 richest people in the world have a combined wealth of more than $1 trillion, representing a doubling of their net-worth in the mid-1990s alone. This is equal to the annual income of the poorest 47 per cent of the world's population, around 2.5 billion people. Just three of the world's richest people and families – the Walton family, owners of the Wal-Mart supermarket and retail chain; Warren Buffett, a leading American investor; and Bill Gates of Microsoft – have between them assets estimated in the region of $140 billion, exceeding the combined GDP of the 48 least-developed countries.

The UN calculated that the additional costs of achieving and maintaining universal access to health care and education for all, adequate food and safe sanitation for the entire population of the world and reproductive health care for all women amounts to only $40 billion per annum, less than 4 per cent of the combined wealth of the richest 225 people. Yet each day an estimated $1.5 trillion is traded on stock markets around the world, 95 per cent of which represent at best a 'bet' on whether interests or currency rates will rise or fall (*New Internationalist*, 2000).

For Marxists there is a clear and direct relationship between poverty and wealth – the increasing accumulation and concentration of wealth in the hands of a few will be accompanied by rising poverty for the many. In a report published in 2000 it estimated that in the last two decades of the twentieth century the number of people living in poverty rose to more than 1.2 billion, representing one in five of the world's population. This included over 600 million children (UNICEF, 2000). While Bill Gates and Warren Buffett are enjoying their vast riches, some 500 million children under 14 are in work with somewhere in the region of 60 million children under 11 working in dangerous circumstances (Lavalette and Cunningham, 2001).

This global picture of increasing wealth concentration and rising poverty is replicated in countries across the world. As noted above, in Russia, whose people were promised by Western leaders in the late 1980s and early 1990s that they would soon reap the benefits of the market, income inequality is at its greatest levels. The share of income of the richest 20 per cent of Russian society is 11 times that of the poorest 20 per cent (UN, 1999). However, it is in two of the leading and richest capitalist societies – US and Britain – that the growth of poverty and rising inequality between rich and poor has been most pronounced in recent decades.

In 1999 President Clinton pronounced that 'Americans are living in an era of unprecedented prosperity'. Yet such a claim is sharply at odds with the picture that has been painted by a series of studies and reports. In 1998 the number of people in the US without health care cover *of any kind* rose to over 45 million, around 16.5 per cent of the population. During the mid-1990s child poverty rates, among the highest in the industrialised world, hovered around 21 per cent. Yet at the same time America's rich found themselves in an even more privileged position. No less than a Congressional Budget Office Study in 1998 pointed to the widening income gulf between rich and poor, and the growing concentration of wealth, which has been has a notable feature of US society during the 1990s (Smith, 1999: 15). In its Annual Report for 1999, *Forbes Magazine* estimated that the net worth of the richest 400 Americans had reached $1 trillion, greater than the entire GDP of China (in Smith, 1999). Since the 1970s the top 1 per cent of US households have doubled their share of national wealth, leaving them with more wealth than the bottom 95 per cent of American society (*New Internationalist*, 2000). In other words, between 1983 and 1989, the top 20 per cent of wealth holders received 99 per cent of the total gain in marketable wealth with the bottom 80 per cent sharing a meagre 1 per cent (*The American Prospect Online*, 1995). It is not simply that the poorest sections of American society did not benefit from economic growth during the 1980s and 1990s, their share of income actually *declined* in real terms. Between 1977 and 1992 the poorest one-fifth of Americans saw their income decline by 17 per cent compared with an increase of 28 per cent for the top 1 per cent and a whopping 91 per cent for the richest 1 per cent.

A similar story holds for Britain. On coming to power in 1997 the New Labour government of Tony Blair inherited a country more unequal than at any time since 1945. During the 1980s and 1990s Britain experienced a massive increase in income and wealth inequalities, reversing the trend towards redistribution, albeit of a limited nature, between 1949 and 1979. Income inequality grew faster in Britain than in any other developed country apart from New Zealand during the 1980s and early 1990s (Gordon, 2000; Labour Research, 2000; Pantazis and Gordon, 2000; Rahman et al., 2000; Shaw et al., 1999).

Statistics on the distribution of wealth in Britain are highly inadequate. Perhaps this is not so surprising when it is remembered that one of Margaret Thatcher's early decisions on coming to power in 1979 was to abolish the Royal Commission on the Distribution of Income and Wealth set up by Labour in 1974. However, it is possible to gleam some sense of wealth inequalities from various government reports. Taken together these highlight a growing polarisation between rich and poor in British society.

In the mid-1990s the richest 10 per cent had 50 per cent of marketable wealth, the top 5 per cent owned 38 per cent and the richest 1 per cent accounted for 19 per cent. By contrast the share of the poorest 50 per cent was only 8 per cent (Labour Research, 2000). The richest 21 people owned wealth estimated at £28.4 billion in 1995 – the richest 1,000 had on average 15,000 times more wealth than the poorest 28 million (Gordon, 2000: 41).

This snapshot picture of wealth disparity is underpinned by a trend towards greater inequality. The annual *Sunday Times* 'rich list' offers one source of evidence of this. By its estimates the wealthiest 200 people were worth £38 billion in 1989 but this had increased to £75.9 billion by 1999 (Labour Research, 2000). Income inequalities point in a similar direction. Between 1979 and 1994 the poorest one-tenth of the population saw their income fall by 17 per cent in real terms while for the richest one-tenth there was an increase of 62 per cent. The consequence was that during the 18 years of Conservative rule the poorest became poorer by £520 per annum while the richest saw their income rise by more than £12,000 per year (Gordon, 2000: 34).

The final part of the jigsaw can be gleaned from looking at trends in poverty over the same period. Once again there are limitations with the available statistics and with the absence of any officially recognised poverty line, researchers are forced to rely on a measure of Households Below Half Average Income. Using this measure in 1996, 25 per cent of the population, some 14,100,000 people, were living in poverty, compared with 8 per cent in 1979. This increase did not end with the election of Labour in May 1997. In the two-year period to 1998 the number of people living on what Catherine Howarth and colleagues refer to as *very* low incomes (defined as below 40 per cent of average income) increased by over one million to 8.4 million, with a further 6 million on incomes below half average (Howarth et al., 1999). One of the clearest indicators of this rise in poverty over the past three decades is presented by figures for the proportion of children living in poverty. In 1979, 9 per cent of children in Britain lived in households with an income below half the average. But by 1996/97 this had increased to 35 per cent: more than 1 in 3 children now live in poverty. The number of children dependent on income support has grown from under 1 million in 1979 to over 2.7 million in 1998 (DSS, 1998). In the final quarter of the twentieth century child poverty had increased more in Britain than in almost any other developed society (Fimister, 2001; Gordon and Townsend, 2001; Vleminckx and Smeeding, 2001).

The consequences of poverty are felt in every area of people's lives. In his hard-hitting investigation into the state of education in Britain under New Labour, Davies reaches the conclusion that:

> This is the secret that everyone knows: the children of poor families are far less likely to do well in school than those whose parents are affluent. For the last ten years, this has been almost buried in denial. 'Poverty is no excuse', according to the Department of Education. Nevertheless, it is the key. As everyone knows. (Davies, 2000: 16).

Similarly, in relation to health, the first major report into health inequalities in Britain since the Black Report of the late 1970s concluded that:

... although average mortality has fallen over the past 50 years, unacceptable inequalities in health persist. For many measures of health, inequalities have either remained the same or have widened in recent decades ... The weight of scientific evidence supports a socioeconomic explanation of health inequalities. (Acheson, 1998: 2).

In the face of this evidence of massive inequality, it is perhaps not surprising that a growing number of social policy and social-work writers now argue that issues of poverty and class need to be firmly located at the heart of discussions of welfare (for example, Becker, 1997; Jones, 1997; Jones and Novak, 1999; Bywaters and McLeod, 2000).

A return to commitment

The crises of the market on the one hand and the glaring evidence of massive inequality on the other have contributed to a deepening intellectual crisis which manifests itself in a number of ways, and which constitutes the third factor in explaining the revival of interest in Marxism. In particular postmodernism, which has dominated many areas of academic life for over a decade, is increasingly recognised as contributing to a moral relativism and a stance of 'ironic detachment' which is untenable in the face of the economic and ecological crisis currently facing humanity (Ferguson and Lavalette, 1999; Philo and Miller, 2000). The comments of two leading activists and theoreticians of the disability movement referring to the problems faced by people with disabilities have much wider application:

We are not convinced that modernity can be dismissed or that postmodernity should be embraced in the ways that are now fashionable. We do not see where we are now as somewhere different from where we were 50 or 20 years ago; rather we are confronted with the same issues that we have always been confronted with, even if the circumstances in which we confront them have changed and are changing. For us capitalism continues to rule OK! Even if it is now global rather than based on the nation state. (Oliver and Barnes, 1998: 4).

The result is a growing return to a politics of commitment concerned with the question of what sort of principles should underpin welfare regimes (Ferguson and Lavalette, 2000). We shall explore some recent attempts to grapple with this issue both in Chapter 8 on globalisation and in the final chapter.

The return of resistance

Finally, after a decade and a half in which trade unionists and movement activists everywhere, from Gdansk to Tienanmen Square, suffered defeat after bloody defeat, the re-emergence of resistance to the ravages of the market on a world scale, including resistance by a working class long since written off by commentators of both left and right, suggests that the tide might be starting to turn. In 1998, for example, Indonesia experienced a revolution in which both students and the working class played a major role and which resulted in the overthrow of the 32-year long dictatorship of President Suharto. In France, the great public sector strikes of 1995 forced the newly-elected Conservative government to abandon its plan to slash public spending, stopped the growth of the far right National Front in its tracks and paved the way for the return of a left-of-centre government under Lionel Jospin. The decade ended with the siege of the World Trade Organisation's annual conference in Seattle by tens of thousands of demonstrators, a siege which resulted in the abandonment of the conference of the representatives of the world's biggest multinationals and richest nations and led commentators to hail the emergence of a new 'anti-capitalist' mood, with its roots in a revulsion against the social and ecological ravages of multinational capitalism (Klein, 2000; Monbiot, 2000; Charlton, 2000b). The fact that similar international mobilisations have since taken place around subsequent WTO conferences at Washington, Prague, Quebec and elsewhere suggests that the movement may have longer-term significance.

Marxism and social welfare

It is against this background that we have written this book. Our central contention is that the ideas of Marx and those who have followed him in what we shall refer to as the classical Marxist tradition are of enormous relevance to understanding the nature of welfare and welfare provision within advanced capitalism. Marxist analyses of the dynamics of capitalism, class, the State, the family, as well as of alienation and oppression are, we shall argue, powerful explanatory tools that help make sense of a whole range of current welfare issues and debates.

Such a project requires some justification. There is already in existence (if not always in print) a corpus of Marxist, or Marxist-influenced, writing within both social policy and social work, much of it stemming from the late 1970s and early 1980s. In social policy, for example, the writings of Gough (1979) and Ginsburg (1979), part of the Macmillan series *Critical Texts in Social Work and the Welfare State* edited by Peter Leonard, were important early attempts to develop a Marxist analysis of the Welfare State. Within social work, Leonard's own *Social Work Practice Under Capitalism* (1978), co-written with Paul Corrigan, explicitly sought to apply Marxist categories to social work practice. While we shall argue below that while some of these texts suffered from important limitations, nevertheless, alongside such texts as Bailey and Brake's collection *Radical*

Social Work (1975), Simpkin's *Trapped Within Welfare* (1979) and Jones' *State Social Work and the Working Class* (1983), they represented an important break with a tradition of Fabian empiricism (in the case of social policy, or social administration as it was then known) and with liberal or psycho-social approaches (in the case of social work). Given the existence of this body of writing, why is another Marxist text on social policy and social work necessary? We believe there are three main reasons.

First, the world of welfare at the beginning of the new millennium differs in important respects from that of ten or twenty years ago. In most advanced capitalist societies, there have been important shifts in the forms of welfare provision and in welfare ideology, with the market, for example, playing a much more central role than was previously the case. Within social work, the development of 'quasi-markets' based on a 'purchaser/provider' split has transformed the role of social work through the growing dominance of care management approaches (Langan and Clarke, 1994; Mooney, 1997; Clarke et al., 2000).

The election of a New Labour Government in Britain in 1997 did not lead to a break with these policies. Instead the commitment to the role of the market in welfare has continued, albeit with some modifications, combined with a moral agenda which sees work as the key to the economic and moral restructuring of the welfare state (Blair, 1998; Ellison and Pierson, 1998; Lavalette and Mooney, 1999). While there have been attempts to understand particular aspects of these changes from a classical Marxist perspective, for reasons that we shall discuss below there has been no attempt to provide an overall Marxist analysis of these changes.

Second, both 'radical social work' and 'critical social policy', the two main critical currents which developed in the mid to late 1970s, were notable for their extreme diversity and eclecticism, broad churches made up of different and often contradictory strands. Alongside the revolutionary socialist position of magazines like *CaseCon*, for example, there was also a strong libertarian or hippie element (though whether this was ever as dominant as Pearson (1988) implies is open to question). The most explicitly Marxist writing of this period, in the series edited by Peter Leonard and referred to above, tended to reflect the Marxism of the Communist Party in Britain and elsewhere, with the main theoretical influence being the French CP philosopher, Louis Althusser.

The relationship between this Stalinist (and its mirror image 'Eurocommunist') version of Marxism and the classical Marxist tradition will be explored below. In terms of the impact of this form of Marxism on social policy and social work literature in the late 1970s and 1980s, however, it is worth noting some of the limitations of this version of Marxism at this stage.

A key characteristic of Stalinist, or Stalinist-influenced, versions of Marxism is a mechanical and determinist 'application' of theory to practice, derived ultimately from the role played by 'Marxism–Leninism' for over 50 years within the USSR. But rather than an engaged science,

'Marxism–Leninism' acted more like a state religion whose primary function was not to analyse critically a changing world but to justify the actions of the Soviet ruling bureaucracy at home and abroad (Molyneux, 1983).

Peter Leonard, for example, whose early writings were clearly sympathetic to the politics of the British Communist Party but who has more recently, albeit critically, embraced postmodernism, now acknowledges that:

> Within orthodox classical Marxism it was argued that everything could be reduced to the economic base, that the characteristics of the mode of production, here late capitalism as a global market, determined the politics of 'superstructure', culture and subjectivity. That such a simple reductionism and economic determinism is no longer convincing is the result, in part at least of the growth of a cultural politics, fuelled substantially by feminist and postmodern critique, which argues for the, at least, relative autonomy, of the cultural and its role in constituting the subject. (1997: 12).

While we shall contest the notion that Stalinism is synonymous with 'orthodox classical Marxism', it is certainly true that much of the Marxist writing of this period often possessed the characteristics which Leonard describes. Similarly, the identification of socialism with the societies existing in Russia and Eastern Europe assumed by writers within this tradition created enormous problems, not least in explaining the continued existence within these societies of women's oppression.

Not surprisingly then, for these writers Althusser's notion of the 'relative autonomy' of different spheres of struggle proved useful. While earlier Stalinist versions of Marxism had often posited a particularly crude and mechanical view of the relationship between the economic 'base' of society and its legal, political and ideological 'superstructure', Althusser 'solved' the problem of base and superstructure by arguing that each of these spheres had their own dynamics, with a purely 'conjunctural' relationship between them. Thus the struggle to understand and combat women's oppression, for example, was only related 'in the last instance' to the trade union struggle or to changes in the mode of production. Rather than being a 'development' of Marxism, however, Althusser's solution in fact amounted to an abandonment of Marxism and pointed the way to poststructuralism and a politics based on identity. As Lee and Raban commented:

> The increasing awareness amongst Marxist theorists of the need to specify the independence of the struggles of women, black people and others from the wider class struggle has led many to abandon Marxism altogether. For thinkers such as Hindess and Hirst, ... it was impossible accurately to assess the degree of relative autonomy of ideological and political practices from economic ones, and from such observations it was but a small step to an intellectual position that celebrated the complete autonomy of all processes! (1988: 206).

Clearly then, a central task for any text asserting the relevance of Marxism for social policy and social work at the beginning of a new century is to demonstrate that Marxism is capable of accounting for oppression, a task we shall address in Chapter 6.

Second, as both Thompson (1978) and Harman (1983) have argued, Althusser's own project was not to undermine Stalinism but rather to salvage it in the face of competition from the New Left of the 1950s and 1960s. Thus, far from Althusserian frameworks challenging Stalinist distortions of Marxism, they often reinforced them. Marx's concept of alienation, for example, potentially one of the most fruitful for making sense of social welfare issues, becomes, through Althusser's discovery of an 'epistemological break' between a young Marx and an old Marx, the work of a young and immature Marx with whom we need not concern ourselves. Consequently, in Marxist social policy and social work texts of the 1970s and 1980s, the concept does not appear.

More generally, a central target of Althusser's work was what he called 'Hegelian Marxism', that group of writers in the 1920s and 1930s including Gramsci, Lukács and Korsch who sought to emphasise the 'active' side of Marxism. By contrast, we shall suggest that the ideas of these writers, particularly Lukács on reification and Gramsci on contradictory consciousness, are of enormous potential significance in making sense of a range of welfare issues.

Finally, the limitations of this form of Marxism on the one hand and the collapse of 'actually existing socialism' on the other mean that many of those within the radical social work and critical social policy tradition who previously identified themselves as Marxists no longer do so. By the late 1980s, for example, Lee and Raban, in the text referred to above, were arguing for 'a fusion of the critical elements of Fabianism with a realistic version of Marxism', 'a "third way" between the Scylla and Charybidis of reform and revolution' (1988: 218). More recently, as we have noted above, Leonard, a seminal figure in the development of radical social work, has referred to 'a socialist politics which is now dead, or at least in its deathbed' (1997: 27) and argued that postmodernism provides 'a now essential ingredient in a revitalized Marxism' (Leonard, 1997: xiii).

In fact, during the 1970s and even during the heyday of Stalinism in the 1950s, there was an alternative Marxist tradition, one which did not ignore structural determinants but which equally emphasised the role of human agency. Supporters of this tradition rejected both the Stalinist caricature of Marxism and the notion that the Stalinist states of Russia and Eastern Europe bore any relation to Marx's idea of socialism. For those who belong to this tradition, the collapse of 'actually existing socialism', far from representing the death of socialist politics, provides the best opportunities since the Stalinist counter-revolution of the 1930s for rediscovering and developing the authentic tradition of Marx and Engels. It is this tradition that we shall outline in the next section and draw on in the chapters which follow to develop a theory and practice of social welfare which goes beyond the relativism and fragmentation of the alternatives currently on offer.

The classical Marxist tradition

The notion of a classical Marxist tradition was first put forward by Trotsky's biographer Isaac Deutscher and later developed by the leading British Marxist intellectual Perry Anderson (1976). Deutscher lamented the:

> ... striking, and to a Marxist, humiliating contrast between what I call classical Marxism – that is, the body of thought developed by Marx, Engels, their contemporaries and after them by Kautsky, Plekhanov, Lenin, Trotsky, Rosa Luxemburg – and the vulgar Marxism, the pseudo-Marxism of the different varieties of European social-democrats, reformists, Stalinists, Kruschevites, and their like. (cited in Callinicos, 1990: 3)

Anderson later went on to contrast this classical Marxist tradition with what he called 'Western Marxism', a strand of thought that developed after the Second World War and whose main representatives – including Adorno, Althusser, Marcuse, Sartre – were located within the universities. Among the key characteristics of Western Marxism – perhaps more accurately described as *academic* Marxism (Rees, 1998c) – were:

- a preoccupation with issues of philosophy and aesthetics, rather than politics or political economy;
- an ambivalence towards Stalinism, reflected, for example, in the attitude of philosophers such as Sartre and Althusser towards the French Communist Party. As Anderson noted: 'To the exponents of the new Marxism that emerged in the West, the official communist movement represented the real sole embodiment of the international working class with meaning for them – whether they joined it, allied with it or rejected it (Anderson, 1976: 92); and
- above all, an often total divorce from, and lack of interest in, the lives and struggles of real working-class people (a lack of interest reflected in the obscure and opaque language which they frequently employed in their writings).

By contrast, Anderson argued, what distinguished adherents of the classical Marxist tradition was their organic involvement in the working-class movement of their day and a theoretical concentration on issues of political economy, forms of bourgeois rule and aspects of class and class struggle.

In relation to the approach pursued in this book, three aspects of the tradition require some discussion at this stage. First, there is the notion of capitalism as a *totality*, a notion which Marx derived from Hegel. Marx's own method developed by grounding Hegel's idealist philosophy in the material world. From Hegel he took three main points: (1) the world is in a constant process of change; (2) the world is a totality; and (3) this totality is internally contradictory (and that it is these internal contradictions that produce change) (Rees, 1998a). Marx 'always pictured capitalist development as a whole. This enabled him to see both its totality in any one of its phenomena, and the dynamic of its structure' (Lukács, 1970: 10).

Viewing the world as a totality means insisting that the various, apparently separate and discrete, elements that compose the modern world are in fact linked and related to one another, that the world is a 'differentiated unity', in Trotsky's phrase. In modern society we face an array of apparently disconnected and separated social institutions and practices – in the academic world this separation is solidified into distinct academic disciplines. In reality, of course, each of these areas is interconnected. For example, we cannot fully understand the modern art world outside the categories of alienation, class division and commodity production (but neither, obviously, can we reduce art to economic criteria); welfare development cannot be adequately understood unless we acknowledge the various elements of control, social wage, commodification and investment in labour power that it involves; the state is portrayed as neutral, yet it reinforces and maintains the power of the already rich and powerful. Rees continues:

> Production is really a collective act – not merely the result of individual effort. The market is a social institution, not the result of individual behavior. Poverty and crime, unemployment and suicide, art and business, language and history, engineering and sociology cannot be understood in isolation, but only as part of a totality ... [W]hen we bring these terms into relation with each other, their meaning is transformed. Once we understand the relationship between poverty and crime, it is impossible to look on either the criminal justice system or those who live in poverty as we did when they were taken to inhabit two separate realms. (1998a: 5)

To see the world as a 'differentiated unity' is to note that each sphere of social life is interconnected. But this does not mean that the diversity of the social structure is eliminated or everything can be reduced to its 'economic logic' – each sphere has its own processes and laws which must be understood and grasped in their own terms while being located in, and related to, the rest of the social world.

For example, the nature of capitalism and the complex division of labour it generates produces a separation between the state and its activities and the direct economic activities of capital (although this is not to deny there are areas where the state and capital have merged). The actions of the state cannot simply be reduced to the economic needs of capital (not least because capital is itself divided into competitive units, and as Marx notes in *Capital* Vol. 3, there is a distinction between 'capital in general', a necessary abstraction, and the 'many competing capitals' of the production process). But neither is it the case that the state is merely a 'superstructural' phenomenon. The state is necessary to protect the interests of capital in general, to aid and facilitate the further expansion of the forces of production, to control and regulate the working class to aid the process of surplus value extraction. What is necessary is a concrete understanding of 'the ways in which capitals and the capitalist state necessarily interact in the course of historical development. Existing national states did arise out of the developing capitalist organisation of production ... But they feed back into that organisation, helping to determine its tempo and direction' (Harman, 1991: 7).

Here we see an example of the process of 'mediation', in other words, the ways in which the parts and the whole mutually condition each other. Thus, as Rees notes:

> Marx's notion of the dialectic ... necessarily requires that he reject reductionist formulations and give full weight to the mediating contradictions between different elements of the totality ... The dialectical method involves analytically separating a chaotic social whole into various constituent economic formulations, classes, institutions, personalities, and so on. It then involves showing how these factors interrelate and contradict each other as part of a totality. (1998a: 107, 275)

Finally, this approach necessarily rules out any form of 'inevitability' in human progress. For Marx, it is real, living men and women who make history (though not, as he noted, in circumstances of their own choosing). While fatalism and determinism have undoubtedly characterised some variants of 'Marxist' thought, they were not typical either of Marx's own thought or practice, or of the practice of his leading followers. As Luxemburg argued:

> Just as in Marx himself, the keen historical analyst, was inseparably bound up with the daring revolutionary, the man of thought with the man of action, supporting and complementing each other, so ... [does] Marxism, as the theory of socialism, pair theoretical knowledge with the revolutionary energy of the proletariat, the one illuminated and fructified by the other. Both aspects belong equally to the inner core of Marxism; separated from each other, each transforms Marxism into a sad caricature of itself. (Quoted in Frölich, 1972: 50)

Similarly, in a polemic against fatalism in theory and practice, Gramsci argued that:

> In reality one can 'scientifically' foresee only the struggle, but not the concrete moments of the struggle, which cannot but be the results of opposing forces in

continuous movement, which are never reducible to fixed quantities since within them quantity is continually becoming quality. In reality one can 'foresee' to the extent that one acts, to the extent that one applies a voluntary effort and therefore contributes concretely to creating the result 'foreseen'. Prediction reveals itself not as a scientific act of knowledge, but as the abstract expression of the effort made, the practical way of creating a collective will. (1971: 438)

The second element of classical Marxism which we wish to emphasise concerns the relationship between theory and practice. Classical Marxism is, in Gramsci's words, the 'philosophy of practice', a theory that helps us understand the world in order to change it. There are two aspects to this. In terms of the *development* of theory, in sharp contrast to academic Marxism which has often seen 'theory' as something that is developed in isolation from the struggles and experience of working people, classical Marxist theory is closely linked to the actual struggles of workers and oppressed groups, learning from the successes and failures of these struggles and generalising from that experience. Thus, Marx's theory of the State, for example, was profoundly informed by the experience of the Paris Commune in 1871; Lenin's understanding both of the role of soviets and of the party were based on his experience of the 1905 Russian Revolution, as was Luxemburg's theory of the mass strike (coupled with her personal experience of the role of German social democracy) and so on. Similarly, in this text, we will frequently refer to, and draw on, a range of welfare struggles with a view to showing how such struggles have often informed welfare theory and policy, be they historical examples such as the Glasgow Rent Strike of 1915 or the more recent anti-capitalist struggles such as the Seattle protests of 1999.

A further aspect of the theory/practice relationship concerns the role of socialist theory. Gramsci's description of Marxism as a 'philosophy of practice' reflects Marx's own early formulation that 'the philosophers have only *interpreted* the world, in various ways; the point is to *change it*' (1845/1975: 423). In similar vein, for Lukács historical materialism was 'the theory of the proletarian revolution' (1970: 9). In other words, in a society riven by class, it is no more possible for theory than for political actors to be 'above the struggle', 'neutral' or 'value free'. Such a perspective does not invalidate Marxism's claim to be a science. While the natural and social sciences are clearly different it is not the case that the natural sciences are 'objective' and 'neutral' (decisions over what is studied, what is developed and what is financed in the natural sciences reflect *in part* the priorities and dynamism of capitalism to expand and develop new commodities) (see, for example, MacKenzie and Wajcman, 1985). Neither is it the case that any of the social sciences are 'value free'. Bourgeois economics, for example, discusses production while trying to hide and deny the very fact of labour exploitation and the creation of surplus value; mainstream works in law and politics ignore the class divisions and unequal distribution of power in society and portray the state as a neutral entity, reinforcing bourgeois ideology but obscuring the real underlying social relations that exist in society. In this respect, Marxism can claim to be *more* scientific than these approaches since its aim is to penetrate beneath the surface appearances of capitalism and reveal the operation of the real relations of exploitation and oppression at work within society. As Lukács argued, it is able to do this precisely because it is 'the science of the proletarian revolution' with no interest in maintaining the outward appearance of bourgeois society but with a real interest in revealing its exploitative and oppressive core (Lukács, 1970).

The final strand running through the text concerns the central role of the working class within classical Marxist theory and practice. In 1879 Marx and Engels wrote:

> For almost forty years we have stressed the class struggle as the immediate driving power of history, and in particular the class struggle between the bourgeoisie and proletariat as the great lever of the modern social revolution ... we expressly formulated the battle-cry: The emancipation of the working class is conquered by the working classes themselves. (quoted in Callinicos, 1983: 141)

Whether or not the working class is still capable of playing this role (or more fundamentally, the extent to which it is still valid to speak in terms of 'the working class') is a question that will be explored in Chapter 3. At this stage, we simply note that the notion of the self-emancipation of the working class is at the heart of the classical Marxist tradition. This formulation both addresses the issue of agency – of *how* society is to be changed – as well as providing us with a yardstick against which we can measure those societies which claim (or have claimed) to be socialist.

In terms of agency, it implies that a genuinely socialist society can only be created by the conscious activity of the working class. To paraphrase the American Marxist Hal Draper (1966/1996), socialism must be brought about 'from below' by the working class collectively taking control of society and democratically planning to meet the needs of all, rather than being imposed 'from above' by Red Army tanks (for example, in the former Eastern Bloc), peasant-based armies of national liberation (for example, in China or Vietnam), an army of intellectuals based in the Sierras (Cuba), or any amount of parliamentary manoeuvring by an 'enlightened minority'.

As regards self-emancipation as an evaluative criterion, during the twentieth century different regimes across the globe have claimed the mantle of 'Marxism', whilst administering systems where some of the most oppressive and exploitative social practices have been maintained and reinforced. Such governments have been involved in arms races with each other (Vietnam and China, for example), used troops to suppress working-class revolts (Hungary 1956, Poland 1981 and China 1989, for example), imprisoned a wide range of political prisoners in slave camps (most obviously, the Soviet Union's Gulag), oppressed minority sexualities (Cuba), uniformly maintained the 'modern' family (and with it the oppression of women), perpetuated and reinforced both nationalism and racism in their institutional practices and ideologies, and through the operation of various 'nomenklatura' maintained a minority ruling class whose wealth and privilege have been obtained and maintained at the expense of, and in opposition to, the interests and needs of the majority. A central theme of this text will be that the collapse of many of these regimes in the late 1980s, far from invalidating a Marxist understanding of the world, for the first time in many decades allows for the re-emergence of an authentic Marxism which sees Marxism and full democracy not as incompatible but as inextricably linked (Callinicos, 1989). As the journal of Marx and Engels' group proclaimed some months before the publication of *The Communist Manifesto* (Marx and Engels, 1848/1973):

> We are not amongst those communists who are out to destroy personal liberty, who wish to turn the world into one huge barrack or gigantic warehouse … we have no desire to exchange freedom for equality. We are convinced … that in no social order will personal freedom be so assured as in a society based on communal ownership … Let us put our hands to work in order to establish a democratic state wherein each party would be able by word or in writing to win a majority over to its ideas. (cited in Draper, 1966/1996: 12).

Within the classical tradition, there is a substantial body of work, beginning in the late 1920s, that has attempted to offer a Marxist analysis and critique, firstly of the Soviet Union and then of the various so-called 'socialist' countries across the globe (see, for example, Trotsky, 1934/1972; Cliff, 1948/1974; Draper, 1966/1996). At various points within this book we shall draw on, or make reference to, this body of thought. Whatever differences they may have, those working within this tradition have argued that socialism is first and foremost a system of prioritising human need over profit, where production is controlled and planned by the direct producers (that is, workers in their factories and offices) and where both these requirements necessitate a system of open and direct democracy – far more democratic than anything seen under capitalism. None of the past or present representatives of 'actually existing socialism' come close to meeting these criteria.

On the basis, then, of these three key ideas – capitalism as a contradictory totality; Marxism as a philosophy of praxis; and socialism as the self-emancipation of the working class – we shall now attempt to develop an analysis of capitalism and welfare in the twenty-first century.

2 'Incentives and punishments': Capitalism and Welfare

In the *The Communist Manifesto*, Marx and Engels drew attention to the vast wealth created by capitalism.

> The bourgeoisie, during its rule of scarce one hundred years, has created more massive and more colossal productive forces than have all preceding generations together. (1848/1973: 72)

The productive forces had been revolutionised, the system was dynamic and expansive, the potential for human fulfilment immense. And this was written in 1848! Now Marx's 'praise' seems almost quaint, for at the start of the twenty-first century the power, wealth and productive capacity of modern capitalism is infinitely greater. As we argued in Chapter 1, however, it is clear that the vast potential and wealth of society is not used to improve all our lives. Modern capitalism has given us the potential to escape misery, disease, ill health and poverty, and to meet human need across the globe. Yet these needs remain unfulfilled and we are witnessing more, not less, inequality. Why is this?

For Marx, the answer to this question was built into the very fabric and nature of modern capitalism. Capitalism, he argued, *is* a dynamic system, but it is a system marked by two great divisions. The first is between that tiny minority of people who own and control the wealth in society on the one hand – the ruling class or the bourgeoisie – and on the other, those who can only survive by selling their skills and their ability to work – the working class. The bourgeoisie own and/or control the means of production under capitalism but require the labour of the working class in the offices and factories to produce commodities that can then be bought and sold on the market. The working class – the overwhelming majority of people in society – have no means of survival without selling their labour power, without entering the wage-labour market. Therefore, the bourgeoisie and the working class are tied together in a relationship – but it is not a relationship of equals. The wealth of modern society is created by the labour of workers but the commodities they produce generates vast profits for the bourgeoisie because there is no mechanism to force the bourgeoisie to pay workers the monetary equivalent of the value their labour creates. To maintain their wealth the bourgeoisie must continuously try to make workers work longer, faster and for less money. For the working class, on the other hand, their interests are for higher wages, shorter hours, longer holidays and less regulated working. Thus, Marx argued, the interests of workers and the bourgeoisie are irreconcilable – they are tied together in a mutually antagonistic relationship of exploitation where the survival of the bourgeoisie as a class depends on the subjugation of workers as a class.

The second great division of capitalism is a division *within* the bourgeoisie. Marx termed the bourgeoisie a 'band of warring brothers', meaning they had a 'brotherly' interest in maintaining capitalism and the exploitation of the working class. This is their general class interest – the interest of 'capital in general'. But they are warring brothers, competing with each other intensely with the aim of putting each other out of business and obtaining a greater share of the surplus product – capitalism, then, is a system of 'many competing capitals'. It is this competition between the competing units of capitals that drives each of them to invest resources in technology, to try and expand production and, at the same time, to attack workers' living conditions, to try and increase the rate of exploitation. The two structural divisions of capitalism therefore are intimately connected.

Finally, although each unit of capital tries to plan their investment, their labour market strategies and the realisation of their profits (that is the actual selling of their commodities), the system as a whole is unplanned and uncontrollable. It is a system that lurches from periods of economic boom to economic bust when all forms of resources, including labour, are left redundant. It is a system built upon the anarchy of generalised, competitive commodity production, whose goal is production for profit, not production for need.

So where does welfare fit into this picture? Is it not a set of provisions concerned with fulfilling human need rather than profit? Is it not an area of social life free from the dominant principles of market capitalism? The ideological claims of welfare clearly suggest that it is a separate and distinct area of social life, geared to combating the worst manifestations of poverty and inequality, and structured by a general society-wide commitment to some shared humanitarian impulse. But is this really an accurate picture of the functions of welfare?

In what follows we start to outline the key themes of a Marxist approach to welfare and introduce concepts which we will deepen and expand upon in later chapters.

Analysing welfare

Most accounts of welfare treat it as a separate sphere of social activity, something distinct from the general dynamic of capitalism. But as Gough notes, Marxist approaches to welfare are distinct from those that suggest that:

> ... the welfare state ... marks the end of capitalism and its replacement with a different and better society, whether the mixed economy, 'post-industrial' society, 'welfare' society or whatever. For almost all writers within [this]

tradition ... the welfare state has as its goals the satisfaction of human needs
and the improvement of human welfare ... Common to all is the view that the
purpose of the welfare state is the enhancement of human welfare ... [Marxists]
adopt a fundamentally different approach by treating the welfare state as a
constituent feature of modern capitalist societies ... [situating] the welfare state
within its contemporary environment: the capitalist economy and its attendant
social relations. (1979: 1, 2, 3)

For classical Marxism, welfare cannot be separated from the wider
social totality. It is intimately tied to the political and economic processes
of capitalism, yet at the same time it cannot simply be reduced to the
needs of economic production. The fact that welfare provision takes
a variety of forms across the globe – but that each exists within the capitalist economic system – attests to the fact that welfare developments
reflect more than 'mere economics' and that a range of historical, political
and social factors are involved in producing different 'welfare settlements'.
     Saville suggests that we can identify three 'strands' which affect and
shape welfare:

   ... the economic and social requirements of an increasingly complex industrial
   society; ... the pressures which have come from the mass of the population as
   the perceptions of economic and social needs have gradually widened and
   become more explicit; ... [and] the political calculations of the ruling groups.
   (1983: 11)

Many elements within these three strands will, of course, overlap. For
example, capitalism's 'social requirements' are, in no small measure,
shaped by the pressure from the masses, which in turn will affect
the various calculations of different sections of capital over what form
welfare should take. In reality all strands merge and thus this division is
primarily for analytical purposes. This noted, let us look at these
'strands' in more detail.

Economic and social requirements of an increasingly complex industial society

In the earliest phases of capitalist expansion the basic problem for
the system is to 'adapt' or 'mould' a free labour force to the requirements of industry, to break 'old' customs and traditions, to enforce the
cash nexus onto social life and to try and coerce people to work hard and
participate in 'appropriate' and regulated social lives. Edward
Thompson (1991) discusses a range of traditional and cultural practices
which, in the eighteenth century, clashed with the requirements of
surplus value extraction and accumulation, leading to conflict over, for
example, the attempt to move work activity from a 'task-orientated' to a

'time-measured' operation and the struggle to break what he terms the 'moral economy of the crowd' and establish market principles based around the 'laws' of supply and demand. Linebaugh (1991) in his study of crime, criminal justice and capitalism in the same period shows how increased regulation, criminalisation and judicial murder (which he suggests amounted to 'thanatocracy' – political rule structured and maintained by fear of death) are used to enforce the new bourgeois moral and legal code on the developing working class.

Similarly, more obviously social legislation such as the Poor Laws in Britain were clearly shaped by the need to enforce 'moral responsibility' and the acceptance of wage labour by the poor and (certainly in the case of the 'new' Poor Law of 1834) to create a national labour market. As Pierson notes of the Poor Laws, their 'intent was clearly coercive' (1991: 53). To emphasise the point, Sir George Nicholls, one of the three Commissioners appointed to implement the New Poor Law, suggested that the workhouse 'compelled them [that is, the poor], *bred* them to be industrious, sober, provident, careful of themselves, of their parents and children'. He went on:

> I wish to see the Poor House looked to with dread by the labouring classes, and the reproach for being an inmate of it extended down from father to son. ... For without this, where is the needful stimulus to industry? (quoted in Novak, 1988: 31, 47)

But poverty, hunger and repression are rather blunt weapons of class domination. For capitalism to stabilise there is a need, both politically and socially, to move beyond the more extreme manifestations of naked class rule. Further, as capitalism develops, the very nature of the system means that if it is to survive and develop, a range of new economic, industrial and technological needs must be met. Welfare provisions partially meet both of these demands. As Saville notes:

> Industrial capitalism requires an increasing range of technical expertise; and that means an improving educational system. A labour force that suffers from a high incidence of disease – the result of dirt, poor housing, inadequate diet – is an inefficient labour force; and therefore the improvement of the physical environment in which working people live, the means of purchasing an adequate food supply, the availability of medical services in sufficient quantity and at a satisfactory level of competence, are all necessary if the industrial machine is to work at full stretch. (1983: 13)

Although welfare cannot be reduced to 'mere economics' it does, nevertheless, meet certain basic economic needs of the system. For capitalism to exist and expand there is a requirement for certain activities to be performed and for certain services to be provided. Capitalism needs relatively healthy workers to labour efficiently in the offices and factories, it needs some sort of support mechanism for non-labouring individuals such as children, the elderly, the unemployed (and this may include basic financial provision) and new workers must be educated and trained in the skills they will utilise while at work (and hence increase their productivity). These provisions can be provided by individual capitalists (or groups of capitalists), be based on some form of 'insurance scheme' with payments being given to private companies to provide these services or they can be provided by the state. Of course, it is not the case that without any of these systems or provisions capitalism would necessarily collapse – indeed there are sectors of the world economy where there is little in the way of health or educational provision, for example. But without these needs being met the system operates less efficiently and given the competitive nature of capitalism it results in units of capital (and indeed national economies) falling behind their international competitors, with the drive for capital accumulation being left to rest on the crudest forms of exploitation – via such measures as lengthening the working day, pitiful wages, intense regulation and policing of workers, all of which can be effective in the short-term but which increase political instability and discontent in the long-term.

Thus, the existence of basic welfare services reflects the recognition that while workers' labour may be commodified under capitalism, it cannot be abandoned completely to the market without potentially affecting present or future capital accumulation.

One central economic problem facing capitalism is related to the daily and intergenerational reproduction of labour. There is some evidence that the process of proletarianisation in the early to mid-nineteenth century was undermining the existence of the working-class family (Engels, 1884/1978). The long hours of work, combined with shift patterns, meant that in some districts 'family life' was completely disrupted. In these circumstances child rearing was problematic and domestic labour was left inadequately fulfilled. This created problems for both the bourgeoisie and the working class. For the bourgeoisie it threatened the existence of a future workforce: while existing profits could be guaranteed on the basis of the cheap labour of men, women and children (at least to the extent that they can ever be guaranteed, given the anarchy of the market system), the creation of surplus value in the future required the existence of a new generation of fit, healthy and disciplined workers. The break up of family life threatened all of this. From within the working class there were concerns that mass proletarianisation was having the effect of 'overstocking the labour market' and hence reducing wages. In these circumstances there were attempts from within both the bourgeoisie and working class to re-establish the family.

From the bourgeois perspective this matched their ideological commitment to the family while providing a network that would be responsible for childrearing, support for the elderly, sick and unemployed and would have a role in maintaining and supporting the existing workforce while socialising future generations of workers. From the working-class perspective it was suggested that by establishing a 'family wage' (that is, a wage earned by men and large enough to support an entire family), first children and then women could be withdrawn from the labour market. This would protect children from the worst horrors of the factory and allow women to engage in domestic labour to support the family. There was then a material reason why such a demand was raised and supported, although the family wage was rarely achieved in practice and represented a significant defeat for women.

Nevertheless, the result was the growth of family-related social policy. These were policies that initially restricted the hours of work and sectors of employment available to children and women but by the end of the nineteenth century such policies had become much more inter-ventionist, attempting to structure and control working-class family life. Today such concerns remain central to government policy strategies. Under both recent Conservative and New Labour governments family policy has taken on a vitally important ideological role (Lavalette and Mooney, 1999).

Here we can identify the linked 'social requirements' of developing capitalism mentioned by Saville. Capitalism must encourage workers to work hard, to be productive and committed to producing good quality work. But this is complicated by the fact that the system depersonalises and alienates individuals. Work is regimented, stressful and controlled, social life isolating and commodified. In these conditions, if the system as a whole is to function it 'must encourage the general sentiment that the future will be better than the present or the past' (Saville, 1983: 13). Welfare expansion (especially state welfare expansion) is part of the attempt to 'legitimise' capitalism, to win people politically to the system. Welfare provision seems to offer workers something for nothing, or it at least offers a collective benefit paid out of taxes for the care of the old, the sick or those unable to work. It seems to represent an arena where the market does not necessarily dominate and it apparently proves that the expansion of capitalism benefits us all – the 'appearance' is of a benign set of services constructed around some uniformly accepted set of values, the essential underlying relations is of a system which is in no small part constructed to meet some vital economic, social and political needs of the system as a whole.

There are two further points worth emphasising. First, the services created by the expansion of welfare remain structured by the general laws of commodity production within capitalism. This is an important point. Many Marxist writers on welfare try to distinguish service provision on the basis of whether it is 'commodified' (that is, provided by private, for-profit companies) or 'decommodified' (provided by the state) (see, for example, Ginsburg, 1992). Such a distinction draws on the work of Esping-Andersen (1990) and is also based on trends within academic Marxism which view the state as in some way relatively 'autonomous' from the needs of economic production.

72185

In his popular and authoritative study of comparative 'welfare regimes' Esping-Andersen (1990) has made extensive use of the concept of 'de-commodification' to explain variation in state welfare provision. He suggests that the expansion of 'social rights' and state provided universal benefits results in a 'loosening of the pure commodity status' of the wage labourer. He continues:

> De-commodification occurs when a service is rendered as a matter of right, and when a person can maintain a livelihood without reliance on the market ... the concept refers to the degree to which individuals, or families, can uphold a socially acceptable standard of living independently of market participation. (1990: 21–22, 37)

The political conclusions of Esping-Andersen's thesis are revealed when he suggests that the ideal-type decommodified welfare regime is the social-democratic welfare state. The argument, in other words, is developed as a sophisticated defence of the politics of social democracy (see below).

But the distinction 'commodified/decommodified' is unhelpful. As should be clear from what we have already said, much state welfare development was a direct consequence of an attempt to manage the problems of capitalism – with its prime goal the maintenance and smooth running of the accumulation process and the system of generalised commodity production. Further, as Guy Standing (1982) points out, Esping-Andersen's concept of 'decommodified labour' rests, rather confusingly, on a general system of commodified labour! In other words, the system rests on exploited wage labourers paying taxes and insurance payments to support themselves and others during periods when they do not have full-time work.

Moreover, as a device for distinguishing modes of welfare delivery, the distinction fails to move beyond the 'surface appearance' of society to address the real relations of welfare under capitalism – it loses sight of the general aspects of welfare within the wider social totality by focusing on a secondary aspect, the specific manifestations of forms of welfare delivery. For example, private and state health or educational provision both fulfil the same basic economic functions of providing relatively fit and educated workers. Both sectors employ commodified labour who neither control their work activity nor provide a service structured around the principle of meeting people's needs. The demands of 'cost management', 'efficiency', 'value for money' and so on affect and shape both service delivery and workers conditions in both the private and state sector. Moreover the distinction between 'commodified' and 'decommodified' services can lead to a misunderstanding of their political content where decommodified, nationalised welfare industries are viewed almost as islands of socialism (or social democracy) in a capitalist sea. But as a whole range of studies over the years have emphasised (see, for example,

Penketh, 2001; Wilson, 2001; Woodward, 2001), within nationalised welfare services, from a service user perspective class inequality, racism and women's oppression remain deeply embedded and institutionalised in the functioning and operationalisation of their service delivery; worker rights are no more advanced than other spheres of the economy; and nationalised welfare services are embroiled within relationships with a range of (national and local) state agencies, private industries (local, national and multi-national) and financial institutions – they are part, to adapt Navarro (1989) slightly, of a an increasingly intricate 'welfare-industrial complex' and are thus deeply embedded in the general production process.

To take just one example, there have been several studies of the often intimate relationship between the National Health Service in Britain and the pharmaceuticals industry. Widgery, quoting the esteemed medical journal the *Lancet*, noted in 1988 (and hence the figures may now represent a significant underestimation) that:

> Doctors have about £3,200 each spent on them per year [by the drug companies], including over a hundredweight of literature and gifts ... At present rates, the average doctor can expect to have £50,000 spent on 'education' by the drug companies during his professional lifetime ... The drug companies provide the most insistent form of postgraduate education most GP's receive ... drug companies have direct links with medical faculties ... [where some] 'professorial chairs and important positions in the medical world also act as paid advisers to industrial concerns'. (1988: 101–102)

Although this relationship is often very 'friendly' the size of some NHS suppliers clearly puts them in a very powerful position in any deals they strike with the NHS. In January 2000 two companies, GlaxoWellcome and SmithKline Beecham, merged to become 'Britain's largest company and the biggest force in world pharmaceuticals' (*Observer*, 16 January 2000). GlaxoSmithKline was expected to earn approximately £15 billion a year from sales of drugs across the globe and in the process became the NHS's biggest drug provider. The company undertakes both drug research and production but the Royal College of General Practitioners suggested GlaxoSmithKline's monopolistic position was leading to substantial increases in drug prices and the NHS being 'held to ransom' by the company (*Daily Record*, 18 January 2000); before merger GlaxoWellcome threatened to curtail research into flu drugs because the NHS was refusing to pay the companies price for their 'Relenza' flu treatment.

It is clear that Esping-Andersen, Ginsburg and others view 'decommodification' of services as a significant element of a more egalitarian and progressive social system. As a consequence they are at best ambivalent about the political basis of such 'decommodified' welfare systems as Cuba, China and the former Eastern Bloc. As we argued in Chapter 1, however, there is nothing 'progressive' about these societies. Like their

Western counterparts the welfare systems of Cuba, China, the former Soviet Union and the countries of the Eastern Bloc are, and were, not primarily concerned with meeting human need but of establishing fit, healthy and educated workers, ideologically committed to the existing state system (part of the attempt to legitimate state capitalism in these countries.)

This does not, however, imply political neutrality when it comes to questions of state versus private delivery of welfare. While it is essential to note the ways in which welfare reinforces various inequalities and forms of oppression and exploitation in society and to acknowledge that state welfare remains embedded within the process of generalised commodity production, it is also important to appreciate that the existence of state welfare institutions and social policies have also brought direct benefits to working-class families. To take an obvious example, the existence of a national health service in Britain represents a very significant gain for the working class – probably the single most important reform of the post-war era. In the US, where health care remains overwhelmingly privatised, somewhere in the region of 60 per cent of the population has no, or inadequate, healthcare insurance (Ginsburg, 1992; Maidment and Dawson, 1999) and during the 1990s 'a million more workers ... lost their health coverage each year ... Last year [1998] the number of people without health coverage rose to 45 million, 16.3 per cent of the population' (Smith, 1999: 15). In the majority of countries across the globe, sickness, illness or injury means workers face a range of medical bills, many of which simply cannot be paid. Despite encroaching privatisation and spiralling prescription charges, the existence of the NHS in Britain at least means that the direct costs of illness are met by the state. More generally, however miserly child benefits and family income maintenance policies may be, the money they provide is often vital to working-class family budgets. The existence of a comprehensive education system, free at the point of use, allows most children at least to read, write and undertake basic mathematics. Similarly, the existence of social, community and welfare services can offer some advice and even limited financial support to families facing the most biting poverty (even if these services have been severely curtailed in recent years).

Such state welfare provision – or more generally those provisions that are free or heavily subsidised at the point of delivery – can be identified as part of a collectively consumed social wage. That is, not a direct wage payment paid by an individual capitalist to a worker but the:

> ... sum of the collective benefits which are transferred to individuals or families in both cash and kind via the state. (Bryson, 1992: 32)

That said, the demand for state provision is not the end of the story. Given the ways in which such state welfare provision reinforce inequality, oppression and exploitation, it is also necessary to argue for state provisions which are universalistic, which are anti-oppressive and which promote equality, and against those which stigmatise, divide and promote selective forms of delivery.

Pierson suggests that Marx thought it may be possible for workers to obtain 'limited social reform' but that 'widespread state welfare ... was inconsistent with the demands of capital accumulation ... [an account which] mainstream classical Marxists saw little reason to amend' (1991: 49). Yet this claim overstates the case. Within the classical tradition, for example, there is Marx's writing on factory legislation and the working day (Marx, 1867/1976) and his writings on the formation of wage rates (Marx, 1865/1996), all of which have direct and indirect implications for analysis of welfare. Pierson also ignores the arguments put forward by Lenin and other Russian Marxists for a state social security system in pre-revolutionary Russia (Lenin, 1912), as well as the practical but far-reaching welfare developments that occurred in the difficult circumstances of post-revolutionary Russia, discussed by Solomon and Hutchinson (1990) and Stites (1989 and 1990).

Together, to quote Rosdolsky, these works emphasise that wage rates, material consumption, and various social and political reforms:

> ... are themselves the products of *history* ... [which in no small part] depend on the demands which the working class raises and succeeds in achieving in its political and trade-union struggle against the capitalist class. (1977: 283)

Marxism, therefore, does not rule out *a priori* the possibility of significant social reforms or welfarism taking place within capitalism – just as it did not rule out the possibility of 'democratisation' of the political process with the expansion of the vote (Draper, 1978). Whether, and to what extent, welfare expands depends on how the class struggle in its fullest sense progresses and unfolds within society can only be seen as the product of history.

Welfare as social control

The expansion of the various 'economic and social requirements' so far discussed does not mean that the state's 'social control' functions become any less important. As Novak notes: 'The maintenance of capitalism ... require[s] a series of incentives and punishments' (1988: 30). Bruce Andersen, for example, advisor to Conservative prime ministers in Britain during the 1980s and 1990s, argued that post-War welfarism had: 'constructed slums full of layabouts and sluts whose progeny are two-legged beasts. We cannot cure this by family, religion and self-help. So we will have to rely on repression' (quoted in Jones, 1998: 16).

Within the criminal justice system in Britain there are continuing attempts to restrict and control accepted civil rights and liberties, including restrictions on the right to trial by jury, and there is a continuing, seemingly inexorable growth of the prison population (Ferguson, 1994; Jones, 1998; Young, 1999). In the US, according to the *Observer* (8 February 1998) there are six million people under supervision within the criminal justice system – including 40 per cent of all young Blacks in Washington, DC. As James notes:

> Currently, some 70 percent of the nearly 2 million imprisoned in U.S. jails, prisons, and detention centers are 'minorities', or (poor) 'people of color'; approximately 200,000 mentally ill people are incarcerated … By June 1977 there were 138,000 women incarcerated in the United States; triple the number since 1985 … Most of the women … are non-violent offenders convicted of economic crimes or drug-related offences. Eighty percent are mothers, eighty percent are poor, and the majority are 'women of color'. … The United States has the highest incarceration rate in the industrialized world. (2000: x, xi)

Jones (1998) suggests that what we are witnessing is a brutalising turn within social policy in both Britain and the US, where:

> [The] increasing use of prisons and the ongoing onslaught on welfare entitlements are part and parcel of the new politics of repression and pessimism by which we are encouraged to understand the most impoverished and vulnerable as being beyond redemption and that their position in society is an accurate reflection of their worthlessness. (1998 : 21)

But it is not just imprisonment that is on the rise. In the US the death penalty was reinstated in 1976 and over 600 people had been executed by the end of the twentieth century. This includes the execution of juveniles, individuals with mental health problems and political opponents. The US is one of only six countries (along with Iran, Nigeria, Saudi Arabia, Pakistan and Yeman) to have executed a juvenile in the last ten years – but it has executed more than the combined total in these other states (*Guardian*, 12 January 2000). In 18 US states the death penalty can be imposed on 16-year-olds and in five more it can be imposed on 17-year-olds (*Guardian*, 10 January 2000) – all of which breaches the UN Convention on the Rights of the Child which the US was centrally involved in creating, although it continues to refuse to ratify the document!

In August 2000 in the state of Texas, Oliver Cruz was executed by lethal injection despite the fact that he had been 'tested as mentally disabled and could barely read or write with an IQ between 63 and 76' (*Guardian*, 10 August 2000). Cruz became the 226th execution in Texas since 1982, his being the 141st death-warrant signed by the then self-styled 'caring conservative' Governor, now President, George W. Bush Jnr.

Left-wing political opponents in the US have always been dealt with in the most brutal fashion by the police and judicial systems (Seal, 1970; Davies, 1998; James, 2000). Early in 2001 the US was still trying to execute Mumia Abu-Jamal, a member of the Black Panther Party from the age of

15 and by the early 1970s a well-known radical journalist known as the 'voice of the oppressed'. In 1981 he was framed by police for murder and waits on death row despite an international campaign for his release (*Socialist Worker*, 8 January 2000; Williams, 2000).

Those on death row in the states are overwhelmingly Black, poor and the victims of a system where 'capital punishment' is a verdict meted out to those with no capital – a point emphasised by Borger who notes that 'courts assign poor defendants lawyers who are often on low pay and have few qualifications. One court [in Texas] assigned 14 death penalty appeals to two former clerks with no experience in capital cases' (2000: 15). This all reinforces the case that: 'There is a good deal of historical evidence to support the [Marxist] social control thesis' (Pierson, 1991: 53).

But social controls also operate, perhaps less spectacularly, within the daily functioning of welfare services and institutions. This includes attempts to control and regulate the behaviour of young people within schools (in part through what Bowles and Gintis (1976) have termed the 'hidden curriculum' of discipline and obedience to authority) or in their locality by implementing curfews and 'anti-social legislation' using a range of agencies such as the police, social services, school educational welfare services (truancy officers) and the wider juvenile 'justice' system (Jones and Novak, 1999; Lavalette and Mooney, 1999). It also includes trying to control the behaviour of strikers by restricting their entitlements to benefits (Jones and Novak, 1985); regulating and controlling family relationships or financial provision for children after relationship break-down via, for example, the Child Support Agency or social work/services departments; and ensuring that 'the conditions that are placed on state benefits ... are often orientated not to the meeting of recipients' needs but rather to the requirement not to undermine the dynamics of the labour market' (Pierson, 1991: 53).

'Social control' also operates at the level of ideology (reinforcing nationalism, racism or sexism, for example), of restricting liberty (the right not to work, for example) or by reflecting the dominant values of society and repressing, oppressing or discriminating against a range of 'alternative' life-styles and modes of living and so on. Social policies attempt to determine how we live our lives, what are appropriate child-rearing practices, what are legitimate families, and how we should behave to qualify for benefits.

Recently, feminist, gay and lesbian and anti-racist histories have drawn attention to the ways in which social policies and welfare institutions attempt to control our lives by operating with a set of assumptions about how we live (or should live) our lives. In particular much welfare policy is based on familial assumptions (Merrick, 1996). It assumes that most women will be at home to raise children and provide domestic labour, that the family unit (of one adult male, one adult female and children) is the best site for child rearing, and hence that gay families are illegitimate (Wilson, 2001) and that families have the responsibility to finance their children's higher education or provide care 'in a community setting' for elderly or sick relatives. It also reflects judgements about who should qualify for welfare benefits or services, invariably including a notion of 'citizenship' that questions the legitimacy of claims for benefits from 'outsiders', such as asylum seekers (Cook, 1998; Mynott, 2000).

Finally in this section, it is important to re-emphasise that welfare provision, its expansion and contraction, is intimately linked to the general process of accumulation. At certain periods the system has the ability to deliver certain reforms or forms of welfare provision. The long post-War boom certainly eased the expansion of the various welfare systems in the advanced economies. In contrast, during periods of economic crisis and slump there is a drive to reduce or cut government expenditure. Whether such cuts are achievable for the ruling class is a political question that depends, more than any other factor, on the collective response of the working class and the activities of the leadership of the labour and trade union movement. Politically, it is not an inevitable process but a potentially risky exercise that may provoke a collective working class response, as the ruling class in France and Italy found out during the 1990s (Bensaid, 1996; Woolfries, 2000).

However, there are also limits beyond which cuts in service provision start to affect economic performance and the accumulation process. Thus all advanced capitalist economies need to invest in education and health systems, for example, to enhance their economic competitiveness, to legitimate the system, and to provide a degree of social control. At times of economic crisis they attempt to reduce social spending but such cuts are fraught with difficulties, which can lead to uncertainty and prevarication within the ruling class. To emphasise the point here, let us mention the social policy strategies of the two main international finance institutions: the IMF and the World Bank. In the 1980s both organisations were committed to Structural Adjustment Programmes (SAPs). Central to SAP's were demands that welfare and social provision should be cut. By the early 1990s, however, the World Bank started to change track slightly, increasingly arguing that economic growth and expansion required investment in 'human capital' via, for instance, investment in education services, some basic forms of social provision and the amelioration of the worst manifestations of poverty. This is not to suggest that the World Bank is 'better' or even 'more progressive' than the IMF but it does indicate that welfare provides some basic needs for the system and hence cutting welfare can create problems for national capitals and their ability to continue with their competitive accumulation drive (see Chapter 8).

Thus welfare provision performs a number of roles in society. It meets economic needs, increases labour productivity and is an essential part of the process of generalised commodity production. It is part of a process of legitimating capitalism and creating an ideological veneer to cover the exploitative and oppressive structures of society. It is built upon, and reinforces, familial ideology, which reinforces women's oppression, and it attempts to structure, control and regulate our lives in numerous ways. But this is still only part of the picture. As we noted, welfarism can also be part of the 'social wage' and in this sense it can bring material benefits to workers. This being the case, it is perhaps not surprising that welfare provision is also directly affected by pressures from below and it is to a consideration of such pressures that we now turn.

Pressure from the mass of the population

The second general strand Saville noted was that welfarism is affected by the presence, demands and pressure of the mass of ordinary people. Once again it is necessary to unpack this. Such pressure can be understood in two ways: through the politics of reformism and through the contentious politics of collective action.

The politic of reformism

The organised presence of the working class movement has been central to the politics of reformism, social democracy or labourism and within this tradition social welfare has been an important element of their goal to 'humanise' capitalism. As ideology and political practice, reformism has many roots and variations but central to most conceptions are the following claims. First, that capitalism has changed significantly since the nineteenth century. The capitalist class has increasingly lost its dominant position in society as it has been brought under control by the state and witnessed the nationalisation of core areas of economic activity. This is a consequence of the 'democratisation process', which reflects the expansion of the vote, the organised presence of a strong and centralised trade union movement and a social democratic political party able to reflect working class demands. Secondly, under conditions of sustained economic growth and enduring social democratic governmental incumbency, substantial welfare improvements can be achieved for the betterment of society as a whole. Thirdly, for these conditions to be met there should be strong class identification and correspondingly weak cleavages along religious, ethnic or linguistic lines (Pierson, 1991: 31). Under these conditions it is thought possible to transform capitalism towards socialism via the institutions of parliamentary democracy – replacing the need for any revolutionary transformation of society. The British Labour Party theorist of the post-War epoch, Anthony Crosland in his book *The Future of Socialism*, suggested:

> Today the capitalist business class has lost ... [its] ... commanding position. The change in the balance of economic power is reflected in, and may be inferred from, three developments. First, certain decisive sources and levers of economic

power have been transferred from private business to other hands; and new levers have emerged, again concentrated in other hands than theirs. Secondly, the outcome of clashes of group or class economic interests is markedly less favourable to private employers than it used to be. Thirdly, the social attitudes and behaviour of the business class have undergone a significant change, which appears to reflect a pronounced loss of strength and self-confidence ... (1956: 26)

Focusing directly on state welfare, Stephens, writing in 1979, argued that in Sweden the social democratic welfare state was:

... developed by a strongly organized and highly centralized trades union movement ... in cooperation with a social democratic government that remained in government for 44 years ... the welfare state is characterized by high levels of expenditure and progressive financing and thus represents a transformation of capitalism towards socialism. (1979: 129)

While Furniss and Tilton argued:

... that a democratic majority, backed by a committed labor movement, can capture and employ political power to create a more decent society along the lines of a social welfare state. (1979: 93)

Finally, from Esping-Andersen:

A theory of welfare-state developments must ... [consider] three factors in particular ... the nature of class mobilization (especially of the working class); class-political coalition structures; and the historical legacy of regime institutionalization (1990: 29).

For these theorists the presence of an organised working class, principally through a centralised trade union movement, gives the party (Labour, Socialist or Social Democratic) the leverage to wrestle concessions out of capital. In the process it can further democratise society and create a 'decent society along the lines of a social welfare state'. Hence, in no small part, they are claiming that the growth and elaboration of various welfare systems is a direct result of social democratic party hold on government.

It would be absurd to deny that parliamentary politics matters or that social democratic or labourist parties have not affected state welfare provision in various countries. Marxists have always recognised that laws passed in Parliament, conflicts between national politicians, the actions of the state both at home and abroad, and the activities of various state officials are all important in shaping the tenor and form of political debate in any particular nation. More specifically in Britain, for example, while a broad 'Keynesian-Beveridgean' consensus was established between the major political parties in the post-War era, if the Conservative Party, rather than Labour, had been elected in 1945 the welfare state would have been significantly different in a number of key areas – most notably in terms of health care provision which would not have taken the form of a nationalised NHS. Nevertheless there are both theoretical and empirical issues which question the potential of reformist parties to deliver social reforms in all circumstances.

First, the theoretical problems. Central to the social democratic case is a claim that the basic drives and goals of the capitalist economy have been tamed to some degree. In Bernstein's writings on Germany at the end of the nineteenth century it was the development of cartels which had overcome the crisis tendency of capitalism, for Crosland nationalisation and state direction of the economy had established a sort of half-way house between capitalism and socialism, while today, theorists of the 'Third Way' like Anthony Giddens suggest that consumerism, the growth of information technology and economic globalisation have transformed the system out of all recognition. We deal with some of these themes in Chapters 3, 8 and 9, but here let's briefly note that while capitalism is constantly changing its organisational forms (from small family firms, to cartels, to multinationals for example) the basic social relations, and with it the horrors of inequality, oppression and exploitation, remain remarkably constant: as we saw in Chapter 1, the rich and powerful enrich themselves even more on the labour of the vast majority. Further, the basic contradictions of capitalism mean that the boom/bust cycle with deepening economic crises has not been overcome, as the severe crises of the last few years in Japan, South Korea, Russia and various Latin American countries testify.

Secondly, reformist parties may be elected to government, but this is not the same as control over the state which is much wider and includes many powerful, unelected interests (such as the police, army, judiciary, top civil service, the central Banks). Further, as Miliband (1972) emphasised in his history of the Labour Party, the government does not control capital but is itself extremely vulnerable to pressure from capital to ensure it follows 'appropriate' pro-business policies.

Finally, the ideological commitment of social democratic parties is to the interests of both nation and class. On the one hand their goal is national efficiency, national economic improvement, success within the capitalist economic system and pursuing national interests both at home and abroad. On the other hand there is a set of values structured around overcoming the worst manifestations of poverty and inequality and expanding social benefits for all. The concern is to 'humanise' capitalism by re-directing some of the wealth created by an expanding capitalism to tackle some of the social problems capitalism creates. Of course during periods of economic expansion it is possible to some extent to pursue both these sets of goals, but at times of economic recession and slump both sets of values clash. During these periods social democratic governments have repeatedly pursued the interests of national capital and national economic efficiency at the expense of the interests of their own working class constituency who vote them into office. 'Old' Labour Prime Minister Harold Wilson, for example, faced with speculative pressure on the pound in 1964 revealed that while devaluation:

> ... would have given us a year or two breathing space ... that would have enabled us to carry through our positive generous programmes of social reform ... the national interest was one hundred per cent the other way ... [further] there are many people overseas, including governments, marketing boards, central banks and others, who left their money in the form of sterling balances, on the assumption that the value of sterling would be maintained. To have let them down would have been ... a betrayal of trust. (quoted in Miliband, 1972: 361–2)

Wilson was not the first Labour Prime Minister, nor was he the last, to put the general interests of capital and of international financiers, governments and others above those of workers. More recently, in the 1980s and 1990s Socialist, Social Democratic and Labour governments in Greece, Spain, France, Sweden, Italy, Germany and Britain have all pursued welfare cutting and public expenditure reduction programmes in an attempt to appease the interests of national and international capital.

In addition to these theoretical criticisms, key assumptions of the social democratic perspective can also be questioned on empirical grounds. Thus, in most states welfare developments were initiated by conservative or liberal parties – rather than social democratic ones – and even at the high point of welfare state expansion conservative and liberal parties were not opposed to welfare settlements. Indeed in Britain, for example, more council houses were built in any four-year period by the Tories in the 1950s than there was by Labour in any equivalent period and, perhaps even more surprisingly, more comprehensive schools were opened while Margaret Thatcher was Minister of Education than at any other time (Lowe, 1993).

Also, in the post-War era the growth and domination of State policies structured around Keynesian economic management was central to the social democratic case that the state (or the government) could control and direct the economy utilising the wealth generated to develop and expand social welfare. But by the late 1970s Keynesianism increasingly went out of fashion as various forms of 'monetarism' became the dominant governmental economic paradigm. With this change government commitment to demand management of the economy and policies of full-employment were abandoned – seriously affecting social democracy's rationale and claims as the vehicle to deliver significant social improvement (see Chapter 8).

Class mobilisation

As noted above Esping-Andersen (1990) does discuss the concept of 'class mobilisation' as a factor shaping welfare formation but in a very particular sense. For him, this conception is used to describe the political activity of the official trade union movement (or the trade union bureaucracy) and the dominant social democratic party and their chances of electoral success, rather than welfare struggles from below involving large numbers of working-class people. Yet as Jones and Novak suggest: 'Welfare has always been at the heart of class struggle ... In the final analysis it is a concern for human welfare ... that has fuelled the struggle for social transformation' (2000: 34). Class struggle and collective action *do* affect welfare, sometimes in an obvious way, while at other times the relationship is less direct.

The general extent, nature and form of the class struggle and how this configures society, in the process promoting welfare, needs to be recognised. Charlton (2000a), for example, notes the way in which a growing and visible working class presence, combined with their increasing class combativity, were central elements of the process of establishing more corporatist forms of welfare in Britain at the turn of the twentieth century. In this case, it is the nature and conflicts of class society that prompts welfarism. It is the potential of working class collective action (or fear of this potential) that motivates social policy. Examples of this process might include Bismarck's social legislation in nineteenth-century Germany which was clearly tied in with his anti-socialist laws, or the cross-party consensus in Britain on the need for reform at the end of the Second World War, reflected in the statement of the British Tory MP Quentin Hogg (later Lord Hailsham) who claimed in 1943: 'If you do not give the people social reform, they are going to give you social revolution' (*Hansard*, 17 February 1943). This is clearly part of what we termed earlier the 'legitimation process' and part of an attempt to divert discontent before it can fully develop.

But sometimes, substantial waves of working class protest can affect social policy more directly and immediately. A few examples drawn from a variety of states will illustrate the point. In France the social welfare settlement was directly affected by working class collective protest and action which were part of the popular front struggles of 1936. In February of that year there were one million strikers in Paris, with mass factory occupations. As a direct consequence wages increased, the working week was restricted and paid holidays guaranteed (including the 'institutionalisation' of a summer holiday in August which remains in place today) (Danos and Gibelin, 1986). Again in France, in 1995/96, it was the threat of cuts in the social welfare budget (the so-called Juppé plan) which brought two million people out onto the streets, defeated the cuts and ignited an atmosphere of class conflict which continues to rock the country (Woolfries, 2000).

In the late 1960s and early 1970s, Italy was in the midst of a substantial wave of protest. As Ginsborg notes: 'As a result, the period from 1969 onwards saw the politicians mediate collective protest by a sudden increase in reform legislation... [these include] political reforms... [and] a number of social ones' (1990: 327). The list of social reforms includes an upgrading of pensions, divorce legalisation and expansion of housing provision. In the US social legislation from the 'New Deal' era of the 1930s (including the Social Security Act 1935) were partially a response to the economic and political crisis of those years, the 'presence' of organised labour and substantial industrial conflict – by dockers, miners, teamsters, autoworkers, textile and mill workers (Brecher, 1997). While in Japan, Gould suggests: 'It was only in response to the rice riots of 1918 that the government introduced the first genuine social security measure' (1993: 35–6) (although he fails to add that the various insurance and worker compensation acts of the immediate post-War years were instigated against the backdrop of what Halliday (1975) terms the 'post-surrender explosion' of the Japanese working class movement).

More directly, because certain forms of welfare delivery or social policies bring material or social benefits to the working class, social movements of the oppressed have often developed to defend particular welfare settlements or demand the expansion of various forms of provision. Again a few examples will illustrate the point.

One of the most notable examples in Britain arose as a consequence of the Rent Strikes which took place in Clydeside during World War One. The move to a war economy meant that there was a rapid expansion of war-related industries in Glasgow. Labour was sucked into the city to work in the shipyards, engineering factories and related industries and as a result there was a severe housing shortage. Landlords now had control of a valuable and scarce resource and put up their rents. The response from sections of the working class in Glasgow was to go on rent strike. These were led and organised by working-class women and quickly gained the support of a wide range of working-class activists and trade unionists. When the strikers were pulled in front of the debtors' courts there was a mass walk-out from many workplaces on Clydeside, the women were released and the Government introduced the Rent Restriction Act which pegged rents to their pre-War level and prohibited landlords from increasing rents for the duration of the war (Damer, 1980; 2000).

Clegg and Gough (2000), in their analysis of the various campaigns to defend abortion rights in both Britain and the US, argue that in Britain the joint action of working-class women and men, from various socialist political parties, women's groups and trade unions have been vital to defend a woman's right to choose, whereas in the US, they suggest, the absence (or at least the weakness) of a generalised class response to the question or reproductive politics has led to significant retreat in this area. Elsewhere Lavalette and Mooney (2000b) have argued that the poll tax in Britain, implemented by the last Thatcher government between 1989 and 1992, met such a fierce response from working-class communities because it was a clear generalised attack on workers' standard of living, on local authority welfare provision and on local government accountability. Thus attacks on welfare represent a potentially explosive source of grievance generating collective action by the oppressed and exploited.

Finally, a less documented area of working class pressure on welfare (at least by theorists of welfare and social policy in the academy) is the extent to which welfare workers can collectively shape welfare delivery. The expansion of welfare services has created a vast army of welfare workers – teachers, social workers, community workers, health care practitioners, benefit workers and a range of 'ancillary staff' throughout the various welfare systems – who are required to sell their labour power in order to survive and without whose work activity the various services would not be provided. The vast majority of these workers do not own or control the various tools they require to undertake their work tasks, and the vast majority of them find themselves subject to the authority of others while at work (various levels of managers who have effective control over both or either of the labour process and service/product delivery system). What we have witnessed, especially in the post Second World War era, is the 'proletarianisation' of vast numbers of welfare workers and linked to this, the growth of a range of trade unions representing welfare workers. For example, the largest trade union in Britain is Unison which represents workers in the National Health Service, local government (including social work and social service workers, workers in housing departments, welfare advice workers, community workers) and a range of workers in the voluntary and privatised welfare services.

Over recent years welfare workers have flexed their industrial muscle – both to defend service provision and to protect and improve their own working conditions: welfare workers in France have been centrally involved in the various disputes that continue to rock the country (Bensaid, 1996); in Britain local government workers in many parts of the country have fought privatisation (Lavalette and Flanagan, 2001), while hospital workers in the early 1980s were involved in organising rolling regional general strikes to defend the NHS from privatisation (Lavalette and Mooney, 2000b).

Thus direct class mobilisations can have an important role in shaping and defending forms of welfare delivery and are an important part of the struggle of the oppressed to obtain a better world.

The political calculations of the ruling class

As we can see, there are a number of tendencies promoting and shaping social welfare. The precise form welfare takes, however, will also reflect the political calculations of, and divisions within, the ruling class – Saville's third strand affecting welfare development. As we have already emphasised, the interests of 'capital in general' promotes some system-wide shared class interests on behalf of the bourgeoisie – for example, to maintain the profitability of the system, to maintain and increase the level of exploitation over the working class and so on. But capitalism is a world of 'many competing capitals' – each with their own specific short-, mid- and long-term interests which creates divisions over a range of political, social and economic questions within the ruling class. For example, when central banks meet to set interest rates within national economies it is not uncommon to hear groups in favour of interest rate cuts (for example, to boost exports), those in favour of raising the interest rate (for example, importers of components) and those advocating no change (for example, to establish 'stability' on the financial markets). In Britain during the 1990s and early years of the twenty-first century there has been considerable division within the ruling class over the question of further European integration, the adoption of European social legislation and whether Britain should sign-up to the single European currency. As we noted earlier, there has been some divergence between the World Bank and the IMF over the appropriate strategies needed to stabilise and develop capitalism in a number of 'Third World' economies – in particular the appropriate social welfare strategies needed to encourage economic growth.

It may, in the abstract, be in the interests of 'capital in general' for certain welfare developments to take place, but in the real world of 'many competing capitals' different capitalists or sections of the ruling class may view their direct economic interests rather differently.

Finally, there are other divisions and aspects of 'ruling elite calculation' that can affect welfare. It is important to recognise that various interest groups within the ruling class can have an input on the political process and social policy development: the Catholic church in Italy or Ireland, or both the openly pro-business parties in the US (the Democrats and the Republicans), for example. Occasionally the input of particular indivi-duals within the state or the state bureaucracy is important: Chadwick, Beveridge and Bismark, for example, have had an important effect in shaping welfare delivery, and not just within their own countries. The form and intensity of the economic and political relationships and competition between states can also affect welfare choices: the effect of the US Marshall Plan on post-War Western European societies (including their welfare settlements) is clearly important, the state structures and welfare commitments of various countries in Latin America, Africa and Southeast Asia reflect their subordinate political, economic and military relationship with the US and various international financial institutions tied to the interests of the advanced capitalist economies. While, more benignly, states and state officials have often copied each others' models of economic and social policy delivery in what is known as 'policy transfer'. For example, Japan after the Meiji Restoration (that is, according to Moore (1973), Japan's 'bourgeois revolution from above') consciously attempted to follow the 'German model' of social and economic development (Gould, 1993). Or, more recently, the formation of various supra-national state bodies and organisations has brought with it increased pressures for policy transfer or harmonisation (for example, the various UN Conventions or EU Directives are a case in point).

Thus the political calculations of different sections of the ruling class (and often the conflict and competition between sections of that class) affect the general political process and this can directly affect the development, expansion and form of welfare delivery. Class and class struggle, therefore, are at the heart of welfare – themes we address directly in Chapters 3 and 4.

Part 2

Marxism and Welfare

---

3 'We are all classless nowadays': The Class Structure Today

As we noted in Chapters 1 and 2, the world is marked by vast and growing inequalities. At the top of the heap are the 450 dollar billionaires, at the bottom the 3 billion who live on less than £1.30 a day. While the minority live with undreamt of wealth and opulence, 840 million people worldwide are malnourished, 2.6 billion people lack access to basic sanitation and one-quarter of the global burden of disease is due to preventable or easily curable diseases such as measles, worm infections and malaria (Health Matters, 2000: 2–3). Such inequalities blight the modern world. Economic inequalities between countries have been widening steadily for 200 years, yet, it is not simply a case of global inequality divided along the lines of a rich North and an impoverished South as inequalities within countries (in the North and the South) are also widening. For example, in America, by far the richest country on the planet, Edward Luttwak has noted that:

> The United States is on its way to acquiring the income distribution characteristics of a Third World country, with a truly very rich top 1 per cent, and a significant minority (roughly 12 per cent) which remains below the official poverty line even though fully employed, forty hours a week, fifty weeks a year. (1999: 67)

Similarly the vast numbers of people living and working in truly appalling conditions in countries in Latin America, Africa or Southeast Asia contrast sharply with the lifestyles of the wealthy within these countries who continue to enrich themselves at the expense of their 'fellow citizens'. John Pilger (2001) notes the contrast in Indonesia between the young workers – working directly or indirectly for multinationals like Nike, GAP, Adidas and Reebok – who can work 36-hour shifts for as little as 72 pence a day, and the indigenous elite who shop in down-town Jakarta and lavish themselves with Jaguar cars, Versace suits, diamonds and the various other trappings of wealth. There are, therefore, growing inequalities across the world – in the 'rich North' and the 'impoverished South' – and these are a direct consequence of the class system and structure of modern capitalism. It is the competitive basis of the system that drives capitalists to accumulate and reinvest – but this, in turn, requires that they increase the rate and intensity of exploitation of those they employ. Wealth and poverty are linked, they are relational – the poor are poor *because* the rich are rich.

The sense of a growing divide and increasing social polarisation is articulated popularly as part of an everyday language of 'haves' and 'have nots', 'us' and 'them' and 'rich' and 'poor'. The findings of numerous attitude surveys and opinion polls highlight that class continues to 'matter' to the majority of people in Britain, for example. Findings from the *British Social Attitudes Survey* emphasise that people think in class terms. In its 1996 Report (Park et al., 1996), two-thirds of those questioned agreed that there was 'one law for the rich and one for the poor' and that 'ordinary people did not get their fare share of the nation's wealth' (quoted in Adonis and Pollard, 1998: 11). In a poll for Radio 4's *Today* programme, conduced by ICM in 1998, 55 per cent of respondents defined themselves as working class and 41 per cent as middle class, while, according to Wilson (1999: 3), between 1966 and 1997 the number of people categorising themselves as belonging to the middle class has risen by only 5.5 per cent in Britain. Finally, Gallup have conducted an annual attitude survey in Britain since 1961 and one question they have asked is: 'Do you think that there is a class struggle in this country?' In 1961, 56 per cent of respondents thought there was, this reached 70 per cent in the 1980s and 81 per cent in 1995 (quoted in Adonis and Pollard, 1998: 3). Of course, people's attitudes to class is not the same as 'class location', as we will argue below, but this evidence suggests that public attitudes and experiences reflect a broad understanding of class and how it shapes social life. The recognition that class remained important to people's lives was also reflected in a number of popular studies that were published in the 1990s (for example, Adonis and Pollard, 1998; Cannadine, 1998; McKibbon, 1998) and in the work of some academics who continued to emphasise its relevance to understanding the growing gap between rich and poor (for example, Joyce, 1995; Lee and Turner, 1996; Devine, 1997; Jones, 1997; Crompton, 1998; Jones and Novak, 1999; Milner, 1999).

There is an objective basis for these findings, for as study after study shows, class *does* matter. It has a direct impact on our health and wellbeing and on our 'life-chances'. If you are born into a working-class family you are likely to end up in a working-class job (Westergaard, 1995). People from the working class are more likely to suffer ill-health and die younger than those from other class backgrounds (Scrambler and Higgs, 1999; Shaw et al., 1999). And if you are from the working class you are likely to live in poverty (or live in poverty at particular points in the life cycle) (Oppenheim and Harker, 1996), face periods of unemployment, perform relatively poorly within education (Adonis and Pollard, 1998; Davies, 2000; Lavalette et al., 2001) and are more likely to be victims of crime (Goldson, 2000) and both domestic violence and sexual abuse (Corby, 2000).

Yet despite growing inequalities and poverty and the continuing popularity of 'class' in everyday discourse, 'class' as an analytical and theoretical concept has been pushed to the margins within academic debate. For example, the academic journal *Critical Social Policy*, which in its early years proclaimed its commitment to developing socialist and feminist theory and practice in social welfare, published only one article with an emphasis on class through out the whole of 1999 and 2000 (and that was co-written by one of the present authors!) (Mooney and Johnstone, 2000). Nick Ellison and Chris Pierson's (1998) edited collection on developments within British social welfare runs to 17 chapters, plots policy developments under New Labour and includes three chapters on various social movements (anti-racist, women's and environmental) and their effects on policy. Yet class gets only the briefest of mentions – in a passage that suggests class is now a declining factor in voting patterns, and in a cursory review of the work of Ian Gough. In cultural studies, Stefan Collini claims:

> In the frequently incanted quartet of race, class, gender, and sexual orientation, there is no doubt that class has been the least fashionable ... despite the fact that all the available evidence suggest that class remains the singly most powerful determinant of life-chances. (1994: 3)

Collini's argument can usefully be extended across a wide spectrum of academic study. Indeed some academics have gone as far as to announce the 'death of class', proclaiming that it 'can no longer give us purchase on the big social, political and cultural issues of the age' (Pakulski and Waters, 1996: vii).

Within academia, then, class is unfashionable and is all too frequently dismissed as 'old hat' – out of touch with the realities of late twentieth and early twenty-first century life. Further, when – or if – class is used, especially within academic social policy and social work, then as Neil Thompson (1993, 2000) notes, it is often defined 'loosely, in a broadly Weberian sense, to indicate different levels of economic power' (1993: 15). In this chapter and the next, we argue that class analysis remains crucial to understanding the social situation of the vast majority in the modern world. But, more than that, we wish to emphasise the potential for transformation which collective social actors have as a consequence of their social location within the dominant relations of production – that the working class, in other words, is not merely an oppressed, suffering class, but has the potential to re-shape society anew. To begin we need to clarify what we mean by class.

The foundations

Marxism offers a materialist analysis of society that places the production process (the various ways human societies co-operate to produce the basic goods and materials necessary for survival) at the centre of its analysis. Within this there is a recognition that in the majority of human societies the surplus product (that is, the goods produced over and above those necessary for daily survival) is taken and controlled by a tiny minority – who use this surplus for their own ends and purposes. This group – the dominant class – has, as a result, been able to lead a relatively leisured existence, while the majority have had to work to provide for themselves and support the lifestyle of the ruling class. In each mode of production it is the dominant class's control over the conditions of production that has been central to the formation of the exploitative relationships on which society is based. These relationships are embedded within the political, economic, ideological and social structure – in short, within the totality – of each society or mode of production. As the historian Geoffrey de Ste Croix notes:

> The most significant distinguishing feature of each ... mode of production ... is not so much how *the bulk of the labour production is done*, as *how the dominant political classes*, controlling the conditions of production, *ensure the extraction of surplus* which makes their own leisured existence possible. (1981: 52 emphasis in original)

It is one's location, with regard to the exploitative relationships, that defines one class. But 'class' is essentially a relationship:

> Class is the collective social expression of the fact of exploitation, the way in which exploitation is embodied in a social structure ... A class is a group of persons in a community identified by their position in the whole system of social production, defined above all according to their relationship (primarily in terms of the degree of ownership or control) to the conditions of production ... and to other classes. (de Ste Croix, 1981: 43)

Thus class, for Marxists, is an objective category, determined by relationship (in terms of ownership and/or control) to the means of production. Hence whether one defines oneself as belonging to a particular class or not is immaterial in these terms – class consciousness is important for Marxists but it is an analytically separate concept. Thus in defining class, Marx, Engels and their followers avoid those approaches that focus on various occupational measures, income, type of work or the outcomes of class inequality or stratification; instead they focus on the underlying factors that generate class divisions in the first place. Conceived in this way class is, to borrow Crompton's phrase, 'strongly relational' in that it stresses the exploitative nature of social relations between different social classes (Gubbay, 1997; Crompton, 1998).

From this starting point we can identify capitalism as a system dominated by two main classes in direct opposition to each other: the bourgeoisie, who own and/or control the means of production but who rely on others to work in their factories and offices to produce goods and create wealth; and the working class, the vast majority, who have no means of supporting themselves except by selling their labour power to the bourgeoisie: to work for a wage. In *The Communist Manifesto* Marx and Engels comment:

Our epoch, the epoch of the bourgeoisie, possesses … this distinctive feature: it has simplified the class antagonisms. Society as a whole is more and more splitting up into two great hostile classes directly facing each other: Bourgeoisie and Proletariat. (1848/1973: 68)

However, this claim has led to criticisms that Marxism provides a simplistic two-class model that is unable to comprehend recent developments in the class structure. In particular the emergence of a new, expanding service class and the decline and fragmentation of the industrial working class, it is suggested, render Marx's perspective irrelevant to understanding the modern world. How should we respond to these criticisms?

Goodbye to the working class?

The idea that class has lost its saliency is not new. In the late 1950s and 1960s, for example, in the context of rapid economic, social and political change, some academic researchers and politicians suggested we were witnessing the creation of a post-industrial society (Bell, 1973) within which the working class was disappearing and the middle class becoming dominant. Sociologists like Ferdynand Zweig argued that:

> … working-class life finds itself on the move towards new middle class values and existence … the change can only be described as a deep transformation of values, as the development of new ways or thinking and feeling, a new ethos, new aspirations and cravings. (1961: ix)

Zweig's 'embourgeoisment' thesis was roundly criticised at the time. In the 1960s the 'rediscovery of poverty' in Britain (Abel-Smith and Townsend, 1965) and the US (Harrington, 1963), the reality of working-class life – portrayed in films like *Friday Night Saturday Morning, Cathy Come Home* or *Kes* – and the fact that the manufacturing sector of the economy became dominant during this period, all undermined Zweig's case.

Within academia, Goldthorpe et al. (1969) attacked embourgeoisment in their *Affluent Worker* studies. This emphasised the continuing relevance of class and the creation of new types of working-class jobs (in their case within the car industry). However, they suggested these new workers had developed a new culture of familialism and instrumentalism – this 'new' or 'affluent' working class was shaped by individualist, much more than collectivist, concerns. This meant, they concluded, the 'new' affluent workers did not express the 'old' class solidarities of traditional sections of the working class like miners or dockers. It was a conclusion that was undermined by the resurgence in industrial militancy in the late 1960s and early 1970s, within which car workers played a leading role.

Attacks on class theory, therefore, are not new. They tend to surface during periods of low class conflict, or when the organised labour movement is in retreat – which is taken as *prima facia* evidence of working class decline. In this sense it is worth noting Lipset and Benedix's comment that discussion of class is never neutral, and that it is 'often an academic substitute for a real conflict over political orientations' (quoted in de Ste Croix, 1981: 31).

Over the past two decades claims about the end of class, and the demise or fragmentation of the working class in particular, have reappeared with even more vigour than in the 1950s and 1960s. Indeed as Richard Hoggart has pointed out:

> One of the most commonly voiced misconceptions is that 'we are all classless nowadays': it has been said for at least half a century – though with mounting irritation in those who assert it. (cited in Adonis and Pollard, 1998: 1)

Liberal and conservative writers wedded to various ideologies of individualism have always dismissed class analysis. Since the 1980s, however, some writers who claim a radical perspective on a number of social and political questions have also rejected 'class'. These writers fall into one of three broad categories. First, class analysis is rejected by a range of academics who formerly adhered to some form of Marxism. Included here are those who could be labelled as ex-Marxists, for example André Gorz (1982), and others who would prefer the label 'post-Marxists' such as Ernesto Laclau and Chantal Mouffe (1985, 1997). Ellen Woods summarises their project. For these writers the struggle for socialism can now:

> ... be conceived as a plurality of 'democratic' struggles, bringing together a variety of resistances to many forms of inequality and oppression. In fact, it may even be possible to replace the concept of socialism with the notion of 'radical democracy'. (Woods, 1986: 4)

The decline of the working class, it is claimed, has fundamentally altered the nature of the struggle for a better world.

A second group to reject class are those associated with theories of the 'Third Way'. In early 1999 Tony Blair announced that New Labour's mission was to make Britain a 'middle-class society':

> A middle class that will include millions of people who traditionally may see themselves as working class, but whose ambitions are far broader that those of their parents and grandparents ... Slowly but surely the old establishment is being replaced by a new, larger, more meritocratic middle class. I believe we will have an expanded middle class with ladders of opportunity for those from all backgrounds, no more ceilings that prevent people from achieving the success they merit. (Tony Blair, 14 January 1999)

Blair's pronouncements, and his dismissal of Marxism as containing a 'time-bound' explanation of class, have been both fuelled and legitimised by fashionable academic and social commentary – important elements of which derive from the writings of ex/post-Marxists (two of the most notable being Geoff Mulgan and Martin Jacques, both former members of the Communist Party of Great Britain). But it has been left to Anthony Giddens, one of Britain's leading sociologists, to provide academic justification for New Labour's claims about class (Giddens, 1998a and b, 2000):

> With the rapid shrinking of the working class and the disappearance of the bipolar world, the salience of class politics, as well as the traditional divisions of left and right, has diminished. (1998a: 18)

In New Labour's 'Third Way' it is clear that there is little room for recognition of class divisions, or the underpinning of inequalities by class relations. The priority has been to combat 'social exclusion', a discourse that both denies the validity of class analysis and the very existence of class divisions and inequalities (see Lavalette and Mooney, 1999; Mooney and Johnstone, 2000).

Finally, within postmodern theorising class is dismissed and replaced with a stress on 'consumerism', 'lifestyle' and 'identity' in processes of social differentiation. Postmodernism takes various guises, but one of its 'radical' interpretations comes from Leonard (1997) who argues (in typically postmodern jargon):

> With the ideological collapse of the organising metanarrative of class struggle, together with the decomposition and restructuring of classes in the post-Fordist era, social movements based upon the identities of class ... appear to have lost the will and resources to mount effective resistance. (1997: 154)

Within each of these 'anti-class' positions – despite their various differences – is a series of shared claims that suggest that modern societies have undergone a radical transformation to a new era of economic development that has brought changes to the social structure, particularly in relation to the labour market. These key themes include the claim that we are witnessing a shift from manufacturing to service employment, a growth in the white-collar middle classes, the development of a divergent 'core' and 'peripheral' labour force, and a far-reaching transformation in the organisation of work – themes we deal with in the following section. But behind these sociological and economic claims is a political point. As a consequence of these shifts, it is suggested, the transformatory potential of the working class has been dissipated. The working class is no longer – if it ever was – an agent for radical social change. We explore this argument in the next chapter.

The growth of services and white-collar work

Notions of an expanding service sector have been tied to perspectives that suggest we are moving towards a 'post-industrial society'. Such theories have their roots in the work of Daniel Bell (1973). For post-industrial theorists the shift to services and white-collar employment was an indicator of a decline in perceived class differences, in particular a disappearing working class, and the emergence of more meritocratic structures and pluralistic lifestyles. For Bell this results in a transition to forms of work that are less alienating and more 'professional', wherein 'information' and 'knowledge' become more important than manual labour. White-collar workers are not subject to the harsh routines of manual labour and low wages and correspondingly do not perceive their interests in class terms. Bell was, at the same time, arguing that we were approaching the 'end of ideology' – his argument was that the basis for class based theories, and Marxism in particular, was being eroded.

The liberal Bell shares with ex-Marxist André Gorz an emphasis upon the role of technological change in processes of social and economic change, with Gorz arguing that one direct outcome of changing technology is the 'end of the working class'. Other theorists have offered very different interpretations of the growth of professional occupations. Notable here is the notion of a 'service-class'. This idea was initially developed by Austro-Marxist Karl Renner in the 1950s but more recently it has been taken up by a range of writers. For Goldthorpe (1987), the growth of a service class of salaried employees reflects not only the expansion of professional and managerial occupations, but also upward social mobility. This service class represents a privileged grouping in the labour market that are in a position of 'trust' and authority from their employers. For Goldthorpe this class is very homogenous in character and is developing forms of class solidarity. Alternatively for Lash and Urry (1987) the expansion of a service class of managers and professionals, which perform certain services for capital in public and private sector bureaucracies, is tied up with the transition to disorganised capitalism, and in particular with the growth of the welfare state. Unlike Goldthorpe, however, they see this class as a more fragmented grouping, socially and politically. But they go further to argue that the emergence of a service class signifies a decline in class politics and an increase in cultural diversity and social fragmentation.

Claims about a widespread transformation in the class structure of advanced capitalist societies such as Britain have been taken up by theorists of social welfare and social policy. Gould, for example, claims that changes in the occupational structure and the shift to post-Fordism, together with rising living standards, have contributed to the emergence of a 'salaried middle class', a class which has not only been the main beneficiary of the expansion of the post-War welfare state, but is increasingly running the welfare state in its own class interests, ensuring that its members benefit in terms of the provision of good quality education, health and so on (Gould, 1993). However, Gould simply takes the existence of a 'salaried middle class' for granted and nowhere does he offer an adequate definition of such a class. Elsewhere Esping-Andersen (1993) has argued that the shift to post-industrial occupational structures varies between different welfare regimes, though the decline in industrial employment and the feminisation of the labour force appears universal. Unlike a number of other post-industrial theorists, Esping-Andersen focuses on the patterns of stratification and social polarisation that emerge in post-industrial societies and while this means that his approach avoids some of the more serious pitfalls of post-industrial thinking, nonetheless he also displays some of the uncritical acceptance of changes in the social structure which befall other theorists.

Despite the claims, the reality of vast swathes of service employment is far removed from the idyllic picture presented by Bell, Lash and Urry, Goldthorpe and Gould. First, it is important to point out that the service sector includes many jobs that would be viewed as 'traditional' working-class jobs: train, truck and bus drivers, refuse collectors, dockers and postal workers, for example, are all service workers. Second, many of the newly expanding service jobs are dominated by poor pay and working conditions. Telesales workers, workers in fast-food outlets on flexible or 'zero hour' contracts, office and shopping centre cleaners and sales assistants, for example, do not generally have privileged working conditions or remuneration packages. Third, even the so-called 'decline of manufacturing employment' only really stands up if we narrow our focus to its relative decline in the advanced capitalist economies. Across the globe, however, there have never been more people employed in manufacturing industries – the numbers employed in this sector remain substantial in Europe and the US, but there are also vast numbers of workers in manufacturing throughout China, Southeast Asia, Africa and Latin America, for example. Hence the claims of the 'post-industrialist' are in danger of exhibiting an extreme 'Eurocentrism'. Finally, the distinction between manufacturing and services in modern capitalism is often not a useful one. As German notes:

> As manufacturing develops, more services are required to make it possible. And since services are far more likely to be labour intensive, the disproportion between the two will continue to grow. But as this disproportion grows, so services become an integral part of capitalism. (1990: 27)

Some Marxists have developed a sophisticated account of the relevance of the manufacturing/service split by drawing a distinction between 'productive labour', which directly produces surplus value, and 'unproductive labour' that does not and is therefore a drain on capital. Here productive workers are all those employed in factories and mines directly producing commodities, or involved in transporting them to the point of sale (for example, train drivers). Unproductive workers would be all those employed in delivering various services such as welfare workers, office workers, bus drivers or refuse workers. This usage, therefore, gives us a 'narrow' definition of the working class, those involved in productive labour only. Yet Marx rejected this approach in his major work *Capital* (Marx, 1867/1976). Here, Marx argues that the increasingly complex division of labour within capitalism makes it difficult to utilise such a rigid distinction between 'productive' and 'unproductive' workers and that all workers involved in the entire process of producing commodities are in reality 'productive'. Thus as various office workers' tasks are essential to the process of commodity production their work is therefore productive labour and, as a result, they are workers subordinated to the process of production. Further, there is little evidence to suggest that Marx thought that even on this wider definition only productive workers were part of the working class. As Wright notes, 'both productive and unproductive workers are exploited; both have unpaid labour extracted from them.' (1979: 49).

Going hand in hand with the emphasis on service sector employment is a sharp distinction between the worlds of white-collar and service-based work, and that of blue-collar manufacturing work. Yet if this distinction ever held true it is certainly now problematic. As Aronowitz points out, such labels are ideological:

> 'White-collar' is a label that *presupposes* an essential difference between the structure of labour in the factory and the office. It is a category of social ideology rather than of social science. (Aronowitz, 1973, quoted in Callinicos and Harman, 1987: 4, our emphasis)

It is true that developments in the occupational structure have resulted in the growth in 'white-collar' work in 'services', but it is important to stress that such categorisation tends to homogenise a diverse range of occupations – white-collar work includes various administrative, managerial and professional jobs, as well as large numbers of low-grade, poorly-paid work particularly – though by no means exclusively – in the public sector. Writing at the same time as Bell, for example, American Marxist Harry Braverman questioned the usefulness of the distinction between white- and blue-collar work in the following way:

> Restaurant labour, which cooks, prepares, assembles, serves, cleans dishes and utensils, etc, carries on tangible production just as much as labour employed in many other manufacturing processes; the fact that the consumer is sitting nearby at a counter or table is the chief distinction, in principle, between this industry and those food processing industries which are classified under 'manufacturing'. Laundry workers, workers in cleaning and pressing establishments, workers in automobile repair shops and in machine servicing or repair work of other sorts perform the same sort of work as many workers in manufacturing industries. (Braverman, 1974: 360)

Braverman argues that there has been a decline in the status of much white-collar work – it has become 'proletarianised'. Historically, this process has been the main tendency within white-collar work since the

1930s. The proletarianisation of white-collar work can be identified in the decline in status and authority of teachers, social workers, welfare workers, health care workers, civil servants and even university lecturers. These are all jobs which may have had some prestige in the past, but are now the jobs of salaried public sector workers. In other words, white-collar work has been degraded, deskilled and controlled in ways that have attempted to both intensify work and management control of the labour process. In this sense white-collar workers have been subjected to the same managerial strategies as workers in manufacturing industry and from this perspective we can identify the growth of this form of working as evidence of the increased homogeneity of the working class rather than its fragmentation.

Post-Fordism and disorganised capitalism

A second set of linked arguments is that we are now witnessing a fundamental change to the organisation of work as we enter a stage of 'disorganised capitalism' (Lash and Urry, 1987) or a 'post-Fordist' society (Murray, 1988), with its post-Fordist forms of welfare delivery (Burrows and Loader, 1994). Alongside the gradual, but long-term, decline in manufacturing employment (in the advanced capitalist economies) and the expansion of employment in the service sector there has been a growth in what are generally referred to as 'flexible' or 'non-traditional' forms of employment, of which part-time, temporary, sub-contracted and self-employment represent the most significant elements. One of the most frequently highlighted features of 'post-Fordism' is the growing divide between what has been termed a 'core' and 'peripheral' labour force. 'Core' workers offer functional flexibility through their multi-skilling whereas, by contrast, low paid 'peripheral' workers, often through part-time and sub-contract work, provide numerical flexibility. These arguments are advanced by theorists who see themselves as sympathetic to a particular version of Marxism. For example, it was the now defunct journal *Marxism Today* which did much to popularise these notions and to claim that 'post-Fordism' represented a fragmentation of the working class. Charles Leadbetter writing in the magazine in 1987 argued:

> The growth of a peripheral workforce of part-timers ... has accompanied rising security and prosperity for those in full-time employment. (1987: 18)

The point to note is that Leadbetter is claiming that those in full-time employment are enjoying benefits accrued at the expense of part-time or numerically flexible workers – there is a growing division between workers, which renders notions of class solidarity moribund. Presumably some of the full-time workers Leadbetter had in mind in

1987 were (the remaining) miners and dock workers – two sectors where, in the five years after he had written, there was mass unemployment and insecurity.

The problem with much 'post-Fordist' theorising is that it focuses on a range of temporary, peripheral or superficial changes to work organisation and argues that these constitute a new era of capitalism, in contrast to an earlier 'Fordist' model. Fordism, it is claimed, dominated the first two-thirds of the twentieth century, a claim justified by aggregating certain trends within manufacturing and state activity in this era – mass production of standardised goods, flow-line assembly techniques, mass marketing and advertising to create demand, mass membership trade unions, state strategies based on Keynesian economics and commitment to state welfare, and the domination of production by a few large multi-national corporations producing for an increasingly global market. These trends are then contrasted against the new norms of 'post-Fordism'. Small flexible firms are said to be more vibrant and responsive to market demands, in comparison to large multinationals. Niche, rather than mass, production is the road to success. Just-in-time techniques, utilising advanced computer technology, it is claimed, allow firms to respond quickly to consumer demand and can off-set crises of overproduction. Trade unions are marginalised as a consequence of core and periphery labour markets. Core workers, it is suggested, have no need for unions as they are valued and well-paid, peripheral workers by contrast are too disposable and cannot be organised. Finally an 'enabling' state, rather than a directing state, is required – committed to establishing the right environment for firms to expand.

Sociologists Scott Lash and John Urry (1987, 1994) offer a slightly different approach to the modern world. They argue that Western societies are undergoing a transition not to post-Fordism, but to 'disorganised' capitalism. Yet the outcome is not substantially different. They claim that changes in the spatial organisation of production and a growing political and consumption based division between public and private sector workers and also between welfare claimants and those in employment has led to the fragmentation of the working class.

The problem with much of this is its superficiality. The main contrast between 'Fordism' and 'post-Fordism' requires that we abstract developments within particular sections or areas of the manufacturing sector and generalise these to the economy as a whole. But as a result the analysis both overstates the prevalence of Fordism in the past and underestimates its continuing relevance today. With respect to the first point it is important to note that Fordism never existed as a total system. It may have been dominant in the car industry but there were always vast swathes of manufacturing where industry operated in different ways (textiles and mining, for example). As Ray Hudson (1988) points out, particularly in the 'older' industrial regions, Fordism was conspicuous by its absence. Secondly, the notion that industry has left all this behind ignores the extent to which 'Fordist methods' remain typical in many industries today (especially those geared to the production of a range of consumer goods, like cars, fridges, freezers, washing machines, tumble dryers, televisions, video recorders and so on). Elements of this approach (mass production for mass consumption, deskilling of labour, fragmentation of work tasks) can even be found in services such as the mass holiday market, or out-of-town shopping developments with their large superstores, or within the 'production line' approach to children's parties at many leisure facilities and fast-food shops. Thirdly, the trend within capitalism is towards giant multinational corporations (rather than small flexible firms) and monopolisation. The interests of these organisations are protected by their own national governments and by various intergovernmental bodies, like the World Trade Organisation. Finally, the distinction between 'core' and 'peripheral' workers is less dramatic than is often portrayed. Anna Pollert (1988) has commented that employers have always sought 'flexibility' from workers. For example, historically employment on the docks – across the world – has been dominated by 'flexibility' in the form of an engrained system of 'casualism'. Dockers in Britain were not guaranteed employment from one day to the next until the National Dock Labour Scheme was introduced in the wake of the Donovan Report of 1968 (Lavalette and Kennedy, 1996). Further, Pollert argues that in the context of the 1980s the claims about increasing flexibility were more prescriptive than descriptive (Pollert, 1988). In recent decades there has been increased use of part-time workers but the majority of these workers have permanent contracts with fixed working hours and most have the same rates of pay (pro rata) and working conditions as their full-time colleagues. Of course employers, including large multinationals, constantly try to utilise a range of labour practices and techniques to obtain control over the labour process and increase surplus value extraction, but it is a grave error to regard any of these techniques as inevitable, static or universal.

What these approaches have in common is an economic and/or technological determinism, reflected in their claim that economic and technological changes, in and of themselves, have eroded class divisions, altered the class structure and changed attitudes away from 'bi-polar' or class-driven perspectives. Put at its most crude, they claim that a decline in 'industry' (the manufacturing sector) represents a 'decline in the working class'. However, not only are these trends and their effects frequently over-exaggerated but quantitative changes in the occupational structure are interpreted as implying qualitative changes in the class structure. There is little doubt that there have been significant changes in the occupational structure of Britain since the 1960s and 1970s. But recognising this is not the same as suggesting the working class has been fragmented, eroded or disappeared.

Occupational measures of class continue to dominate social science and while these do at least discuss changes in employment they represent, as

Erik Olin Wright (1979) has commented, 'static' conceptions of class. The use of such measures blurs class distinctions and underlying relations of production. But of course this does not mean that the class structure has remained unchanged since Marx's day. Central to Marxism is a recognition that capitalism constantly revolutionises the means of production and, as part of this process, the organisation of production and work is also restructured. To make sense of changes in the class structure in the context of the dynamism of capitalism requires a model that understands class as part of the totality of capitalism itself, and explores it in that context.

The class structure of capitalism today

We shall now return to Marx's conception of class, building on the foundations we outlined earlier in the chapter, to offer an account of the class structure of capitalism today. The Marxist approach to class provides a very different perspective to the various sociological approaches high-lighted above. First, let us quickly deal with the claim that Marx offers a simple (simplistic) two-class model. Marx certainly talked about the two major classes of capitalism – the bourgeoisie and the working class – but he also recognised the existence of other classes. In *Capital* Volume III, for example, he emphasised the complexity of the class structure:

> Even [in England] the stratification of classes does not appear in its pure form. Middle and intermediate strata even here obliterate lines of demarcation every-where. However, this is immaterial for our analysis. We have seen that the continual tendency and law of development of the capitalist mode of produc-tion is more and more to divorce the means of production from labour, and more and more to concentrate the scattered means of production into large groups, thereby transforming labour into wage labour and the means of pro-duction into capital. (1894/1974: 885)

But the existence of other classes was, as he himself observed, 'imma-terial for our analysis' (Marx, 1894/1974: 885). The reasons for this are two-fold. First, because the long-term tendency within capitalism is towards an increasing polarisation between the proletariat and bour-geoisie, reflecting the trend towards the increasing concentration and centralisation of capital, and the increasing separation of labour from the means of production. Second, because the central, exploitative social relationship within capitalism is the relationship between bourgeoisie and working class that results in the extraction of surplus value. The key point of this is that within capitalism, for Marx, there are two major classes in a direct antagonistic relationship with each other.

Instead of 'narrow' definitions of the working class adopted by Leadbetter, Lash and Urry, and Goldthorpe, Marx's approach leads to the adoption of a 'broad' definition. As Mandel has claimed:

> The defining structural characteristic of the proletariat in Marx's analysis of
> capitalism is the socio-economic compulsion to sell one's labour power. (cited
> in Callinicos and Harman, 1987: 20)

Thus, in combination with notions of proletarianisation outlined above,
a Marxist approach to class will view the vast majority of wage labourers
in offices and welfare institutions as part of the working class – not a
white-collar service class – with similar objective interests and experiences to workers in factories, docks and mines.

But does this mean that anyone who works for a wage is part of the
working class? Clearly the answer is an emphatic 'no': wage labour is a
necessary, but not in itself a sufficient, condition for determining membership of the working class. The majority of 'top industrialists', for example,
earn salaries but this fact alone does not make them part of the working
class. To understand why this is so we must look at how capitalism has
developed over the last 200 years.

Previously we noted that membership of the ruling class rested in those
who owned and/or controlled the means of production. This means that
members of the bourgeoisie do not need to directly own companies as
long as they have effective control over them. Thus, the Managing
Directors of, for example, British Gas, Barclays Bank, General Motors and
Ford, will be salaried 'employees', although they may also have substantial share ownership in the company in which they work as part of
their perks of 'employment'. But while they do not individually own the
company they work for, they nevertheless have a significant degree of
control over them, their investment and development plans and, as a result,
over the labour of those who work for their companies. Thus the fact that
these individuals earn salaries does not make them part of the working
class, on the contrary they are salaried members of the bourgeoisie.

Historically there have been many changes to capitalism but two
central developments have had a dramatic impact on the class structure.
First, the 'units of capital' have increased dramatically in scale and size.
As a consequence, companies are often 'owned' (that is, the shares
are owned) by a range of financial institutions, individuals and other
companies. The result is that many members of the bourgeoisie do not
legally own the company or companies that they work for (or at least
own them outright) although they do have effective ownership and
control over them. Secondly, the concentration and centralisation of capital
over this period has made it impossible for individual capitalists to have
hands-on control over the daily operation of the production process –
companies have become too large and complex for a single person to take
all decisions relating to their day-to-day activity. As a result, a range of
tasks has had to be delegated to a layer of middle managers and supervisors. This group is not part of the bourgeoisie but nor is it part of the
working class whose labour it directly supervises. The combined effect of
these changes has been to make the class system more complicated and

introduce a layer of intermediaries between the bourgeoisie and the working class.

Thus, while capitalism remains a system divided by the two dominant classes, the bourgeoisie and the working class, the process of social production in the modern world has also created locations within the production process occupied by strata carrying out specific control functions for capital: controlling investment, production and/or the labour of others. In other words, these strata obtain the confidence of capital to carry out a series of important tasks and functions necessary for the smooth running of modern capitalism. In return they obtain higher levels of rewards (pay and perks) and this places them in a materially advantaged position over the working class. Their relative position of power and privilege rests in their ability to keep the working class in its place. Hence, carrying out these tasks, in combination with the rewards they obtain, sets these strata apart from the working class but it does not make them part of the bourgeoisie. Eric Olin Wright (1979) has attempted to locate these groups within the overall system of labour exploitation within capitalism. In his terminology, these groups occupy a 'contradictory class location': at different times and in different situations drawn towards, or pushed away from, the two dominant classes. One final point needs to be emphasised: there is not one contradictory class site but several, some are closer to the working class than they are to the bourgeoisie (line supervisors), some are closer to, or even merge with, the bourgeoisie, and some Wright identifies as being between the working class and the 'petty-bourgeoisie' (for example, small shop keepers, independent farmers).

The basis of Wright's class differentiation is the concept of control: control over investment and the accumulation process, control over the means of production, and control of labour power. The bourgeoisie have control in each sphere, the working class in none and the petty-bourgeoisie control over the first two but not the labour of others:

> Managers, small employers and semi-autonomous workers enjoy varying amounts of control, more than workers but less than the bourgeoisie. Thus, contradictory classes are those who exhibit a mixed pattern of control. (Edgell, 1993: 18)

So, for Wright, workers are 'wage-labourers who also do not control the labour of others within production and do not control the use of their own labour within the labour process' (quoted in Callinicos and Harman, 1987: 27). The bourgeoisie are those who have effective control over the entire process of capital accumulation, while the 'middle class' consists of two groups: those with a contradictory class location between capital and labour and those with a contradictory location between labour and the petit-bourgeoisie. The conclusion of this argument is that the vast majority of the population of the 'advanced' economies are part of the working class, the bourgeoisie remain a relatively small proportion of the population, while those occupying 'contradictory locations' account for perhaps 20 per cent of the population (Callinicos and Harman, 1987).

Rather than a declining class, the working class remain numerically dominant. But the argument about the 'decline' of the working class is also about their decline as a social force. It is this argument we look at in Chapter 4.

4 'A deplorable concession to the shade of Karl Marx': Class as Agency

In the previous chapter, we emphasised that class is an objective category – class position being determined by one's relationship to the means of production – and for the adoption of a 'broad' and dynamic definition of the working class (Gubbay, 1997). At this level, what class you think you belong to is secondary. But for Marxists, class is also the central collective actor with the potential to engage *consciously* with the social world re-shaping it anew. From this perspective the class with which one identifies and one's belief in its ability to undertake collective action is vitally important. To distinguish between these two levels of analysis Marx, in the *Poverty of Philosophy*, drew a distinction between a 'class in itself', meaning the objective location within the class structure, and 'class for itself', meaning the subjective element – class consciousness – that develops at various levels of intensity as a consequence of living under the exploitative conditions of capitalism.

> Economic conditions first transformed the mass of people of the country into workers ... This mass is thus already a class as against capital, but not yet for itself. In the struggle ... this mass becomes united, and constitutes itself as a class for itself. (in Tucker, 1978: 218)

For Marx, therefore, class location and class consciousness are two different (though related) entities.

Marx's comments have often been interpreted as referring to an historical process. That class location came first and then after a few years class consciousness was established. But this leads to a static view of class consciousness and can leave us measuring class consciousness against some mythical set of values from the past. In other words, this approach can lead to the conclusion that class consciousness was something that was achieved in the past but is now fading or disappearing. As an example, let us return to Goldthorpe et al.'s *Affluent Worker* study. Here the researchers undertook surveys of car worker's attitudes, concluding that they were driven by values of instrumentalism, consumerism and familialism, with little apparent interest in wider trade union or socialist politics. These values were contrasted against the supposed values of 'traditional' workers – like mine workers – who were assumed to have much clearer collectivist, confrontational and class-bound values. Yet:

While the study was still at the printers, some union militants handed out summaries of its conclusions. A week later the *Daily Mail* published a report showing Vauxhall's profits ... and this too was circulated through out the plant. An eruption ensued for the next two days ... *The Times* reported ... 'Wild rioting has broken out at the Vauxhall car factory in Luton. Thousands of workers streamed out of the shops and gathered on the factory yard. They besieged the management to come out; singing "The Red Flag"; shouting "string them up". Groups attempted to storm the offices and battled police which had been called to protect them.' (Fantasia, 1988: 7)

The values Goldthorpe et al. thought of as 'old' or 'traditional' and not part of the make-up of the newly-affluent car workers suddenly appear as part of their repertoire of contention – and, of course, over the following few years these collectivist impulses were expressed regularly as car workers moved into the vanguard of the class struggle in the early 1970s.

The problem with attitude surveys is that they record a range of political values as fixed and static. Yet ideas can, and frequently do, change. What seemed impossible yesterday may appear achievable or obtainable today because the context and circumstances have altered in some way. Recognising this simple feature leads us to the conclusion that class consciousness is not static but can form and/or dissipate at different times, to different degrees, in different circumstances. Fantasia argues:

> In Marx's formulation, the working class is 'in struggle', 'becomes united', 'constitutes itself' and these activities of 'struggling', 'uniting' and 'constituting' ought to be considered *processes* of class consciousness. Too often, however, the notion of a class 'in itself' is reduced to an 'objective' matter of determining the relative size of the labour force, the concentration of workers in various industries, the occupational characteristics of the workforce or the level of union membership. (1988: 9)

By suggesting that class consciousness develops at differing levels of intensity we are arguing that it is a dynamic concept, not a static one. Analytically (an earlier) Giddens (1981) suggested we can divide the concept of class consciousness into three levels. First, there is 'class identity', which involves a minimal recognition of shared class membership; second, there is 'conflict consciousness', which acknowledges an opposition of interests between different classes; and finally, there is 'revolutionary class-consciousness', which recognises:

> The possibility of an overall reorganization in the institutional mediation of power ... and a belief that such a reorganization can be brought about through class action. (Giddens, 1981: 113)

The intensity with which these different levels of class consciousness are held by members of particular classes will be affected by the context within which they find themselves and their confidence (or lack of confidence) in their ability to change their world. Centrally that 'context' will be shaped by the class struggle.

Class struggle

As the historian Geoffrey de Ste Croix notes, while some academics and researchers are happy to discuss 'class' as a structural element of society or a determinant of ones life chances:

> ... 'class struggle' is a very different matter. Merely to employ the expression 'the class struggle' ... evidently seems to many people in the Western world a deplorable concession to the shade of Karl Marx. (1981: 49)

To many, the notion of class struggle seems incredibly dated and the idea that the working class could actively shape the world just seems quaint. As Peter Leonard notes:

> The old social movements, based on class and workplace, appear unable ... to mount collective resistance to developments in late capitalism which adversely affect the well-being of large populations. (1997: 154)

Eric Hobsbawm, one of the best-known British Marxist historians, has drawn similar conclusions. In his introduction to the 1998 Verso edition of the *Communist Manifesto* he writes:

> If at the end of the millennium we must be struck by the acuteness of the mani-festo's vision of the then remote future of massively globalised capitalism, the failure of another of its forecasts is equally striking. It is now evident that the bourgeoisie has not produced 'above all ... its own gravediggers' in the proletariat. (1998: 18)

And these claims seem to be borne out by recent strike figures from Britain, which show an incredibly low level of activity, though as Rees (2001) points out, support for trade unions amongst workers and membership of unions has remained remarkably resilient.

The claims of Leonard and Hobsbawm reflect a common set of assumptions about the working class and class conflict prevalent in academic writing. Within much of this literature, 'class struggle' is often thought to be an old-fashioned phrase, something that was perhaps relevant in the nineteenth or early twentieth centuries but is no longer suitable to describe events in the modern world. Academics working in these and related disciplines may note the continuing relevance of social protest, or even collective action, but now these are thought to be the preserve of the 'new social movements' (like the women's movement, the gay movement or the black movement) or even the new social welfare movements (the pensioners or disability rights movements) where issues of diversity and identity dominate. The working class is assumed to be a declining class, not only numerically (as we have already discussed) but also politically.

Yet if we move beyond the borders of Britain, class conflict in its 'traditional' sense would still seem appropriate. For example, towards the end of the year 2000 the Yugoslav revolution saw mass conflict on the streets of Belgrade and other major cities. Central to these events were the miners in the Kolubara region of Serbia (described by Misha Glenny (2000) as the 'Gdansk of Yugoslavia'). As the *Observer* correspondent Jonathan Steele commented:

> [Milosevic's] downfall was not won on a battlefield or by NATO pilots. It was won among the black dust of the Serbian coalfield, under the vast arc lights of Kolubara pit among the miners who had been his most loyal supporters. (*Observer*, 8 October 2000).

Kim Moody surveying the period 1994–97 notes that there were mass or general *political* strikes in:

> France and Canada in 1995 ... [and] in Nigeria (1994), Indonesia (1994), Paraguay (1994), Taiwan (1994), Bolivia (1995), South Africa (1996), Brazil (1996), Greece (1996, 1997), Spain (1994, 1996), Argentina (twice in 1996), Venezuela (1996), Italy (1996), South Korea (1996–97), Canada (1995–97), Haiti (1997), Columbia (1997), Ecuador (1997) and Belgium (1997). (1997: 21)

Leys and Panitch note that:

> By the mid-1990s strikes in France, the USA and Canada once more occupied the front pages alongside reports of strikes in South Korea and the 'IMF riots' throughout much of the Third World from Zimbabwe to Mexico. (1998: 20)

This while the World Development Movement (Woodroffe and Ellis-Jones, 2000) reports various countries within which strikes and demonstrations against neo-liberal policies took place in the first six months of the year 2000. The list includes Argentina, Bolivia, Colombia, Costa Rica, Ecuador, Honduras, Paraguay, Kenya, Malawi, Nigeria and Zambia. The significant 're-birth' of the union movement in the US and the continuing conflicts in France emphasise that these developments are not merely 'second' or 'third' world events. Furthermore, let's be clear about these movements – they involved the active participation of men and women, black and white, young and old, blue- and white-collar workers – they were not simply the movements of some privileged 'labour aristocracy' but, in the words of the *Communist Manifesto*, they represented 'the self-conscious, independent movement of the immense majority, in the interests of the immense majority' (Marx and Engels, 1848/1973: 78).

Additionally the end of the twentieth century saw the birth of a broad 'anti-capitalist movement' whose burgeoning moments occurred on the streets of Seattle in November–December 1999 in a large protest against the World Trade Organisation's Third Ministerial, and developed in a number of significant demonstrations that took place throughout 2000 in Washington, Melbourne, Millau, Prague and Nice. One of the important aspects about the Seattle events was the creation of what has been termed the 'blue–green alliance' – of trade union and working class organisations ('blue'-collar) coming together with 'green' environmentalists (Charlton, 2000b) – an alliance which was, if anything, even more strongly in evidence at the 20 April WTO protests in Quebec some 17 months after Seattle (*LA Times*, 22 April 2001).

Empirically, then, the beginning of the twenty-first century does not seem to be an opportune time to dismiss class conflict from the realm of social theory. There may, at present, be little sign of these conflicts in Britain, but we would suggest the reason for this is to be located in recent history – the extent of the defeats inflicted on the organised working class movement in Britain during the 1980s, the extent to which these have been reinforced by anti-trade union legislation, and the political commitments of the trade union bureaucracy which has led them to accommodation with the law and government. None of these rules out the return of class conflict in Britain, but they do help explain why it has been slower to reappear here than in other parts of the system.

Indeed there is increasing evidence that the Seattle demonstration and the birth of the anti-capitalist movement may mark the start of a new wave of international social protest. The American sociologist of social movements, Sid Tarrow, has drawn attention to the fact that social protest tends to come in waves or 'cycles'. A cycle of protest is:

A phase of heightened conflict and contention across the social system that includes: a rapid diffusion of collective action from more mobilized to less mobilized sectors; a quickened pace of innovation in the form of contention; new or transformed collective action frames; a combination of organized and unorganized participation; a sequence of intensified interaction between challengers and authorities which can end in reform, repression or sometime revolution. (1994: 153)

He identifies three major international cycles of protest during the twentieth century. First, the conflicts of 1934–38 that encompassed the French popular front struggles, the Spanish Revolution and the strikes and conflicts initiated in the US under the New Deal conditions (such as conflicts on the west coast maritime industry, the Teamsters rebellion and the great sit-down strikes in the car industry). Second, the wave of unrest that rocked the world between 1968 and 1972 – the anti-war movement, the growth of the black, women's and gay movements (in the US and then spreading out from there), the Prague Spring, Ireland's civil rights movement, the French strike of May 1968, the Italian 'Hot Autumn' of 1969 and Britain's 'Glorious Summer' of 1972). Finally, the conflicts in Eastern

Europe between 1980 (and the rise of Solidarity) and 1989 (and the dismantling of the Berlin Wall).

There are problems with Tarrow's account of protest cycles. Empirically, he certainly limits the number of waves of protest that took place in the twentieth century (ignoring the Great Unrest of 1910–14, and the revolutionary wave of 1917–23, for example), and his periodisation of the 'cycles' may be questioned – his first cycle omits the biggest general strike in US history (1946) and by ending his second cycle in 1972 he excludes the Greek struggles against the Generals, the anti-Franco movement in Spain and the Portuguese revolution. Conceptually, the language of 'cycles' can lead to assumptions of a regular pattern of oscillation – with its 'inevitable' victories and defeats. Theoretically, we would question his notion that the key actors in each of the three cycles were radically different (labour organisations in the first, students in the second, intellectuals and worker organisations in the third) and that, therefore, these struggles – certainly in the second and third cycle – are distinct from 'class struggles' which must be assumed to occur only in the industrial field. Capitalism is a totality structured by competing, antagonistic classes and society is marked by the 'now hidden, now open fight' (Marx and Engels, 1848/1973: 68) between these contending social groups. But this fight is not simply restricted to the sphere of material production. The forms of protest generated are not static, nor is their location restricted to particular spheres of social life.

Nevertheless there are some very useful insights in Tarrow's work. First, his approach emphasises that periods of apparent calm and social harmony are not unusual. There are periods when grievances are submerged, when collective aspirations are limited and suppressed, when it seems as if nothing will change, except perhaps through gradual incremental reforms. Writing about the explosions of 1968, Chris Harman notes:

> There are periods which seem calm beyond belief to those who look back on them. Such were the years that ended so dramatically in the spring of 1968. (1988: 1)

In the 20 years prior to 1968 the dominant ideas within academia were those which suggested that the world had changed and that the class struggle was over. Even left-wing academics such as André Gorz, for example, wrote in the *Socialist Register* that 'in the foreseeable future there will be no crisis of European capitalism so dramatic as to drive the mass of workers to revolutionary general strikes' (1968: 111) – although unfortunately for Gorz, while his article was being printed the biggest General Strike in world history rocked France.

And this is the second relevant point that Tarrow's analysis points to. However bleak or calm it may seem, the contradictions of capitalism mean that it is increasingly likely that such conflicts will burst out. The competitive drive of capitalism constantly forces each unit of capital to try and increase its rate of exploitation of labour, economic uncertainty forces governments to try and restructure their debt and expenditure patterns, the expansion of capitalism threatens environmental security and the sustainability of the planet, political liberties and freedoms are restricted and controlled, and throughout the world the struggle for daily survival becomes harder for those at the bottom – on various planes the drives of capitalism increase the pressure until somewhere, at some point, the grievances burst out into conflict. Neither the time and intensity of such conflicts nor their outcomes are predictable – but the history of capitalism, and even more so the history of the twentieth century, is a history of class conflict.

A third important element within Tarrow's approach is his claim that protest waves are international. The internationalisation of capitalism has given rise to an increasingly integrated international working class – all subject to the same rhythms of capitalism's economic and political conflicts and crises; learning forms of struggle, strategies and tactics from each other.

Finally, when such protests burst forth they suddenly raise the hopes and visions of participants in numerous ways. These participants generally respond by developing a series of demands, both economic and political. The Polish Marxist Rosa Luxemburg in her discussion of the mass strike (drawing her experience of the Russian Revolution of 1905) noted that during these episodes the separation of 'political' and 'economic' struggle is blown asunder. In these periods ordinary people raise economic demands that flow over into political ones and vice versa:

> [T]he movement on the whole does not proceed from the economic to the political struggle, nor even the reverse. Every great political mass action, after it has attained its highest point, breaks up into a mass of economic strikes … With the spreading, clarifying and involution of the political struggle, the economic struggle not only does not recede, but extends, organises and becomes involved in equal measure. Between the two there is the most complete reciprocal action.
>
> Every new onset and every fresh victory of the political struggle is transformed into a powerful impetus for the economic struggle, extending at the same time its eternal possibilities and intensifying the inner urge of the workers to better their position, and their desire to struggle. After every foaming wave of political action, a fructifying deposit remains behind from which a thousand stalks of economic struggle shoot forth. And conversely. The workers' condition of ceaseless economic struggle with the capitalists keeps their fighting energy alive in every political interval; it forms, so to speak, the permanent fresh reservoir of the strength of the proletarian classes, from which the political fight ever renews its strength. (1906/1986: 50)

In a similar vein Tarrow notes how waves spread out to encompass society as a whole:

Protest waves are characterized by heightened conflict: not only in industrial relations, but in the streets; not only there, but in villages and schools. ... What is most distinctive about such periods is not that entire societies 'rise' in the same direction at the same time (they seldom do); or that particular population groups act in the same way over and over, but that the demonstration effect of collective action on the part of a small group of 'early risers' triggers a variety of processes of diffusion, extension, imitation and reaction among groups that are normally quiescent. (1994: 155–6)

At the high point of protest waves the *possibility* of the working class acting as the self-conscious gravedigger of capitalism becomes real. Nothing is predetermined, nothing is inevitable but a better world becomes possible.

A class struggle approach

Class analysis is largely *class struggle* analysis. (Miliband, 1989: 3)

We end this chapter by giving an example of how a focus on class and class struggle can influence the study of social policy. It is our contention that it is necessary to adopt a 'class struggle analysis' of social policy and social welfare. By this we mean that our analysis needs to recognise that society is based on the exploitation of the majority by a minority and that objectively these two groups have an antagonistic relationship. The ruling minority utilise an array of measures (from ideological domination to physical coercion) to maintain their dominant position and thus the 'shape' of society is deeply affected by the strategies adopted by the ruling class to maintain their rule and the various overt and covert responses to this from the oppressed and exploited. Hence class conflict is built into the very fabric of society. The totality is one that is structured by conflict; social policy and welfare is completely imbued with the practices and effects of class struggle.

To emphasis how this general 'class struggle approach' shapes analysis let us take one example, the growth of the prison population in the US, recently discussed by Jonathan Neale. The prison population in the US has grown from 200,000 in 1971 to over 2 million by the year 2000. 'By 1999, 45 per cent of prisoners were black' and:

At any one time over a third of black men between the ages of 18 and 30 were in prison, on probation or awaiting trial. In the black working class, and in the inner cities, the proportion was even higher. Behind the 2 million people in prison were the many millions more who had been to prison in the previous 20 years. And behind those men were their parents and wives and children, tens of millions of them. Almost every black worker had some relative who had been to prison. (Neale, 2000: 191–3)

Neale argues that in order to understand the ten-fold increase in the US prison population and the demonisation of the black working class we must look at the backlash initiated by the American ruling class in the mid- to late 1970s against the 'progressive movements' of the 1960s (see also Faludi, 1992). During the late 1960s, the civil rights movement, the anti-Vietnam war rebellion (by peace activists and GIs), and the labour, student, women's and gay movements were all able to inflict defeats on the US ruling class. Black workers had been at the heart of the late 1960s movements – both in actuality and by their example – and thus when the movements receded and the ruling class scrambled to reassert their domination they focussed their sights on the black population. As Neale notes:

> The American ruling class ... reacted to the mass union movement between 1938 and 1946 with ... persecution of Communists ... In the 80s and 90s they reacted to the civil rights movement and Vietnam with a persecution of blacks that sent millions to prison. (2000: 94)

There are three important points raised from this example. First, that historical context, the class struggle in its widest sense, is an essential backdrop to our understanding of social policy developments and their consequences. Second, 'class struggle' is conflict between (at least) two antagonistic classes, something that oppressing classes engage in as much as the oppressed. Third, the link between any 'conflict' and state social or public policy or other state developments may not be direct. Often it is the mere presence of the working class that shapes social policy in certain directions or, in our example above, the imprisonment and criminalisation policies have not only involved the arrest of black political activists (although many such political prisoners do exist within the US system) but has spread down to affect many millions of black working-class families – and indeed has spread beyond the black community with increasing numbers of poor white and Latino families facing the same criminalising processes.

The point is, however, that without a focus on the conflictual, class basis of society we fail to fully comprehend the rationale and logic behind policies and their affects on ordinary working people. And without a recognition of the centrality of class struggle to society we also fail to point to the mechanisms whereby we can establish a future free from such conflicts and oppressions.

5 'People have become objects': The Roots of Alienation

Power is a central theme in much current social welfare writing, particularly in the areas of critical social policy and anti-oppressive practice (Thompson, 1998). Reflecting the influence of post-structuralism (Bradbury, 1988; Callinicos, 1989; O'Brien and Penna, 1998), power within this body of literature is usually conceived of as *omnipresent*. The micro-relations of men and women, blacks and whites, gays and straights, are seen as being (in a frequently-used expression) *saturated* with power. It is a view of power which fits with 'common-sense' experience – after all, large numbers of individual men clearly do assault and abuse women, many whites do behave in racist ways towards black people. In this view, it is male power which is responsible for sexism, pornography, rape, child abuse; white power for the racism experienced by black people; and so on. Not surprisingly, as we shall see in Chapter 6, this notion of power plays a key role in current theories of oppression.

Marx's starting point was very different. For, he argued, while there is a group of people in society – the ruling class – who, directly and indirectly, do wield enormous power over the lives of millions, the experience of the vast majority of working-class people is an experience not of power but rather of *powerlessness*, of having little or no control over the major areas of their own lives. It is that lack of power which often leads people to behave in violent and anti-social ways towards others and themselves, and which breeds the despair and frustration that contribute to drug and alcohol abuse, mental health problems and family breakdown. As the journalist Nick Davies (1998) found in his study of 'hidden Britain', it was this lack of power and control over their own lives that fuelled the anti-social behaviour of the young men in Britain's abandoned housing schemes, rather than a lack of father figures or an innate yobbishness as Charles Murray (1990) would have it. Alongside the poverty that coloured every aspect of the lives of those whom Davies interviewed was a deep sense of being trapped, of being completely impotent in the face of vast impersonal economic forces:

> ... they suffered not only a lack of material things but also a deep lack of opportunity to do anything about it. There were many people here who would never escape and who knew that to be the fact of their lives: they felt a deep despair which occasionally erupted in aggression and crime. (1998: 110)

Similarly, in her exploration of the current 'crisis of masculinity', Susan Faludi describes how she began her research by assuming that:

> The male crisis in America was caused by something men were *doing* unrelated by something being done to them, and that its cure was surely to be found in figuring out how to get men to *stop* whatever it was. I had my own favourite whipping-boy, suspecting that the crisis of masculinity was caused by masculinity on the rampage. (2000: 7)

After several months of sitting in on a therapeutic group for men who had been perpetrators of domestic violence, however, Faludi's views began to shift radically:

> There was something almost absurd about these men struggling, week after week, to recognise themselves as dominators when they were so clearly dominated, done in by the world. (2000: 7)

Referring to 'The Power and Control Wheel', a mimeographed chart that enumerated the myriad ways that men could victimise their mates, one man in the group claimed: 'That "wheel" is misnamed ... it should be called the "Powerlessness and Out-of-Control Wheel"' (2000: 9). Faludi comments:

> The men had probably felt in control when they beat their wives, but their everyday experience was of being controlled – a feeling they had no way of expressing because to reveal it was less than masculine, would make each of them, in fact, 'no man at all'. (2000: 9)

As Faludi notes, there are no circumstances that exonerate such behaviour and in seeking to make the men take responsibility for their actions, the counsellors were pursuing a worthy goal. But as both she and Davies discovered, notions of 'male power' do not take use very far in *explaining* such behaviour. Rather, it is an understanding of the *lack* of power and control which working-class people experience over all aspects of their lives that provides the most useful starting-point for making sense of their lives and behaviour; and it is that understanding which is at the heart of Marx's theory of alienation. While that lack of power is experienced most acutely by those whom capital does not regard as even worthy of exploitation – those excluded from the labour market on grounds of age, disability or lack of skills – it is in the process of the production and circulation of commodities that the roots of alienation are to be found. That theory has been described by Istvan Meszaros as 'the central idea of Marx's system' (1970/1986). It is a theory of potentially enormous value to those working in the area of social welfare, where a lack of power, along with a lack of money, is often the common denominator of those who depend, through poverty or through legal compulsion, on the services of the welfare state. In practice, however, within the social policy and social work literature, as in the wider social science literature, the theory of alienation has tended to suffer trivialisation, distortion and neglect.

Rojek, Peacock and Collins (1988) provide an example of this trivialisation in their attempt to apply post-structuralist ideas to social work. They write:

> The Marxist concept of alienation ... explains everything and nothing. For while social workers will find it easy to give examples of isolation, despair and estrangement amongst clients, they are very often tempered with examples of clients who attest to warm and satisfactory relationships with members of their family, friends, co-workers etc. (1988: 74–5)

The courage, resilience and warmth, which many social work clients and poor people generally display in the face of enormous adversity, should undoubtedly be applauded. Not all poor people abuse drugs, become depressed or behave in 'anti-social' ways. A majority do not. However, that ability to resist and to maintain loving relationships in the face of poverty and stigmatisation should not be allowed to obscure the fact that in general, drug abuse, mental health problems and levels of violence and despair *are* much more prevalent amongst the poorer sections of the working class, as the writings of social-work clients testify (see, for example, Holman, 1998). Failing to provide an explanation for that ill-health and despair, of the sort which Marx provides, leaves the door open for underclass theories which seek to blame the poor for their welfare dependency and lack of moral fibre (Murray, 1990).

This particular distortion of Marx's theory of alienation has its roots in a view of alienation as primarily a psychological or emotional state, a feeling of estrangement and unease. Alienation, in other words, is something 'in people's heads', a view of alienation whose theoretical origins lie in the socialist humanist movement which developed in Western Europe and the US in the late 1950s.

Alienation, socialist humanism and Stalinism

Socialist humanism refers to the ideas and the movement developed by those writers, activists and trade union militants who broke with Stalinism following the crushing of the Hungarian Revolution by Russian tanks in 1956 to form what became known as 'the New Left'. For many of these individuals, including the British historians Edward Thompson and John Saville and the psychoanalyst Eric Fromm in the US, the recently translated writings of the young Marx and particularly his writings on alienation provided them in the late 1950s and early 1960s with an invaluable tool with which to criticise both Western capitalism and Soviet 'communism'.

The theory of alienation highlighted the way in which the enormous growth in the productive capacity of humankind during the years of the long boom following the Second World War had led not to an increase in human freedom but rather to massive arms spending in both East and West and to a Cold War which threatened on a daily basis to spill over into nuclear conflagration.

The theory could also explain why it was that, despite rising living standards and the growth of consumerism, millions of people still felt dissatisfied and unfulfilled, estranged from their fellow human beings and members of what one popular text of the period described as 'the lonely crowd' (Reisman, 1959/1969).

The significance of Marx's early writings for those who rejected Stalinism but were not prepared to accept that there was no alternative to Western capitalism is well conveyed by Berman in a recent collection of writings:

> The thing I found so striking in Marx's 1844 essays [*Economic and Philosophical Manuscripts*], and which I did not expect to find at all, was their feeling for the individual. These early essays articulate the conflict between *Bildung* and alienated labour. *Bildung* is the core human value in liberal romanticism. It is a hard word to put into English but it embraces a family of ideas like 'subjectivity', 'finding yourself', 'growing up', 'identity', 'self-development', and 'becoming who you are'. Marx situates this ideal in history and gives it a social theory. (1999: 9)

This reassertion of Marxism as a humanism, in the face of the dehumanised caricature of Marxism which was Stalinism, was important in laying the basis for the development of an authentic revolutionary socialism to which a new generation of activists in the 1960s could relate. But in contrast to Marxist writings that followed in Trotsky's footsteps by attempting to develop a materialist critique of the regimes in Russia and Eastern Europe (Trotsky, 1934/1972; Cliff, 1948/1974), the New Left critique of Stalinism was essentially a *moral* one. In reacting against the economic structural determinism of Stalinism, this critique could easily slide into a kind of sentimental socialism, with an over-emphasis on thoughts, feelings and subjectivity at the expense of any concern with the constraining role of social structures. Such a critique could also give rise to a view of alienation as primarily a psychological phenomenon, which could be overcome if only individuals would change the way they viewed the world. Thus, for example, Berman can write that:

> By picturing themselves as unfree, men make themselves unfree: their prophecy of powerlessness is self-fulfilling. (1999: 45)

In similar vein, Eric Fromm (1989) could entitle his text on Marx and Freud *Beyond the Chains of Illusion* – as if alienation was primarily a kind of *maya*, which could be overcome through psychotherapy, without the need to change the conditions that, as Marx argued, gave rise to the feelings of estrangement or dissatisfaction in the first place. Not only does such a view of alienation lend itself to easy parody but, as we shall argue below, it is very far removed from Marx's own view.

Despite these limitations the socialist humanist insistence that Marxism is a form of humanism is indisputably true in one very important sense: that while for Marx the *agent* of socialist revolution is the working class, its *goal* is the emancipation of all humanity and the end of class society. Thus the possibility of emancipation lies:

> In the formation of a class with *radical chains*, ... [a class] which has a universal character because of its universal suffering and which lays claim to no *particular right* because the wrong it suffers is not a *particular wrong* but *wrong in general*; ... [a sphere of society] which cannot emancipate itself without emancipating itself from – and thereby emancipating – all the other spheres of society, which is in a word, the *total loss* of humanity and which can therefore itself only through the *total redemption of humanity*. This dissolution of society as a particular class is the proletariat. (Marx, 1844/1975: 256)

In contrast, the second approach to alienation, which has dominated much thinking on the academic Left over the past three decades, rejects such concerns. This approach stemmed from the attempt by 'structuralist Marxists' in the 1960s and 1970s, notably Louis Althusser, to claim an 'epistemological break' (a decisive shift in his theoretical conceptions) between the young, allegedly immature, Marx and the mature Marx of *Capital*. In this view, the writings of the young Marx, including his writings on alienation, can safely be ignored since they represent little more than neo-Hegelian juvenilia, a 'humanism' which was superseded by the more scientific approach of the older Marx. We need not concern ourselves here with the intricacies of this now largely historical debate. Most adherents of structuralist Marxism have long since abandoned Marxism in any form, embracing some variety of post-structuralism or post-Marxism (Laclau and Mouffe, 1985; Carver, 2000). In addition, the continuity of Marx's work and the absence of an epistemological break of the sort claimed by Althusser has been convincingly demonstrated by a number of authoritative studies (for example, Nicolaus, 1972; Walton and Gamble, 1972). For our purposes, what is important to note is that much of the Marxist writing of the 1970s and early 1980s, including writings on welfare (for example, Corrigan and Leonard, 1979) was deeply influenced by Althusserian approaches and consequently the notion of alienation barely merits a footnote.

In this chapter we wish to look afresh at Marx's theory of alienation and to argue that this theory, properly understood, provides a basis both for making sense of welfare work and also for understanding the experience of many welfare clients. This will involve both giving an outline of Marx's theory of alienation and also attempting to demonstrate its relevance to current welfare issues.

Marx's theory of alienation

In Chapter 2 we argued that, for Marx, capitalism as a mode of production is characterised by two great cleavages. The first is that between the competing units of capital, be they privately owned or state owned, corner shop or multinational. The second great division is between the tiny number of people who own the means of production and the great mass of people who have nothing to sell but their ability to work – what Marx called their *labour power*. It is clear that for Marx that ability to work includes not only manual skills, but also technical skills, intellectual skills and artistic skills. It also includes helping skills of the sort employed by welfare workers. The appearance over the past decade of textbooks with titles like *Costing Community Care* (Netten and Beecham, 1993) shows that such skills also have their price.

It is this separation of the producers from the means of production that distinguishes capitalism from all previous modes of production. As Rees argues:

> For the first time in human history, the mass of the laboring classes have lost control over the means of production and the products of their labor. The modern working class must go to the owners of the means of production in order to work; it must produce what it is told to produce, at the pace it is told to produce, in the time it is told to produce, by a capitalist class that has sole control over the means of production. (1998a: 89)

It is this loss of control, more severe under capitalism than under any previous mode of production, that Marx describes as alienation. He distinguishes four aspects of alienation, involving the worker's relation to: the product of her work; her productive activity; what Marx called her 'species-being' and her fellow human beings (Marx, 1844/1975: 324–34). Each of these will be examined in turn.

The product of labour

Under capitalism the worker has no control over *what* is produced – the product of her labour – which belongs to and is disposed of by the employer. In previous societies people have used their creative abilities to produce goods which they would consume, exchange or sell. By contrast under capitalism many workers will often be unable to purchase the item that they have produced, be it a pair of designer jeans, a personal computer or a new car. For example, as Sheridan and McCombes note, in Vietnam the sportswear giant Nike:

> Employ around 80,000 workers, mainly young women, churning out running shoes for export to the west. Their average wage last year worked out at the

equivalent of around £15 a month, which means they would have to save every penny of their wages for five months before they could actually buy a pair of Nike Air running shoes. (2000: 49)

Similarly, workers in the service sector, whether they work in call centres, the leisure industry or the banking and finance sector, will often be unable to afford the fitted kitchens, the expensive holidays or the credit deals which they sell day in and day out to wealthier customers. More than that, for most workers, what they produce is often of little or no consequence in itself but is simply a means to an end. In Marx's words:

> The product of his activity is not the object of his activity. What he produces for himself is not the silk that he weaves, not the gold that he draws from the mine, not the palace that he builds. What he produces for himself is wages, and silk, gold, palace resolve themselves for him into a definite quantity of the means of subsistence, perhaps into a cotton jacket, some copper coins, and a lodging in the cellar. (cited in Meszaros, 1970/1986: 122).

Some writers have argued that while Marx's description holds true for workers on the assembly line of a car factory, it is less true for those workers who enjoy a degree of control over what they produce or, in the case of service workers, over the content of their work: they are 'less alienated', in other words (Davies and Shragge, 1990). Social workers and university lecturers, for example, might be seen as two groups of white-collar workers who experience a greater degree of control over both the content and the process of their work than most workers. It might also be argued that they experience a greater degree of job satisfaction. The erosion of control over the work process will be discussed in the next section. In terms of the content of their work, however, the extension of market forces throughout the 1990s into both social services (Mooney, 1997) and into higher education means that, whatever control such workers may previously have enjoyed over the products of their labour, that control is fast disappearing. Within higher education, for example, the increasing regulation of education by government through such mechanisms as the Research Assessment Exercise, or in the case of professional education, by national training bodies which are increasingly employer-dominated (Jones, 1999), means the content of lecturers' activity is increasingly prescribed from without. Similarly, academic staff have less and less control over the products of their labour. The following clause, for example, concerning the ownership of academic copyright, was included in a new contract issued to staff in the new University sector in Scotland in 2000:

> All findings, discoveries, records, drawings, documents, papers, books, computer programmes, computer software products or any other such material made or acquired by you in the course of your employment, shall be the property of the University, which shall retain copyright and other intellectual rights

therein, unless the University intimates in writing that it has decided not to do so. (University of Paisley, 2000)

For staff in social work and social services, the loss of control over the content of their work has gone even further, as the job has been transformed through the introduction of care management approaches (Jones, 2001). As one worker commented in a study of the impact of managerial approaches in social services:

Well, if you want to become a counsellor, don't come into social services. If you want to be an assessor and a purchaser of services and a care manager, which is a more managerial, monitoring, reviewing type of role, then those are the sort of skills that are going to be needed for today's social worker and social workers into the next century or however long we last. You've got to be skilled at using modern technology, you've got to be skilled at managing funds, money and that's all a new skill for me – in terms of costing. (Harris, 1998: 856).

The degree of distaste felt by many social workers towards this managerial ethos is vividly illustrated by a major study of social workers conducted in the mid-1990s in which 44 per cent of those interviewed agreed that 'I feel that my values are different from the Department's values' (Balloch et al., 1995: 87). As the authors of the study noted, 'Perhaps as a reflection of social workers' disillusionment with the increasing amount of administrative work they have to do, almost half, 48 per cent, said they would be interested in becoming an independent counsellor, and in response to a separate item, 29 per cent would like to move out of social services altogether' (1995: 93).

The labour process

The second element of Marx's theory refers to loss of control over the labour process. As we shall see in the next section, Marx conceives of work not in the narrow sense of paid labour but rather as creative, conscious activity, such activity being the major feature that distinguishes human beings from other animals. Under capitalism, however, not only the goal and the end product of such activity is determined by others but so, too, is the work process. This means that such work is usually experienced as anything but fulfilling. The consequence of this lack of control over the work process is that:

Labour is external to the worker i.e. does not belong to his essential being; that he therefore does not confirm himself in his work, but denies himself, feels miserable and not happy, does not develop free mental and physical energy, but mortifies his flesh and ruins his mind. Hence the worker feels himself only when he is not working; when he is working he does not feel himself. He is at home when he is not working, and not at home when he is working. His labour is therefore not voluntary but forced, it is forced labour. It is therefore not the satisfaction of a need but a mere means to satisfy needs outside itself. Its alien character is clearly demonstrated by the fact that as soon as no physical or other compulsion exists it is shunned like the plague. (Marx, 1844/1975: 326).

This aspect of alienation stems not only from the separation of the producers from the means of production but also from the second great split which was noted in Chapter three as characteristic of the capitalist mode of production, namely the split between the producers themselves and the competition to which it gives rise. That competition requires individual capitalists constantly to seek new ways to increase their profits *vis-à-vis* their rivals (on the assumption that they wish to remain in business) and that in turn means constantly seeking new ways of organising the labour process which will increase the productivity of the workforce. It should be noted that as capitalists have no choice in this process, they too are alienated; as Marx cryptically pointed out, however, 'they are happy in their alienation'!

While the *forms* of organisation which predominate will vary from time to time, with Taylorism or scientific management approaches popular in one period and 'human relations' approaches dominant at another, the end – of organising the labour process in a way that ensures maximum productivity – remains the same.

That drive to increase productivity gives rise in turn to what is perhaps the most distinctive feature of capitalism – the division of labour. As Marx emphasised in his development of the labour theory of value, in a society based upon generalised commodity production, the one common element shared by all commodities and the element that gives them their value is the amount of labour time they contain. This means that not only every job, but also every part of a job can be broken down and costed. Since, as Braverman notes, 'in a society based upon the purchase and sale of labour power, dividing the craft cheapens its individual parts' (1974: 80). From the beginning of the industrial system, employers have had an interest in breaking jobs down into smaller and smaller parts. While the result may be to increase profits for the employer, the effects on the workers themselves is devastating. Lukács outlines the process as follows:

> The process of labour is progressively broken down into abstract, specialised operations so that the worker loses contact with the finished product and his work is reduced to the mechanical repetition of a specialised set of actions ... In consequence of the rationalisation of the work-process, the human qualities and idiosyncrasies of the worker appear increasingly as mere sources of error when contrasted with these abstract special laws functioning according to rational predictions. (1971: 88).

There is both a subjective and an objective side to this phenomenon. Subjectively, as we saw above in the quote from Marx, it means that work is experienced not as a source of satisfaction and personal development but rather as alien, as drudgery; the worker is a prisoner of the work process.

> Neither objectively nor in his relation to his work does man appear as the authentic master of this process; on the contrary, he is a mechanical part fitted into a mechanical system. (Lukács, 1971: 88).

Objectively, the drive to accumulate, which is the central dynamic of the capitalist system, leads to the increasing commodification of every area of life. This process has accelerated enormously over the past two decades and now includes not only the sphere of consumption and lifestyle but also, in the area of welfare, the most personal caring skills of welfare workers which, as we have seen, can now be costed by the hour. The extension of market forces to health and social services gives rise to forms of welfare in which as Marx puts it, 'Time is everything, man is nothing. Quality no longer matters. Quantity alone decides everything: hour for hour, day for day … ' (cited in Lukács, 1971: 89–90).

The process of work fragmentation has increased enormously since Marx's day, most obviously through the widespread introduction in the twentieth century of assembly line methods. In addition, as we noted in the last chapter, Braverman (1974) has shown how the 'industrialisation of white-collar work' has eroded the privileged status previously enjoyed by many white-collar workers. Clarke's comments on the implications of managerialism on notions of professionalism within social work have relevance for a much wider range of public sector workers:

> Professionalism has been placed on the defensive by the assertion of customer-centred models of provision, the fragmentation of professional tasks and the expectation that professionals can be disciplined by the creation of devolved managerial systems and new responsibilities for resource control. (Clarke, 1996: 53)

Our human nature

The third aspect of alienation that Marx identifies is estrangement from our human nature (or, as he calls it, our 'species-being'). By this, Marx specifically did *not* mean the allegedly fixed, unchanging human nature so beloved of conservative philosophers and reactionary sociobiologists – that human beings are 'essentially selfish' for example, or that men are always warlike or rapacious. He had dismissed this conception as early as his mid-twenties in his critique of the German philosopher Ludwig Feuerbach when he wrote that 'the human essence is no abstraction inherent in each single individual. In its reality it is the ensemble of social relations' (1844/1975). Since social relations are constantly changing, so too are the characteristics of human beings. Rather, for Marx, species-being meant those characteristics of humans which distinguish them from other animals. Foremost amongst these is the ability to perform conscious labour:

> The practical creation of an objective world, the fashioning of inorganic nature, is proof that man is a conscious species-being … It is true that animals also produce. They build nests and dwellings, like the bee, the beaver, the ant, and so on. But they produce only their own immediate needs or those of their young; they produce one-sidedly, while man produces universally; they produce only when immediate physical need compels them to do so, when man produces even when he is free from physical need and truly produces only in freedom from such need. (Marx, 1844/1975: 328–9).

As an example of what such creative ability might mean, a conclusion of a major study into stress and job satisfaction in social services in England and Wales was that:

> For most staff … the greatest satisfaction came from aspects over which they had the greatest control, which produced rewards attributable to their own efforts. Least satisfying were aspects over which they had least control which were attributable to somebody or something else. (Balloch et al., 1999: 65)

For most workers under capitalism, this capacity for creative labour is often frustrated, fragmented or denied. It is not only on the assembly line that workers are required to engage in meaningless, repetitive, mind-numbing work. For many 'white-collar' workers in typing pools or call centres, there is scarcely more opportunity to work in a creative way. Even within occupations such as social work, where the scope for such creative work may be thought to be greater, the impact of managerialism has often been to bring about a culture of 'never mind the quality, feel the width' which workers often experience as intensely alienating. As a worker cited in a study of the labour process within state social work commented:

> There is the culture now of moving work through and it's seen as good if you can be closing cases. The fact that you might close them this month and the same client might meet you in three months' time doesn't seem material … If you only had 10 to 15 clients that you were doing really good thorough work with, it's really not so important to be doing that sort of work anymore. (Harris, 1998: 858)

In contrast to this denial or distortion of workers' creative abilities, for Marx a socialist or communist society would permit the universal, rounded development of all through the exercise of their skills and talents.

The denial of creative ability is greatest amongst those excluded from the labour process, like the angry young men interviewed by Davies in the study mentioned earlier:

They all had their own dreams, most of them very mundane. They wanted to go to college, get a job or simply to have something to do all day. In real life, as they readily described, there were only two things to do – thieving and twocking [stealing cars]. They wanted much more. Their lives refused to let them have it, so they became frustrated and hopeless and bitterly angry. And they fought their war against the law with a furious rage. (1998: 82)

The disability theorist Paul Abberley (1996) has criticised Marx's emphasis on creative labour as implicitly disablist, arguing that since even in a socialist society individuals would be still valued on the basis of the work that they did, the limitations imposed by physical impairment would continue to constitute a barrier to full social integration. In fact, Abberley's argument rests on a misunderstanding of Marx's position.

It is not work *per se*, let alone alienated labour, that is at the heart of Marx's vision but something much richer and deeper. Berman sums it up as follows:

If Marx is fetishistic about anything, it is not work or production but rather the far more complex and comprehensive ideal of development – the 'free development of physical and spiritual energies' (1844 manuscripts); 'development of a totality of capacities in the individuals themselves' (*German Ideology*); 'the free development of each will be the condition for the free development of all' (*Manifesto*); 'the universality of individual needs, capacities, pleasures, productive forces, etc.' (*Grundrisse*); 'the fully developed individual' (*Capital*). (1982: 127)

For Marx, a socialist society would remove as many of the barriers as possible which prevent individuals being all that they are capable of being. It is, of course, true that since not all barriers are socially constructed, not all are capable of being removed. In respect of physical impairment, for example, some barriers would remain. As Stack has argued:

Some people say you're not disabled, you're 'differently abled'. It's rubbish. I would have loved to have been able to dance, play the guitar and play for Ireland in the World Cup. None of these things were available to me because of my disability. We should recognise what we face in society. We don't bend to it, don't bow to it, don't cringe before it and fight against it. We aim to lead as full but normal a life as possible. We want to overcome every obstacle that can be physically overcome without playing word games that pretends that something is what it isn't. (1995: 15)

That said, the prioritisation of need over profit in a socialist society would, on the one hand, allow resources to be devoted to the kind of high-quality medical services which many disability activists currently demand and which they are currently denied (Campbell and Oliver, 1996). On the other, it would allow for the removal of the structural, economic and social barriers which the disability movement has identified as constituting the major impediments to people with impairments leading a full life (Oliver, 1996; Oliver and Barnes, 1998).

Alienation from our fellow human beings

The fourth aspect of alienation discussed by Marx is alienation from our fellow human beings. Most obviously there is the alienation between those who own or control the means of production and those whom they exploit. The competition which drives capitalism leaves little room for feelings of human solidarity or collective interest between capitalist and capitalist on the one hand, and between capitalist and worker on the other. As Ollman suggests, in words which recall the world of the movie *Wall St.*:

> Competition may thus be viewed as the activity which produces class. Throughout society, calculator meets calculator in the never-ending battle of who can get the most out of whom. 'Mutual exploitation' is the rule. Other people are mere objects of use; their wishes and feelings are never considered, cannot be on pain of extinction. A lapse into kindness for those who have their own knives poised can be fatal. In this situation, hearts are opened only to absolute losers; charity becomes the only form of giving. (1976: 206)

In the face of such pressures, what is surprising is not so much that people sometimes behave in selfish or anti-social ways but rather that people continue to exhibit as much altruism as they do, on a daily basis and in a myriad different ways, from becoming blood donors to contributing to disaster appeals. For as Ollman argues, the selfishness and egotism which conservative theorists love to attribute to human nature and which lead human beings to see other human beings as a threat, find their origins in the most basic social relations of capitalism:

> Among the proletariat, competition first rears its head at the factory gate where some are allowed in and others not. Inside the factory, workers continue to compete with each other for such favours as their employer has it in him to bestow, especially for the easier and better-paying jobs. After work, with too little money to spend, workers are again at each other's throats for the inadequate food, clothing and shelter available to them. (1976: 207)

If, as Ollman suggests, it is this competition which makes it difficult to organise workers, it is also this competition which leads one set of workers to perceive another set of workers as a threat or an enemy. As we shall discuss in more detail in Chapter 6, for Marx this was the root cause of a variety of different types of discrimination and oppression – something of which, he argued, the ruling class was only too well aware and willing to exploit as a tool to divide and rule. In the British context, the hostility shown in recent years to asylum seekers is a case in point. What the theory of alienation highlights, however, is that far from such feelings and behaviours being natural or inevitable, they are the direct product of feelings of despair and powerlessness which the system creates.

Commodity fetishism

So far, we have looked at the ways in which Marx's theory of alienation helps us make sense of the work process under capitalism. But, Marx argued, the separation of workers from the means of production had implications that went far beyond this. The link between alienation in the work process and alienation throughout society as a whole is to be found in his related theory of commodity fetishism.

In contrast to earlier forms of society where goods were produced primarily for personal use or exchange, Marx argued, capitalism is based on generalised commodity production: the goal of production is not use but profit. In this world, everything, including the ability to work, is turned into a commodity. Like so many other aspects of capitalism that Marx identified, be it the growth of the working class or the internationalisation of capital, the process is much clearer in our own times than it was when Marx was writing. It is now impossible to think of any area of life or relationships which market forces have not penetrated, be it the most basic 'natural' resources such as water, the manipulation of the privatised sphere of family and personal life through the 'lifestyle' industry, or the commodification of altruism expressed in the costing of social and health care. A recent extension of this process can be seen in the 'branding' revolution of the 1990s where the symbols and logos of corporate capitalism, be it Nike, Starbucks or Microsoft, seem to take on a role and existence independent of the products they represent (Klein, 2000).

It is this apparent power of commodities, which are after all the products of human activity, to take on a life of their own which Marx describes as commodity fetishism. The process is seen most clearly in the operation of the 'universal commodity' – money.

> The stronger the power of my money, the stronger am I. The properties of money are my, the possessor's properties and essential powers. Therefore what I *am* and what I *can do* is by no means determined by my individuality. I *am* ugly but I can buy the *most beautiful* woman. Which means to say that I am not *ugly*, for the effect of *ugliness*, its repelling power, is destroyed by money. As an individual, I am *lame*, but money provides me with twenty-four legs. Consequently, I am not lame ... Through money, I can have anything the human heart desires. Do I not therefore possess all human abilities? Does not money transform all my incapacities into their opposite? ... The inversion and confusion of all human and natural qualities, the bringing together of impossibilities, the *divine* power of money lies in its *nature* as the estranged and alienating species essence of man which alienates itself by selling itself. It is the alienated *capacity* of *mankind*. (Marx, 1844/1975: 377)

Two aspects of this process are particularly significant. Firstly, relationships between people take on the appearance of a relationship between things, objects of exchange. The social nature of production is made invisible in the circulation of commodities, in a way that is not the case with earlier modes of production, such as feudalism.

> Since the producers do not come into social contact until they exchange the products of their labour, the specific social characteristics of their private labours appear only within this exchange ... To the producers, therefore, the social relations between their private labours appear as what they are, that is, they do not appear as direct social relations between persons in their work, but rather as material [*dinglich*] relations between persons and social relations between things. (Marx, 1867/1976: 165–6)

Secondly, commodities in general and 'the market' in particular appear to operate quite independently of human activity, as powers over which not only individual human beings but even national governments have no control – 'you can't buck the market' (a perception reinforced by fashionable theories of globalisation, see Chapter 8). Markets, currencies, and share prices 'rise' and 'fall' as if by magic, with the language employed to describe their movement often that of the natural world, with economic crises variously referred to as 'storms', 'typhoons' or (following the collapse of the 'Asian Tigers'), 'contagion'.

As Lukács argued, there is both an objective and a subjective side to this process:

> *Objectively* a world of objects and relations between things springs into being (the world of commodities and their movements on the market). The laws governing these objects are indeed gradually discovered by man, but even so they confront him as invisible forces that generate their own power. The individual can use his knowledge of these laws to his own advantage but even so they confront him as invisible forces that generate their own power. *Subjectively*, ... a man's activity becomes estranged from himself, it turns into a commodity which, subject to the non-human activity of the natural laws of society, must go its own way independently of man just like any consumer article. (1971: 87)

Although often neglected or dismissed, as Rees has argued (1998a), the theory of commodity fetishism is central to Marx's theory of ideology. It provides a *material* basis for the fact that most of the time, in most parts of the world, the vast majority of working-class people are prepared to accept, sometimes grudgingly, sometimes enthusiastically, the continued existence of an economic system which ruthlessly exploits them. Of course it is true that the ownership of the press and the media by a handful of individuals who are totally committed to capitalism and whose newspapers and television channels daily extol the merits of the market (as well as sowing racist, sexist and homophobic divisions amongst their readers and viewers) is also crucial to this process: as Marx noted, 'the ruling ideas in every age are the ideas of the ruling class' (1845/1978). So too is the existence of 'bodies of armed men' in the form of the police and the army prepared to brutally suppress resistance to the system, from Seattle to East Timor. By themselves, however, these factors cannot explain the willingness of hundreds of millions of working people, day in day out to accept capitalism and the political institutions which accompany it. The theory of commodity fetishism *does* provide the basis of such an explanation. As Rees argues:

> And so to add to the sense of dehumanisation, passivity and division induced by alienation, commodity fetishism produces a very definite new element: the appearance that class exploitation is not a social product but the inevitable and unalterable result of the functioning of the market ... Starvation in poor countries is as unavoidable as the weather. Cynicism or charity, fatalism or utopianism seem the only possible responses. And, however much one might prefer the latter to the former, they both leave the essential workings of the system untouched. (1998a: 94–5)

In addition, since in principle anyone can buy anything on the market, from a loaf of bread to a night at the Ritz, the workings of the market seem not only inevitable but also fair and just. So too do the political institutions to which it gives rise: after all, within a parliamentary democracy the unemployed car worker from Birmingham has one vote, exactly the same as Stagecoach millionaire Brian Souter. The fact that Souter was able during the year 2000 to bankroll a homophobic campaign to subvert the mandate of the Scottish Parliament is not perceived as undermining the basic 'fairness' of the system.

These same ideas of 'fairness' also pervade the welfare system and allow both Conservative and New Labour governments to launch vicious attacks on 'scroungers' and social security 'fraud' while at the same time, and without a blush, cutting corporation tax for wealthy companies, spend billions on wars in Iraq and the former Yugoslavia and boast of having a government 'war chest' of several billion pounds while hospital waiting lists grow longer.

Critics have sometimes accused Marx's theory of commodity fetishism of determinism and fatalism. It is deterministic, it is argued, to suggest that the economic structures and relations of capitalism give rise to specific forms of consciousness, fatalistic since, if this is true, then there is no way that workers can ever escape the web of 'false consciousness'. As Rees (1998a) has demonstrated, both points are mistaken. In respect of the first point, the alternative to seeing the roots of ideology as lying in the material conditions of everyday life under capitalism is to see such ideas as somehow free-floating, or as 'put there' by the ruling class, as if workers were simply passive automatons. In this sense, what the theory of commodity fetishism does is provide the essential basis for a materialist theory of ideology.

With regard to the second point, certainly, if capitalism always functioned smoothly, then one might with justification wonder how such false consciousness could ever be challenged. Far from running smoothly, however, the whole history of capitalism is one of booms punctuated by slumps, crises and wars, wrecking millions of lives and leading to enormous social upheavals. During such upheavals, many who were previously passive and acquiescent can begin to challenge the system on a mass scale. Following the First World War, for example, the Russian Revolution inspired waves of mass struggle in Germany, Hungary and even Britain, for example, leading the French premier Clemenceau to write to the British prime minister Lloyd George: 'The whole existing order, in its political, social and economic aspects, is questioned by the masses from one end of Europe to the other' (cited in Carr, 1966: 136). In such situations, the veil of commodity fetishism is ripped aside and people can see the exploitation and brutality underpinning the apparent 'fairness' of the market.

It is not only during such periods of social cataclysm, however, that people question the system. The day-to-day experience of exploitation in the workplace or of oppression on grounds of 'race' or gender or disability leads many to question the alleged 'fairness' of the system and from time to time, to actively resist. In fact, most of the time, most people experience the world in this contradictory way. The media stigmatisation of lone parents, for example, contrasts with many people's experience of the struggle of a daughter or sister or mother or neighbour trying to bring up her children in a decent way on ever-decreasing state benefits. The social work client's experience of having her life controlled and monitored by a supposedly caring social work department, mirrors the social worker's growing disillusionment with a service which, despite the rhetoric of care, is in reality far more concerned with rationing scarce resources. The experience of black unemployed youth at the hands of a racist police force gives the lie to the notion that British justice is impartial. It is this everyday experience which begins to penetrate the veil of commodity fetishism and gives rise to what the Italian Marxist Antonio Gramsci referred to as 'contradictory consciousness':

> The active man-in-the-mass has a practical activity, but has no clear theoretical consciousness of his practical activity, which nonetheless involves understanding the world in so far as it transforms it. His theoretical consciousness can indeed be historically in opposition to his activity. One might almost say that he has two theoretical consciousnesses (or one contradictory consciousness): one which is implicit in his activity and which in reality unites him with his fellow-workers in the practical transformation of the real world; and one, superficially explicit or verbal, which he has inherited from the past and uncritically absorbed. (1971: 333)

Gramsci is referring to the way in which individuals, groups and classes can hold differing, even contradictory, ideas in their heads at the same time. An example would be the way that large numbers of people would be opposed to any form of racism but would nevertheless see immigration controls as necessary to maintain good 'race relations', as if immigrants (for which read 'black immigrants') were in some way responsible for the level of racism in society.

The ideas which predominate in the heads of individuals at any one time – those which see refugees as a threat to homes and jobs, to be loathed and feared for example, or those which recognise these same refugees as bruised and battered fellow human beings and which reach out a hand of friendship to them – will depend on a range of factors. These include: the state of the economy, including the availability of jobs and houses; the level of confidence within the working class movement; and the extent to which racist ideas are actively challenged or promoted within the workplace and society. Where racist or nationalist or sexist ideas predominate, then not only will the stigmatisation and persecution of oppressed groups be left unchallenged but the divisions which these ideas create in workplaces and communities mean that there is unlikely to be resistance to employer or government attacks on working conditions or community resources. Where, however, ideas of solidarity and common interest prevail, then the outcome can be very different. Not only is it possible for those involved to protect or improve their material conditions but they can also begin to overcome alienation and commodity fetishism and develop a sense of their own collective power. For Marx, it is in the process of collective struggle, above all in a revolution, that this overcoming takes place:

> This revolution is necessary, therefore, not only because the ruling class cannot be overthrown in any other way, but also because the class overthrowing it can only in a revolution succeed in ridding itself of all the muck of ages and becoming fitted found society anew. (Marx, 1845/1978: 193)

A glimpse of this process can be seen not only in the mass struggles which occur during revolutionary periods but also in the more frequent struggles of workers and community activists, including welfare struggles. Marx's theory of alienation provides us with an indispensable starting point for understanding the roots of these struggles and their potential to both change individual human beings and the apparently fixed world in which they live.

6 'The complexities of social differentiation': Explaining Oppression

So far we have argued that class and class struggle are central to an understanding of the formation of welfare policy under capitalism. Class runs like a fault line through every aspect of daily existence, determining life chances in a wide variety of areas such as health, housing, education and occupation. That said, class is clearly not the only division within capitalism. Other divisions, such as gender, 'race', sexual orientation, disability and age also form a basis for discrimination and oppression.

Three examples demonstrate the continuing reality of such oppression. In respect of women's oppression, despite repeated claims over the years by the right-wing media on the one hand and 'post-feminists' on the other that women have now achieved equality with men, the first in the series of reports on *Social Inequalities* showed that women still receive 42 per cent less pay than their equivalent full-time male colleagues, more than 25 years after the passage of the Equal Pay Act (Office of National Statistics, 2000).

Then there is racism. While there is a much higher level of contact between black and white people in workplaces and in communities than was the case 30 years ago, and while the overt expression of racist views is now largely considered unacceptable, racism continues to be endemic in British society. In recent years the issue of asylum seekers, for example, has given rise to a Dutch auction between the New Labour and Conservative leaderships as to who can be seen to be the most 'tough-minded' on this issue. Thus, in response to a speech denouncing asylum seekers in May 2000 by Conservative leader William Hague, which was widely compared to Enoch Powell's infamous 'rivers of blood' speech of 1968, the New Labour minister for immigration proudly announced that a record number of asylum seekers had been deported the previous month. The effect is to make racism respectable and give enormous encouragement to racists everywhere. In an interview with the *Guardian* following Hague's speech, for example, Nick Griffin, leader of the Nazi organisation the British National Party, boasted that 'The asylum seeker issue has been great for us. We have had a phenomenal growth in membership. It's quite fun to watch government ministers and the Tories play the race card in far cruder terms than we would ever use but pretend not to. It legitimises us' (*Guardian*, 20 May 2000).

Finally, there is the persistence of homophobia. A decision by the Scottish Executive in 1999 to repeal the homophobic section 28 (clause 2A) of the Local Government Act 1988 which forbids the 'promotion' of homosexuality in schools, led to a high-profile advertising campaign in favour of retaining the section, funded by a millionaire businessman and supported by the Catholic Church whose leading Scottish representative described gays as 'perverts'. While the clause was eventually repealed, the campaign to maintain it showed the extent to which homophobic feelings and ideas continue to exert an influence.

Such persistent and widespread discrimination and oppression cannot be explained in terms of the words or actions of a few prejudiced politicians or church leaders but rather is embedded in every institution of British society, including the welfare state.

This chapter will explore the relationship between oppression, class and welfare. Our central argument – that Marxism can make sense of specific oppressions and that these oppressions have their origins in the social and economic relations of capitalism – goes very much against the grain of current critical welfare thinking. A variety of social, material and ideological shifts during the 1980s and 1990s has resulted in a consensus that, at best, Marxism is incapable of explaining oppression, unless perhaps supplemented by another worldview such as feminism or postmodernism; at worst, Marxism is seen as a 'totalising', Eurocentric 'grand narrative' which is in itself a major source of oppression.

A number of factors have contributed to this negative view. First, there was the (rather belated) discovery by many of those who regarded the former USSR, its Eastern European satellite states, China, Cuba and so on, as 'socialist' of the extent of continuing oppression within these societies. Second, the decline in working-class struggle in Britain and elsewhere in the late 1970s led to a shift in the focus of the women's movement away from class-based issues such as abortion and equal pay and towards areas where women were much more clearly victims, such as rape and domestic violence (German, 1989). This shift was mirrored in other movements, such as the gay movement where it was accompanied by a move towards lifestyle politics (Field, 1995) and, in several of the 'new social movements', where there was an increasing emphasis on *identity* as a basis for organising (Aronowitz, 1992; Smith, 1994). Finally, these shifts coincided with, and were fuelled by, a variety of theoretical currents, usually labelled poststructuralist or postmodernist, which both challenged the 'privileging' of class over other social divisions and also located oppression (and resistance) at the level of micro-relationships, rather than at a structural level.

Bradley has summarised the now dominant view as follows:

> The recognition that social inequalities and divisions could not be subsumed under one monolithic theory, that of class, led to a growing appreciation of the

complexities of social differentiation in multi-cultural, post-colonial societies, where any sources of difference – class, gender, ethnicity, 'race', age, region, dis/ability, sexual orientation – intertwined to produce multi-faceted and intricate forms of social hierarchy. (2000: 478)

The limitations of this view of social inequality will be explored in some detail later in this chapter but three points are worth noting about it at this stage.

First, it bears a striking resemblance to classical sociological pluralism, with its emphasis on 'multifactorial' explanations of inequality, as against the Marxist emphasis on class. This would not necessarily matter were it not for the fact that those who adhere to the view outlined by Bradley often purport to be presenting a more radical explanation than that offered by Marxists. The authors of the key text of 'post-Marxism', for example, suggest that in the 'democratic revolution' spearheaded by the 'new social movements' – the women's movement, the ecology movement and so on – 'what we are witnessing is a politicisation far more radical than anything we have known in the past' (Laclau and Mouffe, 1985: 181). Neither critics nor adherents of pluralism have ever made such a claim for pluralist approaches.

Second, there is the emphasis on the notion of *difference*, which has increasingly replaced the concept of *oppression* in much contemporary social thought. The limits of 'difference' as a way of making sense of social inequality will be explored below.

Third, the suggestion that Marxism cannot account for the 'complexities' of social differentiation and inequality reflects what is perhaps the most commonly-made charge against Marxist explanations of oppression – namely that they are inherently reductionist, in seeking to 'subsume' all forms of oppression under class.

Later in this chapter we shall attempt to address some of these criticisms and argue that Marxism is capable of providing both an analysis of oppression and a strategy for challenging it, which is superior to those theories that are currently dominant within critical social theory and welfare. Before doing so, it is necessary to look at the two currently most influential theoretical approaches to the questions of oppression, identity and difference – *essentialism* and *social constructionism* (Woodward, 1997).

Essentialism

Essentialist theories typically seek to explain (or justify) the existence of power and oppression in terms of a set of allegedly unchanging characteristics (or essences) possessed by one group of human beings which form the basis for their domination of another group (who in turn similarly possess unchanging, albeit different, characteristics). Historically, essentialist theories have tended to be favoured by conservative theoreticians and political groups. Thus, for example, Nazi anti-Semitism was based on the notion that Jewish people by virtue of their membership of the Jewish 'race' possess certain characteristics – greedy, money-grabbing and so on – in contrast to 'Aryan' people who are 'naturally' superior.

During the 1960s, proponents of sociobiology such as Konrad Lorenz and Desmond Morris argued that characteristics such as human aggression were evolutionarily determined so that wars could be seen to be 'natural', rather than the product of a particular social system. Psychologists such as Han Eysenck and Arthur Jensen similarly argued that intelligence in the form of IQ was innate and that differences in educational attainment between the 'races' could be explained in terms of these inherited differences. More recently, adherents of evolutionary psychology have argued that human behaviour (including, according to some its adherents, rape – Thornhill and Palmer, 2000) is rooted in a human nature which, in all essentials, has remained the same for over 100,000 years.

Such essentialist theories share four main characteristics. First, they are *ahistorical*. In order to make their case, they are forced to ignore the fact that the most striking characteristic of human behaviour is its malleability. Second, these theories are *reductionist*, with human behaviour invariably being reduced to some innate characteristic, be it a primeval drive, intelligence, genes or 'human nature'. Third, they are usually based on very poor science. As Steven Rose and his colleagues have argued, the notion, for example, that a specific gene – a 'gay' gene or a 'schizophrenic' gene – can give rise to specific behaviours rests on a profound ignorance of how genes work (Rose et al., 1984). Finally, they are frequently used to justify the *status quo*. In *The Bell Curve*, for example, Herrnstein and Murray (1994), like Eysenck and Jensen before them, have sought to locate the educational and occupational disadvantage of black people not in poverty or institutionalised racism but rather in hereditary intellectual factors.

Within welfare such arguments are far from new and in fact serve the same purpose now as those of the eugenicists in the early twentieth century. Discussing 'experiments' such as the American Federal Violence Initiative, which aimed to identify 100,000 inner-city children 'whose biochemical and genetic make-up will make them prone to violence in later life', Jones and Novak rightly note:

> The violence that is a consequence of poverty, the rage and frustration that can lead people to destroy their own relationships and communities, is obscured under pseudo-scientific explanations that reveal the extremes of a view of the poor as a group that is qualitatively different and incapable of integration into normal society. It does not require too great a grasp of human history to realise that once groups of the population are defined as less than human this provides legitimation for policies of neglect and other more ruthless interventions and treatment. (1999: 8)

That said, the political right does not have a monopoly on essentialist explanations of oppression. In her influential 1970s text *Against Our Will*, for example, the feminist theorist Susan Brownmiller (1976) argued that all men were potential rapists on the basis that they have the necessary biological equipment to carry out rape. In a more favourable appropriation of essentialism, sections of the women's movement involved in anti-nuclear activities at Greenham Common during the 1980s put forward a view of women as 'natural' carers and peacemakers, in contrast to the 'natural' aggressiveness of males (a view reflected in the title of a book published during the 1980s called *Fathering the Unthinkable: Masculinity, Scientists and the Nuclear Arms Race*) (Easlea, 1987).

While there are important and obvious differences between left- and right-wing essentialist approaches, not least in respect of the aims and values of their adherents, what they nevertheless share is a tendency to reduce all behaviour either to biological/genetic factors or to a fixed 'human nature', which is impervious to social or cultural influences. While left-wing essentialism may superficially seem more progressive, like its right-wing variant it is profoundly pessimistic about people's capacity for change and in fact mirrors many of the assumptions of its right-wing counterpart.

Social constructionism

While left-wing essentialist theories do exist, in general the dominant explanations of oppression within current social theory are hostile to essentialism and are more likely to view oppression as *socially constructed*. While understandings of oppression and difference based on social constructionism draw on a range of different theoretical perspectives, what they have in common is 'their stress on the way in which collective or shared understandings, interpretations or representations of the world shape our actions within it' (Clarke and Cochrane, 1998: 29).

As an example, the social construction of physical impairment over the centuries, variously seen as punishment from God, as medical condition, as personal tragedy or more recently as socially imposed disability, has profoundly shaped societal responses to individuals with social impairments, both at the level of the provision of services and also in terms of the reaction of other non-impaired members of society (Hughes, 1998a).

Given the ways in which stigma and stigmatising ideas shape the day-to-day experience not only of disabled people but of most oppressed groups, be they lone parents, unemployed black youth or people with mental health problems, the recognition that ideas can become a material force is a powerful and valid one. Adherents of social constructionism, however, particularly those influenced by poststructuralist/postmodernist ideas, often go further in arguing that social construction is all that there is, that there is no 'reality', material or otherwise, outside of social constructions, or if there is, it cannot be known. Social antagonisms or oppressions therefore cannot exist outside of the context of specific discourses. The 'post-Marxists' Laclau and Mouffe, for example, argue that:

> 'Serf', 'slave' and so on do not designate in themselves antagonistic positions; it is only in the terms of a different discursive formation, such as 'the rights inherent in every human being', that the differential positivity of these categories can be subverted and the subversion can be constructed as oppression. (1985: 153–4).

From here, it is a short step to replacing theories of structural oppression, rooted after all in a material reality which can never be known, with the notions of *identities* which, in contrast to structural oppression, are free-floating and often self-defined:

> The post-structuralist approach allows no necessary connection between social positioning and identification. Identities are seen as fluid, contingent and chosen. (Bradley, 2000: 482)

The weaknesses of explaining oppression in this way are threefold. First, it leads to an *extreme subjectivism*. As Smith notes:

> In place of systematic analysis, we are given impressionism. By this method, oppression is something which is self-articulated and self-defined, having no objective basis in larger society. This approach can and does result in trivialising human suffering – by lumping it together with all in society who define themselves as 'oppressed' – such as middle-class consumers and anti-authoritarian or counter-cultural middle-class youth, whose complaints may be valid, but who hardly constitute specifically oppressed groups within society. (1994: 28–29)

Second, like essentialist explanations, social constructionism is often *ahistorical*. Identities are chosen or ascribed, embraced or rejected, but the really interesting question of *why* particular identities and/or forms of oppression arise or gain adherents at particular times is seldom posed. Williams, for example, following Barrett and Phillips (1992), notes the 'paradigm shift' within the women's movement in the early 1980s from an ideology which stressed commonality with men towards a 'political identity rooted in difference' (1996: 67). One aspect of this shift involved a return to an essentialism which saw women as more caring, more nurturing than men. What is striking about Williams's discussion of this shift is that there is no attempt either to *evaluate* this shift – in terms of challenging women's oppression, is it a step forward or is it a step backwards? – nor to seek its roots, other than in the influence of changing ideas, including postmodern ideas, within the women's movement. Asking why these ideas (which would have been anathema to most supporters of the women's movement only a decade earlier) should have gained a degree of support would imply recognising some relationship between the ideas in people's heads and material reality, a relationship which, as we have seen above, most social constructionists reject.

Finally, social constructionism can lead to an extreme *relativism*, particularly in its postmodern variants. Interestingly, one of the most powerful critiques of this relativism has come from Vivian Burr, the author of a widely-acclaimed introduction to social constructionism (1995). Following what appears to have been a period of intense and painful reflection on the limits of this world-view, Burr now argues that:

> After a while I, like others, began to feel frustrated with constructionism and somewhat disillusioned. The extreme relativistic views that were often espoused under the banner of social constructionism seemed to lead down a road to social and personal paralysis ... How can we say, for example, that certain groups are oppressed, if these 'groups' and their 'oppression' are constructions which have no greater claim to truth than any other? How can we claim that some groups and not others should be given a social 'voice'? If our concern is to give greater social space to marginal groups, does this include, for example, the National Front, and if not, why not? And who is in a position to arbitrate such choices? (1998: 14)

What the above discussion suggests is that neither essentialist nor social constructionist approaches can adequately account for the oppression experienced by different groups of people. To what extent can classical Marxist approaches provide a more satisfactory account?

Marxism and oppression

There are four key elements to the Marxist theory of oppression:

  i)   Oppression has material roots and is historically specific.
 ii)   Oppression exists across classes but does not affect all of the oppressed equally.
iii)   No section of the working class benefits from the oppression of any other.
 iv)   Only the working class has the capacity to end oppression.

Each of these propositions, which differ radically from the ideas about oppression currently dominant within critical social welfare discussion, will be considered in turn.

i) Oppression has material roots and is historically specific

Within the Marxist tradition, oppression is seen as historically specific (Korsch, 1937/1971). In other words, whether it exists at all, and the particular form that it takes, differs markedly from society to society in different historical periods. In contrast to essentialist approaches, oppression is seen to arise not from any biological imperative but rather from the material and social relations of class society. While human beings have certain basic needs which must be addressed if they are to survive, there is no fixed, unchanging, 'essential' human nature to which behaviour is reducible. If males were 'naturally' sexist, whites 'naturally' racist and straight people 'naturally' homophobic, then we should expect to see evidence of all these forms of oppression in every society. In fact, there is ample evidence that systematic discrimination and oppression on the basis of skin colour is a product of the rise of capitalism and was not a feature of, say, early Roman society. As Fryer has argued in his classic study of the experience of black people in Britain:

> The primary functions of race prejudice are cultural and psychological. The primary functions of racism are economic and political. Racism emerged in the oral tradition in Barbados in the seventeenth century, and crystallised in print in Britain in the eighteenth, as the ideology of the plantocracy, the class of sugar-planters and slave merchants that dominated England's Caribbean colonies. It emerged, above all, as a largely defensive ideology – the weapon of a class whose wealth, way of life and power were under mounting attack. (1984: 134)

Similarly, as we shall argue in more detail in Chapter 7, while feminist theories often present women's oppression as the inevitable product of a patriarchy which floats above society, there is substantial anthropological evidence to suggest that many societies have existed in which women were not oppressed in the ways that they currently are (Leacock, 1981). Again, while homophobia is widespread within contemporary Western capitalist societies, the first legislation in Britain to criminalise male homosexuality was only passed in the nineteenth century, as part of the wider attempt by the State to impose the middle-class ideal of the stable monogamous family on the working-class (Weeks, 1977).

The historical specificity of oppression means that its nature and extent will vary enormously depending on a wide range of economic and political factors. The rapid growth in support for the far right National Front in France in the 1980s and 1990s, for example, and the concomitant increase in racial attacks and harassment can only be understood against the background of the disillusionment produced by the behaviour of the French Socialist Party in government from 1982 onwards (Fysh and Woolfries, 1998). Thus, in contrast to some anti-racist theories which see whites as inevitably racist, or poststructuralist theories which see relations of power and oppression as both inevitable, eternal and omnipresent, for Marxists the nature and extent of racism or any other form of oppression needs to be concretely analysed in the context of the overall political and economic situation prevailing at any particular time.

If, however, oppression is not fixed and unchanging, neither is it the free-floating, self-defining matter of identity that current academic discussions often imply. In the wake of recent attempts by right-wing politicians to stir up racial hatred against refugees and asylum seekers, Michael Billig's comments on the limits of such identity theorising have a particular resonance:

> Not all identities should be considered as equivalent and interchangeable. Perhaps the post-modern consumer can purchase a bewildering variety of lifestyles. Certainly the commercial structures are in place for the economically comfortable to change styles in the Western world … [but] national identity cannot be exchanged like last year's clothes … One can eat Chinese today and Turkish the day after, even dress in Chinese or Turkish styles. But *being* Chinese or Turkish are not commercially available options. (cited in Davidson, 2000: 16)

In fact, *pace* the postmodernists, one might argue that, for poor white economic migrants at least, the scope for changing national identity was much greater during the period of 'modernity' than it is now, as evidenced by the massive waves of migrants from Eastern Europe and the poorer regions of Western Europe to the US in particular during the first part of this century.

More generally, as Billig's statement suggests, the choice and desirability of identities on offer will depend, as with any other choice in a market society, on the spending power of the consumer. Few homeless people, for example, would actively choose the identity of 'rough sleeper' over that of 'resident at the Ritz'. Few 'jobseekers' would not prefer to be in an occupation which provided them with a reasonable income and accorded them some social status. Few women would choose the identity of 'battered wife' or 'lone parent', given the stigma attached to these identities. In fact, the notion that identities are 'chosen' in this way rests on a view of a consumerist society in which material inequality has been largely overcome, in which the State does not harass and coerce the poor and in which people are now free to choose the lifestyle that they prefer. As we argued in Chapter 1, such a society bears little resemblance to Britain or other Western capitalist societies today in which the identities on offer to the vast majority of people are often unappealing and/or imposed.

Finally, the view that oppression has material roots and is historically specific has one very important consequence. It implies that oppression is not inevitable, that it is possible to envisage a future society free of racism, sexism, homophobia and other forms of oppression, a point to which we shall return.

ii) Oppression exists across classes but does not affect all of the oppressed equally

Oppression affects people from different classes, including the ruling class. In a league table of the pay of British executives in 1999, for example, only one woman, Marjorie Scardino, was included amongst the 110 senior company executives whose pay reached or exceeded £1 million in that year (*Guardian*, 23 September 2000). Further down the social scale, there is substantial evidence showing that even in professions which are over-whelmingly dominated by women, such as social work, men still far outnumber women in management positions (although the gap has been narrowing in recent years). That said, it is clear that not all women experience oppression in the same way. To take just one example, for the growing number of middle-class couples who employ nannies and domestic servants, it is possible for *both* partners – male and female – to escape the drudgery of housework by passing it on to other people, usually working-class women. In an article on domestic cleaning services in the US, for example, Barbara Ehernreich notes that:

> The cleaning industry is booming. Among my middle-class, professional-women friends and acquaintances, including some who made important contributions to the early feminist analysis of housework, the employment of a maid is now nearly universal. Strangely, or perhaps not so strangely, no one talks about the 'politics of housework' any more. The demand for 'wages for housework' has sunk to the status of a curio. Among former sociologists, housework has lost much of its former cachet – in part, I suspect, because fewer sociologists actually do it. (*Guardian*, 20 August 2000)

'Post-feminism' or 'the new feminism' (Walter, 1998) can be seen as the theoretical expression of this new layer of women. Barrett defines this new feminism as being:

> … above all, about reinstating feminity. This is partly, but not exclusively, about heterosexuality. It is more importantly about a feminine presentation of self … The corporate executive is stunningly dressed, the financial expert gorgeous. What is desired is both the economic and social success of women in breaking through the glass ceiling and the retention of the classic tropes of feminity. (2000: 48)

As Ehrenreich observes, the concerns of the women who work for large cleaning chains with quaint and comforting names like Merry Maids, Maids International, Mini Maids, Maid Brigade and so on, are very different. For them at least the nature of housework (not to mention the miserable wages paid for doing it) continues to be a very live issue:

> Turnover is dizzyingly high in the cleaning-service industry, and not only because of the usual problems that confront the working-poor; childcare prob-lems, unreliable transportation, evictions and poor health problems … this is a physically punishing occupation, something to tide you over for a few months, not year after year. The hands-and-knee posture damages knees, with or with-out pads; vacuuming strains the back; constant wiping and scrubbing invite repetitive strain injuries even in the very young. (*Guardian*, 20 August 2000)

For these and most other women, the option of achieving a degree of liberation through employing other people to undertake domestic drudgery simply does not exist.

It would be wrong, of course, to assume that all those men and women who employ such cleaning services either do so through choice or are themselves wealthy. For some at least employing a cleaner (and the point applies with much greater force to the use of childminders) is likely to represent an attempt to manage a situation where both partners *have* to work, a reflection in other words of *increased* exploitation, rather than greater leisure. As Walter Mosely has argued in a powerful polemic against contemporary American capitalism, in the middle years of the twentieth century:

> The one-job household was common. Often one worker made enough for food, the mortgage, the Christmas club, the college fund, and the ten-dollar doctor and dentist visits. Today that worker makes many more dollars but the one-job household is a thing of the past. The expenses of life have risen much more quickly than the one job salary. Both parents have to work now. Three kids in good colleges is a fortune that few pocketbooks can bear. (2000: 89)

Similar divisions to those described by Ehrenreich exist within the gay community, with the 'pink pound' rather than collective struggle being seen by some wealthier gays as the key to liberation (Field, 1995), and within the black community where the interests of middle-class blacks will similarly often fail to coincide with those of their working-class brothers and sisters.

In fact, not only are the interests of middle-class women, gays and blacks often very different from those of their working-class counterparts but where there is a clash between them it is invariably the latter who lose out. New Labour's landslide victory in the 1997 General Election, for example, was hailed by some feminists as a great step forward for all women, as it resulted in the highest ever number of women elected to Parliament. When some months later, however, the (female) Minister for Social Security pushed through substantial benefit cuts for lone parents – one of the poorest sections of society and overwhelmingly women – not one of these women newly elected in 1997 voted to oppose the cut (*Socialist Review*, January 1998). When it came to the crunch, their ideological commitment to 'prudent finance' and the 'disciplines of the market' proved to be a much more powerful consideration than solidarity with their poorer sisters.

iii) Who benefits from oppression?

The notion that men benefit from the oppression of women, whites from the oppression of blacks, straights from the oppression of gays and so on is now so widespread as to constitute an almost unchallengeable 'common sense' within critical social policy and social work thought. By contrast the argument that the only beneficiary of oppression is the ruling class and that no section of the working class benefits from the oppression of another is at the heart of the Marxist theory of oppression. Oppression, in other words, is a means by which workers can be divided, one against the other. Discussing the antagonism displayed towards immigrant Irish workers by English workers in the nineteenth century, for example, Marx argued (in terms which could equally apply to asylum seekers today):

> This antagonism is artificially kept alive and intensified by the press, the pulpit, the comic papers, in short all the means at the disposal of the ruling classes. This antagonism is the secret of the impotence of the English working class, despite its organisation. It is the secret by which the capitalist class maintains its power. And that class is fully aware of it. (quoted in Callinicos, 1992: 18–19)

A vivid example of the way in which racism is consciously employed by sections of the ruling class as a means of dividing workers is provided by a recent history of the Ku Klux Klan in the 1930s, written by Diane McWhorter, the daughter of a Klansman. In her study, McWhorter found that:

> The Klan was not a redneck aberration perpetuated by poor whites. In Birmingham, it was resurrected from its 19th-century reconstruction-era grave by the city fathers, the coal and steel tycoons who called themselves the Big Mules, and who used the Klan as an underground army fighting the 'socialism' of President Franklin Delano Roosevelt's New Deal … In particular, the Big Mules feared the government guarantees that FDR's New Deal offered to organised labour. 'The worst fear of the heavy manufacturers was that their labour force might organise into a union and exercise self-determination in the workplace'. (*Guardian*, 7 May 2001)

Not surprisingly, therefore, the Big Mules 'promoted a covert battle to prevent the CIO union federation from bringing black and white workers together'.

Nor are the supposed ideological 'benefits' flowing from the oppression of particular groups any more real than the alleged economic benefits. Seeing gays as inferior, for example, may provide a degree of psychological relief for those with a poor sense of their own worth and a need to repress their own sexual feelings but the only real beneficiaries are those conservative forces who wish to bolster up the nuclear family as the only 'normal' way for men and women to live.

Other forms of stigma and discrimination are equally damaging, both to those discriminated against and to those who are discriminating. In recent years, for example, the tabloid press have run frequent campaigns against people with mental health problems, usually portraying them as violent and dangerous, despite the very substantial evidence to the contrary (Philo, 1996). As with homophobia, the object of these moral panics is to create a fear of 'the outsider' and reinforce a sense of the 'normality' of those who do not experience these problems. Yet as one of us has argued elsewhere:

> With one in seven people likely to experience mental health problems at some time in their lives ... and stress identified by 6,000 health and safety representatives in a TUC survey as the single major health and safety issue experienced by workers ... stigmatising people with mental health problems creates a climate in which working-class people are afraid to seek help, while the structural roots of these problems within the capitalist family and work process is obscured and unchallenged, removing the possibility of a collective response. (Ferguson, 2000: 247)

The specific argument that men benefit from women's oppression will be discussed at length in Chapter 7.

v) Only the working class has the capacity to end oppression

For many people who are involved in the struggle against their own particular oppression, the notion that the working class has a central role to play in challenging that oppression will often seem abstract and unrealistic. Not only is there no obvious reason why a white, able-bodied industrial worker should be concerned with the struggles of blacks, gays or disabled people but the fact that that same worker may hold racist, homophobic or disablist ideas may make them appear to be part of the problem rather than part of the solution. There are, however, three very good reasons for seeing the working class as central to the struggle against oppression.

First, there is the question of shared interest. We have argued above that the oppression of women, gays and black people, along with other forms of oppression, is not inevitable, eternal or purely socially constructed. Rather, it has its roots in the social and economic relations of capitalist society. While some members of oppressed groups may be able to escape the worst aspects of their oppression by moving up the social ladder, for the overwhelming majority this option does not exist. Ending their oppression, therefore, will involve replacing capitalism with a society that does not depend on the oppression of women within the family in order to produce the next generation of workers, which is not threatened by sexual diversity and which does not divide workers on the basis of skin colour. In common then with the vast majority of people who can only live through the sale of their labour power, members of oppressed groups have an interest in the overthrow of capitalism.

Not only do oppressed people share a common interest with the rest of the working class in a new society, but for the workers themselves, defence of the oppressed is a *necessity*, not an optional extra. As workers realised long before Marx, only through combination, through standing together against the employer, did they have any chance of making any improvements to wages or conditions. Anything that threatened that unity could only benefit the individual employer or the ruling class. As we saw above, it was for that reason that Marx saw anti-Irish racism as the Achilles heel of the English working class, its biggest weakness both ideologically and materially since a divided working class would prove no match for the wily British bourgeoisie. The argument holds no less true today. Opposition to the stigmatisation of asylum seekers, for example, is important both because of the inherent racism which such stigmatisation involves and also because the exclusion of asylum seekers, from key welfare provisions including cash benefits and the provisions of welfare legislation such as the Social Work (Scotland) Act, is a dangerous precedent which if left unchallenged is likely to be extended to other sections of the poor (Mynott, 2000). In other words, workers have a material as well as an ideological interest in fighting racism.

A third reason for seeing the working class as central to the struggle against oppression concerns the question of power. When groups of oppressed people organise themselves to challenge their oppression, they can often achieve a great deal: one only needs to look at how much attitudes towards women, gays and black people in most Western societies have changed over the past three decades, for example, to see the importance of the struggles that have taken place. There are, however, real limits to such struggles. Not only is there no natural unity *within* oppressed groups – between the female asylum seeker struggling to survive on a degrading voucher system, for example, and the female shadow Home Secretary intent on making her life even more difficult – but there is also no natural unity *between* oppressed groups. The persecution of the Palestinians by a government representing a people who have perhaps suffered more than any other people – the Jews – makes the point only too clearly. In addition, alongside the impossibility of achieving unity is a lack of economic power.

The working class by contrast is a *collective*, rather than simply a *collection* of individuals. The nature of the work process brings people together in a collective enterprise, whether it is in a factory, a call centre or a large hospital. When these workers act together, by withdrawing their labour for example, not only are they able to hurt the system where it is at its most vulnerable but they also begin to gain a sense of their own power.

To assert the central role of the working class in bringing about social change is not to minimise the significance of the struggles of oppressed groups, nor does it require us to ignore the fact that sections of workers are often influenced by racist, sexist or homophobic ideas. Rather it is based on the recognition that in a society whose driving force is profit, the most effective countervailing power to that of capital is the collective action and response of those whose labour produces that profit – that where the chains of capital are forged, as Rosa Luxemburg argued almost a century ago, there must they be broken. Furthermore, it is precisely at such moments when working-class men and women feel less threatened by 'the other' – be it women, gays or blacks – that the possibilities for challenging the old racist, sexist and homophobic ideas is greatest. When the French government of General de Gaulle tried to weaken and divide the massive movement of students and workers which swept through France in May 1968, it resorted to anti-semitic and xenophobic sniping at one of the movement leaders, Danny Cohn-Bendit. The response of hundreds of thousands of demonstrators was to chant 'We are all German Jews' (Harman, 1988). The feeling of confidence and strength was such that racist ideas had much less impact than they would have had when these same demonstrators felt isolated and weak.

For most of the time, of course, struggles against oppression will be at a much lower level than this. Anti-oppressive welfare practice will often involve encouraging small groups of service users or even individual service users to begin to question and challenge their specific oppression. For many people, and particularly women, that questioning will often begin with an assessment of their immediate relationships with their partners (a process of awakening beautifully portrayed in the 1980s film *Shirley Valentine*) or with the welfare professionals involved in their lives, whose control is often exercised through what Foucault conceptualised as 'the clinical gaze'. If that challenge is to be continued and is to be successful, however, then an understanding of the roots of oppression and of the need for oppressed groups to be part of the much wider struggle against a system which systematically and often consciously reproduces that oppression is vital.

7 'The bedrock of a decent, civilised and stable society': Capitalism and the Family

As we noted in the previous chapter, the family is a key site for the oppression of women and gays. In this chapter we expand this discussion to look at the family and welfare policy. Family-related policy is a central area of state social welfare activity. Social work agencies structure much of their work around notions of 'family support' or 'family intervention' to manage a range of social problems. Health visitors and community nurses visit families to check on the health and progress of young children or the elderly, taking account of their home environment and family situation in their general assessment of the individual's 'ability to thrive'. More directly, a range of income benefits such as child benefits and various family tax allowances apparently provide some transfer of income to poor families, married couples or people with children. In these terms, for much 'traditional' social policy analysis, state family policy was unproblematic. It was a gradually expanding area of activity where the family's 'welfare functions' were gradually being taken over by the state. The family was a consumer of welfare resources, but the benefits of such consumption were shared equally within the family and benefited society as a whole.

These perspectives, however, represent an idealisation of the causes, impact and consequences of family policy. First, it is clear that family policy has an explicit ideological role – emphasised most obviously in Britain by the New Labour government's sponsorship of a guide to married life that claims marriage is the best and most appropriate mode of co-habitation, promotes social stability and makes people healthier (*Observer*, 5 November 2000). As Frank Field, who was brought into government by Tony Blair to 'think the unthinkable' on welfare reform, argued the increased incidence of lone parenthood and divorce was a central cause of a range of social problems.

> The family is the bedrock of a decent, civilised and stable society. But it is under enormous strain. Divorce and separation have increased, lone parenthood has risen and child poverty has worsened. The reasons for this may be varied, but the impact is clear: more instability, more crime, greater pressure on housing and social benefits. (Blair, 1998: 13)

Family policy is shaped by notions of what an 'appropriate' family will be like – and thus lone parenthood and divorce for example are viewed as major social problems undermining the 'moral fabric' of society. And while some New Labour ministers have argued for a more tolerant attitude to some 'non-traditional' relationships – like *stable* gay families – this should not blind us to their continued adherence to 'heterosexual normativity' (Wilson, 2001).

Conservative perspectives on the family and state social policy's role in promoting certain familial values form a central part of New Labour's welfare ideology and project.

From the end of the nineteenth century onwards in Britain, family social policy has been promoted as a means of espousing certain values concerned with the nature, role and 'appropriate' activities of the family and its constituent members (Woodward, 2001). It has developed as a significant mechanism whereby the state and government attempt to regulate certain forms of behaviour or promote and support particular models of family life. Given this historical background, a number of feminist academics and writers on social policy have been suspicious of 'family policy' seeing it essentially as a mechanism for reinforcing women's oppression (Barrett and McIntosh, 1985), or a key prism through which the changing relationship between women, the state and men is established and reproduced (but always in ways that are detrimental to women) (Lewis, 1993), or by supporting a 'dubious universalism' that ignores the particularist demands and needs of different women in society (Williams, 1996). Thus, it is argued, since family policy represents the state's intervention into family life to reinforce women's oppression and the domestic division of labour, the state should have no role in determining intra-familial relationships. Family policy necessarily discriminates (either overtly or covertly) against those living in 'non-traditional' families – and hence all forms of family policy should be rejected as a manifestation of 'patriarchal values and power'.

But while the ideological role of family policy is central it is also the case that state-provided family benefits and services offer some (albeit limited) material provision which can help meet the basic costs of social living faced by working-class families. In the 'classical era' of the welfare state in Britain these took the form of cash payments such as maternity, death and clothing grants and child benefits or 'collectively consumed' services like nursery provision, free education, free school milk or meals and so on. In the early twentieth century socialists (both men and women) actively campaigned for the introduction and extension of these types of services and these and similar forms of provision brought real benefits to working-class families. At the start of the twenty-first century, socialists continue to demand the extension of state provision of services and in one area in particular – state provision of free access to abortion facilities – they stand shoulder to shoulder with feminist campaigners (Clegg and Gough, 2000).

The abolition or real-term cuts in grants, benefits and services over the last 20 to 30 years has increased the problems of providing adequate care from 'cradle to grave'. Over this period there have been a whole range of welfare and benefit cuts that have increased the costs of maintaining a family and bringing up children: child benefit cuts, restrictions on nursery care facilities, the increased costs of school milk and meal provision, abolition of higher education grants and the imposition of tuition fees on students, 'community care' policies, lack of facilities for elderly relatives, cuts in death grants – all mean that the daily care costs of raising and looking after relatives are increasingly burdensome for working-class families. The material costs of meeting the benefit and service shortfall may impact on all family members, but the cuts have a disproportionate impact on working-class women who are expected to step in and cover the welfare gap. The domestic division of labour means that it is women who are viewed as carers and nurturers within the family, roles which reinforce their oppressed position within society. Thus family policies and benefits reinforce familial ideology and women's oppression; cuts in services and benefits have a similar effect and indeed increase the oppression working-class women face. This clearly emphasises the contradictory nature of both the family and state family policy and the fact that capitalism both sustains and undermines the family.

To understand this contradiction we must look at the roots of the family and of family-related social policy within capitalism. It is often suggested that the family is an eternal, permanent institution in society, but even a cursory glance at history suggests this is not the case and that the family is intimately tied to the dominant social relations of exploitation within society. In particular, the family under capitalism is markedly different from the family under feudalism and other pre-capitalist class societies because it is not a *directly* productive unit within the production process.

In this chapter we argue that to understand fully the role of the family and family policy under capitalism it is necessary to uncover the reality behind the ideology of the family and locate the family in a changing historical context. By looking at both of these together we can see that the family is the central cause of women's oppression and that the problems of daily and intergenerational reproduction under class societies are at the heart of a Marxist understanding of the changing family form. We start, however, by briefly looking at feminist theory of the family and women's oppression before going on to look at family life in capitalist society.

Feminist perspectives on family life

Feminism includes a long tradition of theorising about women's condition and position in society. Central to these concerns, especially to the concerns of what is often termed 'second wave feminism', has been a concern with family and gender relations. As we noted above, included within this is a suspicion of family policy and its assumptions and the way in which it reinforces 'traditional' gendered values. But the feminist writers referred to above also include one other claim. They suggest that not only does the state use family policy to oppress women but that this process brings direct benefits to men: men benefit from women's oppression, and historically, the state and men have forged an alliance of interests to oppress women. We touched on this issue in the previous chapter, but let's look at the argument in more detail.

At first glance, the claim that men benefit from women's oppression seems to make some sense. It is clear, for example, that women *do* perform the majority of domestic labour tasks. Although figures suggest that men do more housework than they did in the past, nevertheless women spend much more of their time looking after and rearing children, cooking and cleaning and so on than men (*Guardian*, 16 January 2001). As a consequence, women have less leisure time than men and, so it is argued, 'less power'. In a discussion of domestic violence, Mullender argues that:

> Both masculinity and male sexuality are rendered synonymous with power and hence are socially constructed to be oppressive. Men's abuse of women can be understood *only* in this context. It is an extension of normal condoned behaviour. Men wield power over women and all men benefit. (1996: 63)

The idea that all men benefit from women's oppression and that women's oppression precedes capitalism are key elements of what is usually called 'patriarchy theory'. In one definition:

> By the patriarchy we mean a system in which all women are oppressed, an oppression which is total, affecting all aspects of our lives. Just as class oppression preceded capitalism so does our oppression. (*Scarlet Women*, cited in German, 1988: 21)

Notions of patriarchy are very common within academia – indeed they almost form an 'academic common sense'. The basis for these ideas is the assumption that the family is an isolated and separate arena of social life – certainly quite separate from the 'economic sphere' of human productive activity. Juliet Mitchell claims: 'We are dealing with two autonomous areas, the economic mode of capitalism and the ideological mode of patriarchy' (1975: 11), while for the French feminist Christine Delphy:

> There are two modes of production in our society. Most goods are produced in the industrial mode. Domestic services, child rearing and certain other goods are produced in the family mode. The first mode of production gives rise to capitalist exploitation. The second gives rise to familial, or more precisely, patriarchal exploitation. (1977: 69)

These perspectives lead to claims that whilst men are dependent upon their employers for a wage and sustenance, women are totally dependent upon their husbands, they have a 'serf-like' position of subordination to their husbands (Delphy, 1977) or they form a separate and distinct class (see German, 1988). Patriarchy is viewed as an ideology, distinct from any direct link to the material world (Mitchell, 1975), sometimes seen as based on biologically determined features (Firestone, 1979), and/or the institutional structures of male power (Hartmann, 1979). On occasion, it has led to essentialist celebrations of 'motherhood' in contrast to the claimed essentialist nature of men – a predilection towards violence and rape (for example, Brownmiller, 1976).

There are a number of problems with the feminist approach. First, in the work of Mitchell or Delphy the theory fails to account for the fact that the majority of women in Britain have paid jobs on the labour market. It is certainly true that women will face various forms of discrimination at work, will overwhelmingly be ghettoised within certain types of employment, will face various 'glass ceilings' which will restrict their promotion prospects, will be more likely to be employed on a part-time basis and, on average, will be paid less than men – we are not denying the fact of women's oppression, nor the way discrimination affects their labour market participation. But we are suggesting that approaches that only portray women as locked into familial relations of subordination do not capture the full range of experiences women face in modern capitalism.

Second, the approach assumes all women have the same interests – but class divides women as we noted in Chapter 6. As we argued there, the affluent women who hire nannies, domestic helps, cleaners or cooks exploit the cheap labour of working-class women.

Third, one of the main causes of the discrimination women face in the labour market is their familial roles. Women face a dual burden of paid and domestic labour, but their domestic role is one that ties the family completely into the dominant drives of capitalism. The family's main role is in the sphere of reproduction, that is the daily, intergenerational and social reproduction of labour power. The labour of the housewife does not directly produce surplus value for capital, but it aides the process of surplus value extraction *indirectly*, by refuelling, regenerating and reproducing labour (including her own) which will then be employed by capital.

Fourth, despite their intentions, the theorists above actually portray women as relatively passive victims of male authority, not as active participants in social processes – an approach which history shows to have no basis in reality. According to Sheila Rowbotham: 'By the mid-1970s ... instead of self-activity and freedom, we had ended up with the paralysis of the victim in a Manichean world of male evil and female suffering' (1999: 6).

The source of many of these problems lies in the concept of patriarchy itself. As Rowbotham has argued:

> ... 'patriarchy' ... [has been] expounded in countless meetings, redefined again and again in internal documents and buffeted to and fro at conferences. It has

had articles written about it, books based on it and is still being occasionally reinvented as if nothing had dented its reputation. As a definition of a particular household structure, 'patriarchy' is well and good, but as a general term to describe women's oppression it produces confusion. If it is being historically defined it is not clear when and where we are talking about, and if it is being conceptualised as a timeless universal structure we are left with no indication of how we might get out of it ... It implies a universal and historical form of oppression, which returns us to biology. ... [It] implies a structure which is fixed ... It does not carry any notion of how women might act to transform their situation ... 'Patriarchy' suggests a fatalistic submission which allows no space for the complexities of women's defiance. (1999: 5–6, 100)

Similarly with 'male power'. Many feminists argue patriarchy is an expression of male power and this is the problem. But for the working class as a whole their social position is one of *powerlessness* (as we argued in Chapter 5). They do not control their labour, or the products of their labour, alienation dominates society and they face a fragmented existence in all sphere of social life – including home life.

Finally, this takes us directly to the question of 'male benefits'. The sexual division of labour creates an unequal relationship between the sexes and within the family and this is the source of women's oppression. This division creates an *expectation* that women will provide the bulk of domestic labour and men will have the primary responsibility of providing financially for his wife and children – and this means that the vast majority of overtime work, for example, is undertaken by men. But it is not clear why this straitjacketed world of family relationships benefits men. In what way, for example, do men benefit from the fact that there is insufficient state childcare provision and that what is available is very expensive? Or that their partner is employed in 'poor work' (Brown and Scase, 1991)? Or that they live in a house that is too small and overcrowded? Or that their partner has to provide care for an elderly relative?

Capitalist society is, as we argued in Chapter 1, a totality, a differenti-ated unity. Capitalism shapes and affects all areas of social life, including the family, which is tied into the system through its role in the reproduc-tion of labour power. It is in the interests of the working class – men and women – to get rid of the system of oppression and exploitation in all its forms – and that involves freeing women from oppression and liberating women (and to a lesser extent men) from the drudgery of domestic labour. Men do not benefit from women's oppression but capitalism as a system does (a claim which neither denies the realities women's oppres-sion, nor the fact that many men have the most horrible sexist ideas). The liberation of women is possible – but only when the working class in its entirety fights to break its chains and establish a world free from oppression and exploitation. History emphasises that when such system-threatening confrontations develop women, as much as men, play an equal role to try and establish a better world.

But to develop this argument more fully, however, we must confront one of the great myths of modern society – that the family is a haven, rather than the site of oppression.

The family – haven in a heartless world?

For conservative theorists, the family is portrayed as an enduring 'haven'. It is somewhere safe, secure, reliable and protecting where people, tied through bonds of affection, look after each other. In this way it contrasts with 'the outside world' – an unsafe, insecure, unreliable and dangerous place, populated by strangers, criminals, drug-takers and thugs. At the heart of this picture are a number of both idealistic and pessimistic accounts of human society: idealism about the nature of familial relationships and their moral worth combined with a deep pessimism about society and the activities of an amoral 'residuum' (on whom a range of policing, law and order activities must be enforced by state agencies). Yet any such contrast fails to match the contradictions of family life.

In one sense the family is a remarkably enduring institution. The vast majority of people are born into, brought up within and die within families. The majority of people will marry at some stage in their life – while increasing numbers will co-habit in families that mirror the 'legally defined' institution. Those that defy the 'family norm', like gays and lesbians, suffer prejudice as a consequence – but many of them also form 'mirror families' (Wilson, 2001). In this sense the family is a 'universal' institution existing across the classes within modern capitalist society (though as we will see this universalism hides significant differences between the classes).

The family is an institution that people cling to in an uncertain world. The alienating, atomised existence of capitalist society means that families can offer a network of support that is not available elsewhere and these are clung to partially because there are tendencies within capitalism that operate to undermine the family. The constant restructuring of the labour market breaks up families and communities forcing people to migrate (both near and far from their 'home' where existing support networks may not be available). The history of capitalism is a history of forced migrations from land to town, from region to region and country to country. Secondly, there are trends towards 'universal proletarianisation' – of breaking up family life by dragging men, women and children into the labour market and in the process destroying home life by making the very process of 'daily reproduction' much more difficult. These processes have brought significant changes to family life over the last one hundred years but at the same time there are ideological pressures to recreate family structures and promote the family as the embodiment of a range of 'traditional values'.

The notion of the family and the home as a haven – of home centredness and privatism – is reinforced by the vast range of consumer goods targeted on home life, the DIY industry and the increasing number of television programmes devoted to home improvement, gardening and cookery. The family and the home are increasingly commodified entities and central to such perspectives is an ideological notion of what the *family ideal* should be like – with the mother at home caring for and rearing the children and the father at work. This is an ideal which the politicians of the majority political parties across the globe are happy to promote – it was central to the 'family values' of Thatcher, Major and Blair, as well as those of Reagan, Bush and Clinton. It is of course an ideological construct which confronts those who don't match the ideal and which exists alongside stigmatising, workfare-orientated approaches to lone-parent and poor families, where mothers are expected not to stay at home but rather to work and not rely on state benefits.

Despite such pressures to marry and form families, however, family life rarely matches the conservative ideal that depicts carefree parents with a couple of healthy kids living in spacious homes crammed with consumer goods. At best this is a middle-class ideal that a small minority of households can aspire to. For most, the reality is quite different and class impacts on family life in myriad ways. In Britain the majority of women do not stay at home but work in paid employment – although for working-class women, unable to buy in domestic help, this becomes a 'double burden' which must be combined with their expected domestic role and which impacts upon their labour market participation (German, 1989). For working-class families, having young children coincides with a period of life marked by poverty (Oppenheim and Harker, 1996), with debt in one form or another becoming more prevalent throughout 'family life'. The Bank of England, for example, estimated in September 1999 that in Britain '£109 billion [was] owed on credit cards, personal loans and other forms of consumer debt ... an average debt among borrowers of £6,363' (*Guardian*, 26 September 1999). Homes are likely to be cramped rather than spacious, emotions strained rather than carefree and the time needed to enjoy the wide array of cultural pastimes available in society is likely to be in short supply.

The family is also a dangerous place. It is the site of child abuse, domestic violence, elder abuse and murder. Data relating to the extent of child abuse comes from both official statistics and a range of 'prevalence studies'. In Britain there was no official national data on the extent of child abuse prior to 1988. Since that date the Department of Health has produced annual figures of the numbers of children on child protection registers in England. These figures are open to a variety of criticisms but they do give an indication of the levels of abuse taking place and are reproduced in Table 7.1 below.

Corby, extrapolating from various sources, suggests that between 1984 and 1991 'there was a fourfold increase in numbers of children on child

Table 7.1   *Total number of children on child protection registers (England only), selected years*

Year	Number on register
1988	39,200
1989	41,200
1990	43,600
1991	45,200
1992	38,600
1995	35,000
1999	31,900

Source: Corby, 2000: 88

protection registers' (2000: 88). Children on registers may be there because of physical neglect or physical, sexual or emotional abuse. These figures relate to cases reported to social services departments and followed through to registration. There are other 'prevalence studies' that suggest the picture is even more grave. Summarising the qualitative research on the physical abuse of children, Corby notes:

> A longitudinal study of 700 families in Nottingham ... found that two-thirds of parents had smacked their babies by the time of their first birthdays. By age 4, more than nine out of ten children were smacked at least weekly. By the time children were 7, almost one-quarter of parents were regularly hitting their children with straps and sticks and other implements ... [a similar study found] that 35 per cent of children aged 11 had been subjected at some time to 'severe' punishment. (2000: 94)

A broadly similar picture exists in the US and while there have been few prevalence studies of child sex abuse in both countries the picture again suggests official figures underestimate the extent of the problem (Corby, 2000).

Families are also the site of domestic violence against women. In Britain 'Acts of domestic violence are committed every six seconds and 999 calls reporting attacks are made every minute' (*Guardian*, 26 October 2000), the consequence is that 'one in four women suffers domestic violence at sometime during their lives' (*Guardian*, 19 July 2000) and two women a week are killed by a partner or former partner (*Guardian*, 9 December 2000). In the US the figures are similar; a woman is beaten every 15 seconds (US Dept of Justice, 1983), while domestic violence is the leading cause of injury to women between the ages of 15 and 44 (totalling more than car accidents, mugging and rapes combined) (FBI, 1991). While there is increasing evidence of the existence of 'elder abuse' within the home – made worse as pressures mount on families to 'care' for elderly relatives when institutional and day-care services are in decline (Bytheway, 1995).

Finally, the family is the site of murder. Most murders take place at Christmas – a time when the family myth is at its strongest. Yet it's a period when financial and emotional strains burst out in friction, antagonism and occasionally murder. In the US, family members were the most likely perpetrators of murder of young children, while a friend or acquaintance was most likely to murder an older child age 15 to 17. Amongst adults, 45 per cent of murder victims were related to or acquainted with their assailants (US Department of Justice, 2000). The picture is not that different in Britain.

> Every year, between 70 and 100 children in England and Wales are murdered, the majority of them under one and by their parents. Neonaticide, the killing of a baby in the first 24 hours of life, is most commonly perpetuated by the mother, but in the first year of its life there is an even divide between babies killed by the mother and father. By the time a child is in infancy, however, there has been a shift towards the culpability of the father ... Your ex-partner is more likely to kill your children than a stranger in the park. (*Guardian*, 19 April 2000)

The failure of the 'ideal' to match the reality has meant that increasing numbers of people choose to live within 'non-conventional' arrangements – at any one time in Britain the majority of people will not be living within 'nuclear families', single households are increasing, co-habitation has become significantly more prevalent and increasing numbers of women are choosing not to have children. According to Clare Dyer in the *Guardian* (25 October 1999) 'more than 70 per cent of women cohabit before marriage, compared with fewer than 5 per cent in the 1950s and early 1960s'. She continues:

> What's gone wrong with marriage? In one generation the number of people getting married has halved, the number divorcing has trebled and the proportion of children born outside marriage has quadrupled. (*Guardian*, 25 October 1999)

The figures make the point more sharply; in 1996:

> ... 33 per cent of all births in England and Wales were outside marriage, though for 80 per cent of these births there was joint registration. In 1996 lone-parent families constituted 21 per cent of all families with dependent children in Great Britain ... In 1991 there were half-a-million step-families in Britain involving a million children (both birth children and step-children). (Corby, 2000: 223)

It is into this often violent and emotionally-charged arena that state family policy penetrates and attempts to regulate behaviour. It does so by trying to enforce behavioural patterns and 'accepted' modes of living onto families. It regulates, through criminal law, to try and control the worst manifestations of violence – though the police remain reluctant to investigate 'domestics' and there is acceptance that some violence – the smacking of children – is not only acceptable but necessary to control their misbehaviour. It tries to control via financial penalty through, for example, the Child Support Agency, which chases parents for financial support for their children to avoid the state paying through miserly benefits. And it tries to enforce acceptable behaviour by such measures as introducing curfews, determining when children should be in the home at night or setting school homework norms in order to ensure parental involvement in education.

The family is not a haven but an often emotionally strained, violent, 'privatised' – yet state-regulated – institution where the reality and 'the ideal' fail to match in any real sense. Yet given this reality, the obvious question is: *Why does the family continue to exist?* To answer this question we need to look at the origins of the family in class society and its specific role within capitalism.

The origins of the family in class society

Much sociological and feminist writing about the family, in effect, separates the family from productive life. The family is viewed as encapsulating a separate mode of production (Delphy, 1977; Mitchell, 1971), as functional to the needs of industrial society with regard to its educative and socialising role (Smelser, 1974) and as geared towards meeting the needs of men over those of women and children (Hartmann, 1979). In contrast to these positions, if we see all social life, including the family, as rooted in social production, then we can start to comprehend the ways in which family form and family activity alter over time in relation to how production itself is organised. This was the position developed by Marx and Engels in their writings on the family.

Central to Marx and Engels's position on the family are three key points. First, they insist that the family arose with the development of class society (Engels, 1884/1978). Basing his claims on anthropological research Engels argues that in primitive communist societies the rigid gendered divisions that appear in later class divided societies did not exist – a point that more recent anthropologists like Eleanor Leacock (1981) and Evelyn Reed (1975) provide support for. As Engels notes:

> The first class antagonism that appears in history coincides with the development of the antagonism between man and woman in monogamous marriage, and the first class oppression coincides with that of the female sex by the male. (1884/1978: 75)

The importance of this point cannot be overstated. If there was a period in human history when relations between men and women were much more equal ('egalitarian societies' as Leacock terms them) then there is nothing biological determining the relative position of men and women in society – it is a social question – and hence the possibility of women's equality in the future becomes real.

A second related point is Engels' claim that there is a close connection between family and private property. The monogamous family developed to ensure that men could guarantee their property would be passed on to their children.

> Monogamy arose from the concentration of larger wealth in the hands of a single individual – a man – and from the need to bequeath this wealth to the children of that man and of no other. For this purpose, the monogamy of the woman was required, not that of the man, so this monogamy of the woman did not in any way interfere with open or concealed polygamy on the part of man. (1884/1978: 87)

Finally, there is the claim that there is a connection between material production and the reproduction of immediate life. Thus Engels notes:

> On the one side the production of the means of subsistence, of food, clothing and shelter and the tools necessary for that production; on the other side, the production of human beings themselves, the propagation of the species. The social institutions under which the people of a particular historical epoch live are conditioned by both kinds of production: by the stage of development of labour on the one hand and of the family on the other. (1884/1978: 4)

In other words, neither the forms of material production nor the forms of family relationships are static – both vary over time.

Yet despite the strengths of Marx and Engels' account, on occasion they went on to suggest that because the working class owned no (productive) property, the working-class family was likely to disappear. In *The Communist Manifesto*, for example, they argued that:

> On what foundation is the present family, the bourgeois family, based? On capital, on private gain. In its completely developed form this family exists only among the bourgeoisie. But this state of things finds its compliment in the practical absence of the family among the proletarians. (1848/1973: 83)

Such conceptions were partially based on empirical research. Engels's *The Conditions of the Working Class in England* (1845/1973) graphically portrayed the horrendous living and working conditions workers faced in Manchester and other cities in Britain and Ireland in the 1840's; here any notion of 'family life' as understood today was quite absent as men, women and children were forced, wherever possible, to enter paid employment for excessively long hours. Their claims concerning the disappearance of the working-class family, however, were clearly wrong as by the end of the nineteenth century the working class family, far from having disappeared, had become deeply embedded within society.

Jane Humphries in her analysis of the family has developed Marx and Engels' thesis in important ways that explains why the family remained so central to working class lives. She has noted the family's 'primitively communal aspect' (1977a: 247) and argues – in traditionally Marxist terms – that humans are social animals whose productive activities involve them in social relations with others that must generally provide for the *maintenance* and *reproduction* of both individuals and society. This, she notes, requires:

> ... the existence of some surplus labour over and above the necessary labour, as traditionally defined, in all modes of production because the conditions of reproduction of the individual labourer are not equivalent to the conditions of reproduction of the economy as a whole. (Humphries, 1977a: 28)

The family is the site for three inter-linked processes of reproduction: daily, intergenerational and social. *Daily reproduction* means the requirement to feed, clothe and provide a home for all family members. *Intergenerational reproduction* refers to the processes of biological reproduction of the species and the provision of support for those too young or too old to fully support themselves. While *social reproduction* refers to those aspects geared towards reproducing the social structure, of social consumption, socialisation and ideological domination.

Historically, the most obvious groups to identify as the consumers of surplus labour have been, and remain, the dominant classes of each epoch who gain access to the surplus via particular exploitative relationships. However, Humphries points out that there are also 'non-labouring individuals' in each society who require support drawn from the product of surplus labour. These non-labouring individuals include the elderly, the sick, the infirm and children.

To develop her point Humphries attempts to analyse how surplus is distributed within primitive communistic societies. The redistribution of the surplus in these types of societies requires a communal network through which is decided the amount and type of labour required by individuals and their share of the social product. 'The historical basis for such a network of definite relationships is kinship': in class societies, the family acts as a mechanism to redistribute resources to its members both labouring and non-labouring (Humphries, 1977a: 246).

Humphries is arguing that the family acts as a mechanism to redistribute resources to, and provide support for, its non-labouring members in the face of the difficulties caused by social existence in class divided societies. In the abstract the family is not the only possible method of meeting such needs or of providing the surplus required to ensure the survival of those non-labouring members of the family unit, but within class societies, where the majority of surplus is extracted from subordinate class(es) via exploitative relations, the family has been maintained and defended because it represents the best possible way to meet the whole family's needs. These points generally are applicable to all class societies – but they become particularly important within capitalist societies as the separation between productive life and family life becomes more rigid and the problems of meeting family members' needs more acute.

Capitalism and the family

As we noted above, with the expansion of factory production there was a period when the working-class family seemed to be being undermined (Engels, 1845/1973; 1884/1978). There was a growing separation of the 'domestic' and the 'productive' spheres in society (Tilly and Scott, 1987) and this, combined with the move towards individual wage payments (Seccombe, 1986), long working hours and homogenisation – a process of the generalised cheapening of labour – meant that the family's role in the redistribution of surplus to non-labouring individuals, or those who do not produce enough to ensure their own maintenance, was obscured. The operation of *laissez-faire* capitalism in the nineteenth century created immense problems for working-class families in terms of meeting their *daily* and *inter-generational reproduction* needs. It also created problems for the bourgeoisie who required a fit and healthy workforce to work in their factories and a labour force that accepted, to some degree, the legitimacy of capitalism as a social system – they needed to ensure the *social reproduction* of capitalism as a system.

If we take the first of these, the problems as they affect working-class families, Humphries draws attention to two features in particular. First, the issue of domestic labour. She argues:

> The working class family constitutes an arena of production, the inputs being the commodities purchased by the family wages, and one of the outputs being the renewed labour-power sold for wages on the market. Neither the material aspect nor the social forms of household productive activity, family relations and family activity are capitalistic. But household activity is welded to the capitalist mode of production through the reproduction cycle of labour-power. (1977a: 242)

Under conditions of general proletarianisation, with men, women and children working long hours at arduous factory labour, domestic tasks get left unfulfilled or inadequately fulfilled. Similarly issues of child-bearing and rearing are particularly problematic under capitalism. As Brenner and Ramas have argued:

> Biological facts of reproduction – pregnancy, childbirth, lactation – are not readily compatible with capitalist production and to make them so … require[s] capital outlays on maternity leave, nursing facilities, childcare and so on. (1986: 48)

Thus the trends towards universal proletarianisation in the nineteenth century created immense problems around fulfilling the demands of domestic labour and daily reproduction as well as those of child birth and rearing.

For the working class family in nineteenth century England, kinship ties provide a major source of non-bureaucratic support in conditions of chronic uncertainty ... [the] ... cyclical fluctuations in industrial output and employment, which, in a mode of production where the direct producers are separated from the means of production, imposes considerable insecurity. Wage dependence also aggravates other 'critical life situations' that is, situations in which the individual is unlikely to be competent to cope without help such as sickness, death, disaster, old age, marriage and childbirth. (Humphries, 1977a: 248)

The second issue Humphries notes is the potential of universal prole-tarianisation to lead to the replacement of (more expensive) adult male labour with that of (cheaper) women and children. This *tendency*, she argues, provided the working class with a strong motive for defending their traditional family and kinship structures. The belief was that, by so doing, families could control the supply of labour by withdrawing some of its members from active competitive participation in the labour market. This feature, combined with demands for a 'family wage' (albeit largely unsuccessful ones) would, it was thought, allow the level of real wages to rise and this would improve the standard of living of the working-class family. Re-establishing and protecting the family would also allow domestic labour production within the family to be more easily fulfilled, again improving family resources. The difficulties associated with child bearing and rearing would be made easier, while children could be removed from the most exploitative work experiences. Thus:

... kinship ties were strengthened because they provided the only framework controllable by the working class, within which reciprocation could occur that was sufficiently defined to provide an adequate guarantee of assistance in crisis situations. (Humphries, 1977a: 250)

The demand to re-establish the family and obtain a 'family wage' can thus be explained in material terms, in relation to the perceived benefits it would bring to the family's standard of living but, of course, not only was the family wage demand generally not fulfilled, it also meant accepting and reinforcing the subordinate position of both women and children within the home. Nevertheless, from within the working class, the combination of these factors does help to explain support for the family wage demand and various forms of factory and industrial legislation (Davin, 1982).

It was not just the working class, however, who moved to 'defend the family'. Similar concerns motivated 'philanthropists' and sections of capital concerned at the immoral behaviour of Britain's 'lower classes', their uncontrollability, their political independence and organisation and the full range of activities they undertook during their free time (but there were, equally, sections of capital who benefited directly from employing 'cheap' child and women workers and who were opposed to restrictions of their employment, for example). The operationalisation of capitalism creates problems of valorisation, control and labour discipline for the bourgeoisie. There is the need for a relatively fit workforce to fulfil the functions of exploitative labour and there is the long-term need for a future generation or supply of workers. Institutional care (whether via the workhouse, the system of live-in apprentice or homes run by voluntary organisations) was tried with a minority of the working class during the nineteenth century but it was problematic:

> Institutional care was found to be more expensive, to exacerbate problems of labour discipline, to lead to poor physical health and development, and, above all, to provide poor character training … institutional care … [was viewed as] inferior to the family as regards physical and emotional development and the inculcation of independence and initiative. (Creighton, 1985: 197, 199)

Further, for work tasks to be undertaken effectively there is a requirement for the existing workforce to have a degree of commitment to the labour process and to be flexible enough to adapt to differing tasks. However, in a context where workers are 'free' to leave a particular employer, organise with co-workers and spend their free time as they wish, coercive means of control are, on their own, inadequate. In these circumstances, Creighton argues that the family was identified as a socialising agent that would promote certain values beneficial to capitalist social relations.

> The family … encourages close emotional bonds between the parents (or other adults) and children. The psychological reason for the success of the family in this respect is due to the ability of humans to respond to love and affection, but also to the 'union of love and discipline in the same person', for this permits children to accept authority without being cowed by it, and to outgrow it without total rejection of the values that it has inculcated … [Hence] the family plays its part – along with other institutions – in preparing people to function in a wide variety of roles in civil society: as consumers and savers, as voters, as parents, as men and women, as members of religious, political and cultural organisations, to give but a few examples. These are subjects of diverse kinds, but we can sum them up … as aspects of being a citizen. (1985: 200–201)

This may, in part, reflect a degree of idealisation over family relations but it emphasises the motivation for establishing a 'bourgeois family model' onto the working class as a means of appropriately socialising its members to accept the 'benefits' of capitalism.

Thus, as the nineteenth century progressed we can see an accommodation between sections of the bourgeoisie and the working class over the issue of family form and family relations. The motivation for re-establishing the working-class family was different for the bourgeoisie and the working class but there was a growing set of shared assumptions about home and social life that began to develop. These assumptions included expectations about the appropriate role of women and children and suitable activities that each should perform. Such a perspective does not deny the existence of women's oppression, indeed it locates the roots of that oppression within hierarchical family structures, but it does emphasise the link between the family and social production.

State intervention into family life

Towards the end of the nineteenth century, there was a more aggressive state intervention to control and order working-class family life. As Callinicos has remarked, this was a conjuncture:

> ... where it was widely agreed in the British political elite that two challenges confronted the established order. One was the external threat presented to British industrial and naval supremacy by such rising powers as Germany and the United States; the other was the prospect of domestic social conflict raised by the emergence of an increasingly powerful and assertive labour movement. (2000: 89)

At this period the dominant philosophy of state activity altered from one based primarily on notions of self-help and *laissez-faire* towards one of liberal collectivism, a perspective based on the notion that the state itself should take a more directing role in shaping and maintaining social relations (see, generally, Mooney, 1998; Lavalette, 1999).

The social policy 'solutions' reflected the dominant class-based assumptions of the day and in particular were formed with a clear picture of the type of family that needed to be established within the working class. In this sense it was attempting to direct and shape working-class family life. In particular we can note state activity in three areas that was part of the attempt to establish 'legitimate' working-class families. First, there was the growth of family policy. In general terms the role of families in the provision of social care and support is implicit within social policy in Britain rather than open and explicit. But at the end of the nineteenth century a range of welfare, medical and educational professionals were given powers of intervention and control over working-class families: social workers, truancy officers, teachers, doctors and various health workers were given increasing authority to try to determine and organise working-class life in circumstances where it was deemed that the 'new' rules, norm and 'codes' of social living were being infringed in some way. Further, since the Poor Law of 1601 there has been an obligation on parents to support their children, for husbands to support their wives and for children to support their elderly parents. While state provision of pensions, unemployment and sickness insurance relieved some of the burdens for working-class families, 'the legal responsibility of families for their dependent members was not significantly altered' (Muncie and Wetherell, 1997: 42). The growth of family-related social policy had clear implications for women – it was they who were expected to raise and nurture children and provide an appropriate home life for all the family members.

Second, the identification of women as primarily mothers has been a recurrent theme of state social policy. Motherhood and the creation of a working-class 'childhood' went hand in hand – as child-specific activities were established, mothers were expected to regulate and control their children and enforce their attendance at schools and other child-appropriate institutions (Lavalette, 1999; Lavalette and Cunningham, 2001). The developing welfare regime included a number of important pieces of child-specific legislation. Legislation attempted to define 'legitimate' activities for children (schooling), to establish appropriate ways of 'treating' children and their legal position (and relationships) with regard to parental authority (The Childrens Act 1908). This legislation also brought with it the creation of welfare and educational bureaucracies whose remit included work with children and the establishment of recognised welfare and medical professionals with official powers over working-class children. Other government departments and agencies maintained a role in defining, and controlling, children's lives and activities, for example, the Home Office had a part to play in the area of juvenile crime and the regulation of child labour and the police had a prime controlling function.

Finally, there was increasing control over sexual relations. The end of the nineteenth century witnessed increasing attacks on those groups whose sexual activities were deemed threatening to dominant familial values. In particular gay men and prostitutes were subjected to increasing harassment and regulation. Gay men were viewed as a social threat with the potential to affect the birth-rate adversely and to undermine the family. As Weeks (1977) has shown, the trial of Oscar Wilde was part of the process of establishing negative images of homosexuality. The consequence, according to Woodward, was to:

> … put pressure on men to marry and have children in order to be seen to be heterosexual, thereby creating a notion of 'normal' sexuality as heterosexual and taking place within the traditional family. (1997: 84)

The criminalisation of gay sex between adult men was not matched by similar legislation with regard to lesbians – in part because women were portrayed as asexual. However, there was increasing attempts to control 'fallen women' – prostitutes. Through various Contagious Diseases Acts (1864, 1866, 1869) prostitutes were identified as responsible for spreading venereal disease and were subject to substantial police harassment. Indeed the powers of the law enabled the police to 'stop and caution' women out alone at night – allowing for considerable harassment of working-class young women. The increasing control of sexuality was part of the attempt to enforce the 'bourgeois family' model onto society as a whole.

Thus within the legislation there is a set of contrasting and conflicting images of women both 'Virgin Mary' – pure, passive, 'moral', devoted to her children and family – and 'Harlot' – dangerous, immoral and without scruple. At the beginning of the twentieth century, in other words, state social policy was expanding and promoted a number of core values about women and family life – values which reinforced women's oppression within the family setting.

Beveridge, the family and the welfare state

The pattern of state family policy was laid down at the end of the nineteenth century: its aim was to reinforce social reproduction and provide limited resources that would allow the family to fulfil its role in the daily and inter-generational reproduction of labour power. At some periods, and in some pieces of legislation, the controlling and ideological role of family policy is clearer, at others the provision of limited material benefits to working-class families means that the ideological role is more covert, yet both these elements are always present and are thus both intimately connected. In this way we can see that familial assumptions continued to shape social policy throughout the twentieth century. Beveridge was quite explicit with regard to the assumptions shaping family policy in his report:

> During marriage most women will not be gainfully employed. The small minority of women who undertake paid employment require special treatment differing from that of a single woman. Since such paid work will in many cases be intermittent it should be open to any married women to undertake it as an exempt person, paying no contributions of her own and acquiring no claim to benefit in employment or sickness. If she prefers to contribute ... she may do so but will receive benefits at a received rate. (1942: 50)

For Beveridge, married women's main role was to raise and support children and carry out domestic labour within the home. He argued that women should form a distinct and dependent insurance group (qualifying for benefits via their husbands contributions), that their 'sole occupation' should be marriage and that a woman should gain 'a legal right to maintenance by her husband' (1942: 44). Child rearing should be seen as a vital function, 'ensuring the adequate continuance of the British race and of British ideals in the world' (1942: 53). Pascall (1986) suggests The Beveridge Report contains three main assumptions about women and family:

1. Women have a duty to provide domestic labour for free (this includes care of children and elderly relatives);
2. Families consist of one couple consisting of one full-time wage-earner (usually the male);
3. Women can look to men for financial support. (1986: 198)

The consequence is that unemployed married women, for example, cannot claim income support but will be assumed to be receiving adequate support from their husbands. Women's dependent status within family policy even affects single women cohabiting with a man who are also assumed to be reliant on their male partner's earnings.

Yet, even at the time the report was written, Beveridge's picture did not fit the dominant pattern of women's employment in Britain. As German notes:

> The widespread assumption that women are peripheral to the labour force is ... erroneous. Throughout the history of capitalism many women, including many married women, have taken paid work outside the home. Since the 1930s, however, the number doing so has expended on a scale undreamt-of by their mothers and grandmothers. And the areas where they work have become increasingly central to the economy. (1989: 102).

Muncie and Wetherall provide some figures to emphasise the point:

> By 1943 two out of five married women were in employment, compared with one in ten in 1931. In 1946, the year the National Insurance Act was passed, there were 875,000 more women in paid employment than at the beginning of the war. Between 1951 and 1971, 2,500,000 *more* married women joined the labour market and much of this was on a full-time basis. By 1987, 68 percent of married women were in employment. (1997: 45)

While today in Britain 'both parents go out to work in two-thirds of two-parent families with children' (Shirley Lowe, *Guardian*, 14 December 2000).

Once again the reality – the majority of women, including married women, in paid employment – does not match the ideological construct that continues to portray women as first and foremost housewives and mothers. Yet it is this construct that continues to shape state family policy and can be seen underpinning elements within taxation, social security and various benefit policies and provisions.

Although Beveridge's principles were modified in various ways in the post-War years, the assumptions of family policy have remained more or less unchanged. Indeed, the attacks on state welfare, the move towards a more residual form of welfare delivery and policies of privatisation have all increased the burdens on working-class women and working-class families.

From 1979 onwards successive governments in Britain have pursued policies of 'helping families' – which essentially means 'helping' families become less dependent on state welfare by promoting the family as a self-reliant alternative to state welfare. Changes to welfare provision, away from aspects of universalism towards increasingly selective (and residualised and stigmatised) provision are part of wider trends towards increasing inequality in countries like Britain and the US. The consequence is that cuts in state welfare have reinforced working-class women's oppression. When the state withdraws it is women (overwhelmingly) who step in unless the family has the money to purchase their caring and domestic services (usually from low-paid working-class women). The cuts in state welfare have coincided with increased disposable income through tax cuts for the rich, which have benefited some women at the expense of their working-class 'sisters'.

The consequence of welfare cuts has been to increase the burden on working-class women and families, with married women facing an increasingly daunting dual burden: combining their domestic role with paid employment – and this in turn is one factor in the growth of part-time work amongst married women as this allows women to combine these two roles (for example, as German notes (1989: 107) 70 per cent of working mothers work part-time). But the difficulties of meeting the costs of family life, in an atmosphere of welfare cuts, has also resulted in a growing role played by grandparents in aspects of child care and 'generational reproduction'.

> More than a third of grandparents spend the equivalent of three days a week caring for their grandchildren ... 36 per cent said they spend more than 21 hours a week looking after their grandchildren; more than a quarter said they spend in excess of 26 hours .... Harriet Harman, chairwoman of the childcare commission, said 'women are having to go back to work sooner than they would like after having a baby, for the sake of family finances. Grandmothers are taking over childcare, but this is putting a huge burden on them. (*Guardian*, 14 December 2000)

And true to form, the New Labour Government has not been slow to promote grandparents as providers of both caring services and 'morality'. As Shirley Lowe notes, New Labour:

> ... wants us all to be more involved with our grandchildren. New Labour has launched numerous schemes, including promoting grandparent mentors, getting grandparents into classrooms, housing them next to their grandchildren and having them adopt someone else's family. (*Guardian*, 14 December 2000)

Dominant government strategies, then, use family policy to promote a moral agenda which stigmatises and problematises working-class families and relationships. It promotes an ideology of the family as a 'haven' where family members have a responsibility to each other, to provide care and support for each other and to be self-reliant and independent of state support. Yet the ideology and the reality do not match – the family is often an emotionally-strained, violent and oppressive institution built upon hierarchy and women's oppression.

To understand the contradictory nature of the family we must locate it in its appropriate context. The family is not an eternal or permanent institution. It has changed historically in each mode of production. Under capitalism there is a separation of home and productive life but the family remains tied to capitalism through its role in the reproduction of labour power. The family is a direct producer of labour power and hence indirectly a producer of surplus labour. This is the basis of the sexual division of labour within society and of women's oppression.

Part 3

The Neo-Liberal Assault

8 'Apocalypse now': Globalisation, Welfare and the State

For most of the past one hundred years, the state has occupied the central role within the dominant ideologies – liberal-collectivism and social democracy – that have underpinned welfare provision in Britain and most of Western Europe. In the British context, for example, both the Conservative and Labour governments of the 1950s, 1960s and early 1970s shared a view of the state as *the* major provider of welfare and as having a key role to play directing the economy.

Within the social democratic tradition, in fact, socialism has often been equated with such state intervention in all areas of social life, particularly in relation to economic and social activity. The notion that the state is the agency which can reform unbridled capitalism along socialist lines runs like a thread through social democratic thought from the days of the Webbs and the early Fabians, through the heyday of Keynesianism and the theories of Tony Crosland in the period of the post-1945 long boom, to the neo-Keynesians of the 1990s, such as Will Hutton and Larry Elliott. Indeed Crosland, the principal thinker of social reformism in post-War Britain, went as far to argue that as a consequence of the interventionist state, capitalism had been transformed and humanised (Crosland, 1956).

Since the late 1970s, however, this view of the state as a reforming vehicle has come under sustained ideological attack. Neo-liberal theorists and policy makers have argued that capitalism has undergone such a profound transformation in its mode of operation that the basis for state intervention, the mixed economy, nationalisation and the provision of public services, has been radically undermined. In particular it is argued that the nation-state is now relatively impotent in the face of the forces of 'globalisation'. The implications for the welfare state are only too apparent. As John Clarke notes:

> The most pessimistic and apocalyptic view is that the new global economy has sounded the death knell for the developed (Western European) welfare state. Policies of economic and social management are not sustainable by national governments in the face of deregulated capitalism. (2000: 204)

For John Gray, Professor of Political Theory at the London School of Economics:

> Bond markets have knocked away the floor from under post-war full employ-ment policies. No western government today has a credible successor to the

policies which secured western societies in the Keynesian era ... Social market systems are being compelled progressively to dismantle themselves, so that they can compete on equal terms with economies in which environmental, social and labour costs are lowest. (cited in Clarke, 2000: 204)

We share Clarke's scepticism regarding such apocalyptic understandings of the effects of globalisation on welfare and in this chapter we argue that the primary significance of the globalisation debate is *ideological*, in that it provides a convenient rationalisation for those politicians and their intellectual supporters who wish to see market forces extended to all aspects of welfare provision.

Acceptance of globalisation ideology has, nonetheless, become widespread amongst both politicians and theorists of the 'new' social democracy. Ironically, many of those who now seek to stress the weakness of the nation state were previously amongst the most emphatic and enthusiastic advocates of the state's reforming role and its ability to engineer social change and social equality. For Tony Giddens, for example, support for the reforming role of the state has been overtaken by the view that the state represents inefficiency – an argument that was central to Thatcherite attacks on the public sector in the 1980s and 1990s (Giddens, 1998b). As a consequence, the state's reforming role is now seen as secondary: its main activity is to maintain economic competitiveness. In the words of Tony Blair:

Old Labour thought the role of the state was to interfere with the market. New Labour believes that the task of government is to make the market more dynamic, to provide people and business with the means of success. (quoted in Heffernan, 2000: vii).

Thus, the state's role is now seen as an enabling and developmental one, less concerned with the direct provision of public goods and services. As globalisation 'sceptics' Hirst and Thompson put it:

It is widely asserted that a truly global economy has emerged or is emerging ... the world has internationalisation in its basic dynamics, is dominated by uncontrollable global market forces, and has as its principal actors and major agents of change truly transnational corporations, which owe their allegiance to no nation state and locate wherever in the globe market advantage dictates. (Hirst and Thompson, 1999: 195)

Faced with this process, nation states, it is argued, must provide attractive location sites for Multi-National Capital (MNC) and this requires turning their economies into low wage, low taxation enclaves. Here welfare 'retrenchment' – cuts in public expenditure – is the only feasible strategy governments can adopt.

This is an argument that we reject. It is certainly the case that the internationalisation of capital and the integration of production and finance on a world scale have increased in recent years. But rather than seeing this as something radically new or different we wish to argue four things. First, that the recent internationalisation of capital represents the deepening of tendencies that have been inherent within capitalism since its earliest days. Second, that the implications of the increased globalisation of recent decades have been exaggerated, often for ideological reasons. Third, that in one sector of the global economy – the newly industrialising and undeveloped countries – international advocates of neo-liberalism have tried to implement the globalisation agenda, via structural adjustment programmes, with devastating consequences for urban workers and the rural poor. Fourth, that the flip-side of globalisation is the emergence of a global working class – and more recently a globalised resistance – which has the potential to challenge the ravages of international capital in respect of both welfare retrenchment, global inequalities and the destruction of our physical environment.

To develop our argument, however, it is necessary to outline in more detail the major elements of the globalisation thesis, to assess this against what has *actually* happened to the world economy in recent times and to explore the implications of these changes for welfare provision.

The globalisation thesis

An immediate difficulty facing anyone seeking to evaluate the globalisation thesis is that, as a perspective on the world today, 'globalisation' often appears to be less a coherent theory and more a collection of (frequently disparate) arguments that come together in different configurations (Pugh and Gould, 2000). Thus there are 'hyperglobalisers', 'transformationalists' and 'sceptics' or 'revisionists' (see Held et al., 1999: 2–3). This means that there is no single universal definition of globalisation itself. Instead what is usually stressed is that globalisation involves a number of separate but interrelated trends and processes. Despite this, it is useful to try and summarise the main claims that are made about the impact of globalisation. Let us begin by considering a definition of globalisation that is provided by one of the central organisations involved in its advocacy, the International Monetary Fund (IMF). The IMF claims globalisation reflects 'the growing economic interdependence of countries worldwide', this being the result of:

> ... the volume of cross-border transactions in goods and services, ... of international capital flows, and through the more rapid and widespread diffusion of technology. (quoted in Mullard and Spicker, 1998: 120)

This definition suggests a world where there are growing interconnections and networks between different countries, which are driven by the almost relentless rise of multinational corporations who roam the world in search of investment opportunities. In this process, it is argued, national economies are 'dissolved'. It is a 'borderless world' (Ohmae, 1990): trade, markets and technology increasingly operate beyond national boundaries. New technology and improved communications help to 'shrink' the world, obliterating geographical distance, while enhancing the mobility of capital and encouraging the growth in financial markets (O'Brien, 1992). In turn what Castells (1996, 1997, 1998 and 2000) refers to as 'informational labour' becomes more central.

Globalisation, however, is not only about increased trade and global financial flows. One of its key features is said to be the increasing propensity for production to be organised on a global basis. This is reflected in the idea of a global 'assembly line' with different elements in the production process increasingly organised across the world. It is a persuasive argument and one which is accepted, at least in part, by some left-wing critics of globalisation. In a recent powerful critique of neo-liberalism, for example, Sheridan and McCombes note that:

> Ford UK ... has recently announced that it will buy its components on-line, rather than from local supply industries. In practice, it will mean that the company can trawl the Internet searching for the cheapest suppliers of the hundreds of different parts that are required to assemble a car ... windscreens from China, upholstery from India, brake discs from the Philippines and so on. (2000: 51)

Here the consequences for employment in the advanced industrial societies are seen as particularly disastrous, with multinational firms presented as 'footloose' operations, able to transfer production with relatively little trouble to the newly industrialising countries and the Third World – to wherever labour is cheap and unions weak. They continue:

> Even semi-developed countries like Brazil and the Philippines are being spurned by the transnationals as they search for even cheaper labour and even lower rates of taxation. Over the past decade or so, Nike ... has flitted from the US to South Korea, to Indonesia and now to Vietnam in a never ending quest for cheaper labour, lower production costs and higher profits ... The ships that were once built on the Clyde are now built by cheap labour on the Yangtse ... The textile mills in the borders [of Scotland] fall silent and empty, their work taken over by industrial concentration camps in Jakarta and Manila. From Clydebank to Selkirk ... the price of globalisation is mass long-term unemployment. (Sheridan and McCombes, 2000: 49–50, 52)

In the 'post-industrialised' first world as a result, deregulated markets, poor work and labour market flexibility become a necessity if mass unemployment and economic degeneration are to be avoided.

While globalisation is usually presented as primarily an economic process, it is also seen as involving cultural processes. Thus the growth in communications and media-related industries, reflected in the rapid expansion of the Internet and of satellite broadcasting, is seen as leading to global homogenisation. We are entering what Barber (1996) terms a 'McWorld' in which corporations such as Microsoft, Nike, MTV, McDonalds and Coca-Cola are increasingly dominant.

Alongside these economic and cultural dimensions of the globalisation thesis are the political and ideological dimensions. The collapse of the Soviet Union and its satellite countries in the last decade of the twentieth century was widely heralded as signifying the emergence of a 'new world order'. With the success of the free market assured, so it was claimed, a period of renewed economic growth and prosperity was promised. We had now reached the 'end of history' according to Fukuyama (1992), capitalism had triumphed and there was no further basis for any 'ideological struggles' against capitalism. Globalisation and the triumph of the market would benefit us all. In 1997, for instance, Yukaita Kosai of the Japan Centre for Economic Research claimed that there was a 'global shift towards prosperity' (quoted in the *Independent*, 10 February 1997). Bizarrely, as late as 2000, World Bank Researchers were continuing to argue that economic growth would eventually trickle down to more and more sections of the world population leading to rising incomes for everyone – despite the collapse of the Asian Tiger economies, the major economic problems facing Japan and Eastern Europe and the prospect of recession in the US (Dollar and Kraay, 2000).

The globalisation thesis is, therefore, part and parcel of neo-liberal ideology. To expand and deepen capitalism, the free-flow of capital, the 'opening up' of national economies and markets, the deregulation of economies and labour markets and the marginalisation of illegitimate monopolies (such as trade unions) are seen as vital – they are the guiding principles of economic activity. These principles in turn require only minimal state 'interference' and where there has been state intervention this should be dismantled or 'rolled back' – markets represent the most efficient distributive mechanism and any interference in markets brings disequilibrium into the system which, in turn, will increase the probability of breakdown and short-term economic crisis.

Globalisation – a new phenomenon?

Proponents of the globalisation thesis often present globalisation as something entirely new, or at the very least, as a distinct phase of capitalism. In fact, however, since its inception, capital has scoured the globe in search of new markets, while its apologists in each century have argued (in language very similar to that employed by contemporary supporters of neo-liberal policies) that attempts to place constraints on the free movement of capital will result in a decline in economic growth and lower living standards for all. As early as 1821, for example, the economist David Ricardo was arguing that the state should not try to protect jobs by interfering with investment since:

> If capital is not allowed to get the greatest net revenue that the use of machinery will afford here, it will be carried abroad [leading to] serious discouragement to the demand for labour. (cited in Harman, 1996: 5)

It was precisely this dynamic aspect of capitalism – it's insatiable need to accumulate which drove it beyond national boundaries and frontiers – that Marx saw as the system's central characteristic. In words which mirror contemporary descriptions of globalisation, he wrote in *The Communist Manifesto* of 1848 that:

> The need of a constantly expanding market for its production chases the bourgeoisie over the whole surface of the globe. It must nestle everywhere, settle everywhere, establish connections everywhere.
>   The bourgeoisie has through its exploitation of the world market given a cosmopolitan character to production and consumption in every country. All old established national industries have been destroyed or daily are being destroyed. They are dislodged by new industries ... that no longer work up indigenous raw materials, but raw materials drawn from the remotest zones, industries whose products are consumed not at home, but in every quarter of the globe ... In place of the old local and national seclusion and self-sufficiency, we have intercourse in every direction, universal inter-dependence of nations. (Marx and Engels, 1848/1973: 71)

The half-century that followed the publication of these words saw an expansion of capitalism that easily rivals the expansion of the past few decades. By 1914 world trade had grown by 900 per cent – an average growth rate of 3.4 per cent a year in the 40 years preceding the First World War (Hirst and Thompson, 1999). The same period also saw a massive growth in international finance, with about half of investment from Britain flowing overseas.

The expansion of international trade was even greater during the 'long boom' of the 1950s and 1960s – by about 9.9 per cent until 1973. In the 30 years since then, however, which includes the period when the new era of globalisation is alleged to have come into existence, the picture has been a very different one. As Harman has noted, the share of inputs and exports in total output for the three major parts of the advanced world – the US, Japan and the European Union – remained more or less constant between 1980 and the mid-1990s (Harman, 1996: 6). Given that the period since then has seen the collapse of the Asian Tiger economies, the Russian economy and the slowdown of the US economy, it is difficult to sustain the argument that we are currently seeing an unprecedented *increase* in the flows of international trade.

That said, much of the case for the globalisation thesis rests less on the increase in international trade than on the increase in global investment and the ease with which it is alleged that capital can take up and move from country to country, seeking the lowest wage levels and least restrictions on its operations. Here too, however, the reality is both different and more complex. As Hirst and Thompson note, most trade continues to take place within 'the Triad', that is in the three leading investment and trading blocs: North America, Western Europe and Japan/East Asia – with Africa and much of the Third World loosing out, despite offering very cheap labour as an inducement to MNC. As Harman notes:

> The pattern of investment by the multinationals certainly does not provide a picture of massive investment in cheap labour countries at the expense of jobs in the advanced countries. Quite the opposite ... the bulk of direct foreign investment by multinationals is in the advanced countries. This is for the simple reason that the multinationals have found these the most profitable countries to invest in. (1996: 15)

Further, most corporations continue to organise production on a regional basis or in countries where their respective 'home states' exercise political and strategic influence. In the case of ex-colonial powers such as Britain, both the old and new commonwealth represent important areas of investment.

The notion of the 'footloose' multinational is also exaggerated. Manufacturers have always relocated, and this has meant shutting plant and making workers redundant. In recent years some multinationals have clearly relocated to the Third World, but it is not the case that multinationals can quickly and easily transfer production across the globe. Each site of production is, in reality, part of an 'industrial complex' (Ruigrok and van Tulder, 1995). Companies have long-established, formal and informal, links with the national and local state, component manufacturers, power companies and so on. They require access to appropriately skilled and trained workers, to an appropriate transport network, to a continuous, uninterrupted, power supply, for example. And thus, before moving, they have to be sure the new site can meet their needs with regard to these and other important strategic and logistical questions – and this takes years of planning. Even when transfer does take place, there are many risks – will the component manufacturers meet the company's quality thresholds and delivery schedules? Will the low wages (apparently the main feature attracting the multinationals) lead to industrial and political conflict in the short- and/or long-term? Thus moving can be 'risky' and for all capitalists, risk is something that they try to minimise in their relentless pursuit of profit.

Further, as Ruigrok and van Tulder show, the idea of the global assembly line and of globalised production remains largely wishful thinking. From the early 1970s Ford, for example, have pursued this strategy, but with very little real success – the global Ford car remains a distant objective. Most large corporations continue to concentrate production within one state while the vast bulk of research and development and other leading edge work are done at home (Ruigrok and van Tulder, 1995). For some critics of the thesis, there are in fact more signs of regionalisation or localisation than of globalisation.

Finally, the state remains absolutely central to the activities of modern multinationals. Most multinationals remain firmly embedded within their 'home' or 'base' country. Most rely on state contracts of one kind or another for a significant part of their productive output. State's promote the interest of 'their' multinationals and often secure contracts with other states on their behalf – for example, South Korea promotes Dawoo, Britain the interests of British Aerospace or British Telecom, the US looks after McDonald Douglas, while Sweden supports Volvo and so on. The state is also vital because it provides a 'safe' and appropriate environment for multinationals to operate within – including, for example, the regulation and control of their population, and a suitably 'modern' and appropriate infrastructure and both public and social service network (including the provision of education, training and basic health services). Crucially, states also provide military protection to multinationals and their interests. Since the early 1990s the major imperialist powers have fought two wars (in Iraq and Serbia) where the protection of oil interests and the giant oil companies – the most powerful of all multinationals – has been a central concern.

What the above discussion suggests, then, is that capitalism, as a dynamic system, is constantly changing and seeking to expand. To reject the globalisation thesis, therefore, is not to argue that 'nothing has changed' but is rather to assert that the newness of the internationalisation of capitalism, its extent and its implications for welfare have been exaggerated to meet the ideological needs of neo-liberalism. It is these supposed implications that we shall explore in the next section.

Globalisation and the end of the welfare state?

The portrayal of the modern world as a free-floating global economy has revived earlier debates about the 'crisis' and the 'dissolution' of the welfare state. Pessimism regarding the implications of what might be called the logic of globalisation is widespread and has affected some rather unlikely people. During the 1980s, for example, Ramesh Mishra was a stout defender of the welfare state who argued, in the face of the Thatcherite assault on welfare, that the cure to Britain's economic and social malaise would come from a *deepening* of welfare, by establishing a fully integrated welfare state, based on the Scandinavian model (Mishra, 1984). By the 1990s, however, perhaps because retrenchment was reaching even Scandinavian shores, Mishra was much more fearful about the prospects for welfare states:

> The pre-eminence of the economic sphere means that not only full employment but also universality can no longer be seen as sacrosanct in the modern world ... once we bid farewell to full employment as well as to universality, the 'welfare state' as a distinct phase in the evolution of social policy in the West will have come to an end. (1993: 36)

By the end of that decade, globalisation was seen as creating immense pressures which were being expressed in some areas a 'race to the bottom' in terms of social legislation: social protection and standards were being ditched as countries tried to compete for MNC investment:

> Three major developments in recent decades have altered the economic, political and ideological context of the welfare state ... the collapse of the socialist alternative, the globalisation of the economy and the relative decline of the nation state ... for the *foreseeable future* ... the prospect of a viable and progressive systemic alternative to capitalism seems to have disappeared ... the opening up of economies has curtailed the policy autonomy of nation states ... pressures – in part political and ideological – stemming from globalisation have impinged significantly on labour markets, taxation, social spending and systems of social protection. And the arrow points downwards. (Mishra, 1999: 1, ix)

Similarly, Peter Leonard, a leading figure in the radical social work movement of the 1970s, notes that:

> ... the old ideas which ruled the modern welfare state – universality, full employment, increasing equality – are proclaimed to be a hindrance to survival. They are castigated as ideas which have outlived their usefulness: they are no longer appropriate to the conditions of a global capitalist economy where investment, production, labour and consumption are all characterised by flexibility, transience and uncertainty. (1997: 113)

Leonard believes these developments have undermined the basis for reformism in the classic social democratic mould. The commitment to 'competitive taxation' policies necessitates a cut in the social wage and reduced public expenditure, with the result that privatisation and the increasing role of the market in the delivery of public services is left as the only viable alternative for 'reluctant welfare dismantlers' (as opposed to the more ideologically driven 'enthusiastic dismantlers') (Leonard, 1997: 114).

These concerns are dramatic, the issues important. In the face of a globally mobile capitalism, the dominant argument runs, each state must compete to attract MNC investment. This involves the 'race to the bottom': creating an economy with the lowest wages, the fewest rights at work, the most pliable health and safety systems, the cheapest welfare, the lowest tax rates, the most compliant and craven trade unions and the least resistance. Of course there will still be a role for aspects of the traditional welfare state – especially in the area of education and training for work to provide a workforce with the knowledge skills required by MNC, and in the more enforcing and authoritarian aspects of social control – but social provision will have to be cut, stigmatised and, if necessary, abolished.

Such concerns have led Mishra to identify seven propositions regarding the implications of globalisation logic for welfare. Globalisation, he argues,

1. undermines the ability of governments to pursue the objectives of full-employment and economic growth through reflationary policies. 'Keynesianism in one country' is no longer possible;
2. leads to increasing inequality and a downward shift in wages and working conditions;
3. exerts downwards pressure on 'systems of social protection and social expenditure' by prioritising reduction in tax and government debt reduction within state policy;
4. undermines notions of 'social solidarity' and social protection by increasing inequality;
5. undermines tripartism and shifts the balance of power from organised labour and states to capital;
6. constrains policy by excluding 'left-of-centre' approaches;
7. will increasingly lead to conflict between the economic logic of globalisation and the 'logic' of national community and democratic politics. (1999: 15)

How accurate are Mishra's propositions? Reviewing welfare developments in a number of countries, he argues that there is substantial evidence to support propositions 1, 4 and 5 – there are increasing trends towards neo-liberal labour market strategies, growing inequality within countries (which undermines notions of 'solidarity'), and increasing marginalisation of trade unions and states.

As we have argued above, the growth of inequality on an international scale as a consequence of neo-liberal policies is indisputable. The evidence for other two propositions, however, is more open to challenge. In terms of the alleged growing trend towards neo-liberal policies, for example, it is noteworthy that the prospect of a recession in the US in 2001 was met by the Bush administration not with an extension of market forces but with barely concealed Keynesian demand management policies. In terms of popular support for neo-liberal policies, the experience of privatised public services in Britain over the past decade has led to a situation where opinion polls now show an overwhelming majority of people – including Conservative voters – supporting the argument that public services should be run on a not-for-profit basis (*Guardian*, 21 March 2001).

As regards trade union militancy, it is certainly true that ruling classes throughout the world have often been successful over the past two decades in marginalising organised labour, particularly in Britain and the US. What is less clear, however, is the extent and the permanence of such marginalisation. As we noted in Chapter 4 (and the US must be included here), the years 2000 and 2001 saw a substantial revival in trade union militancy and organisation internationally. While this revival is very uneven and much more evident in some countries (such as France) than in others (notably Britain), nevertheless, the years 2000 and 2001 seemed to mark a revival in organised working class politics.

Mishra himself expresses doubts regarding the other propositions. In respect of proposition 2, for example, comparative data suggests that not all countries adopt the cheap labour, flexibility, low social cost model to attract inward investment. As he notes:

> Germany ... shows [that] a dynamic, competitive economy is apparently quite compatible with a well-regulated labour market, centralized collective bargaining, high wages, good working conditions and strong entrenched workers' rights. (1999: 95)

Further, in terms of proposition 3, there are wide variations in tax levels within OECD countries, and many countries find immense difficulties in cutting their social expenditure, not least because of the political costs this can bring. For Mishra, these facts both highlight the ideological basis of globalisation logic and also hold out some hope for a (reduced) social democratic agenda at national level (proposition 6) and at the international level (proposition 7) – two themes we look at below and in Chapter 9.

His key point, on the basis of an examination of substantial comparative data, is that that some of the main claims made for globalisation logic may be flawed. This is important. Notions of globalisation have produced deep pessimism on much of the academic and political left. Despite being influenced by aspects of the globalisation thesis, overall Mishra's arguments suggest that things may be less bleak, and global developments less inevitable, than some other theorists have suggested.

Nor is Mishra alone in reaching this conclusion. Several prominent theorists have argued that globalisation has not resulted in any form of welfare convergence (Esping-Andersen, 1996; Pierson, 1996; Taylor-Gooby, 1997; Wilding, 1997). Taylor-Gooby, for example, argues that the nation-state continues to play a major role in generating divergent responses to globalisation, while for Esping-Andersen diversity continues to be a notable feature among welfare states today (Esping-Andersen, 1996: 2). Nation-states are not mere 'passive victims' of globalising economic forces. Different governments have adopted divergent political and ideological positions with regard to welfarism over the last 20 years. As Mishra (1999) notes, it is really only in the 'Anglo–American' regimes that the neo-liberal globalisation agenda has been pursued – and even here opposition has hindered the full implementation of the neo-liberal agenda (Lavalette and Mooney, 2000a).

In this connection, Rhodes is one of several commentators who stress the importance of the 'welfare constituency' (Rhodes, 1996). In Britain as elsewhere in Western Europe there has been protest and opposition to some of the retrenchment and privatisation strategies. In the first year of the New Labour government, for example, strong opposition to its plans to cut benefit to lone parents and other groups, for example, forced the resignations of two key ministers (Frank Field and Harriet Harman), while massive extra-parliamentary opposition from pensioners' groups and the trade union movement later forced the government to significantly increase their miserly 75p-a-week pension increase (while still refusing to restore the link broken by Margaret Thatcher between pensions and earnings). In France the massive strike wave of 1995 was initially caused by government attempts to restrict pension entitlements.

For other theorists, it is the *resilience* of state welfare in the face of globalisation logic, rather than its disappearance, which should be emphasised (Burchardt and Hills, 1999). Rhodes, for example, has argued that globalisation can be interpreted as leading to an expansion in welfare, albeit in the context of a system that is 'leaner and meaner' (1996: 318). Clarke, meanwhile, makes the important point that in many accounts of welfare retrenchment the welfare state is conceived narrowly as an 'income transfer machine', neglecting the central role that the welfare state plays in the reproduction of inequalities and social differentiation (2000: 203). This is only too apparent when we consider the case of 'welfare refugees' in Britain and in Western Europe where state-sponsored racism and oppression have been notable features in recent times, or in the case of New Labour where the pursuit and imposition of a strong law and order regime has been a significant ideological goal (Lavalette and Mooney, 1999; Mynott, 2000; Lavalette et al., 2001). In this respect it makes little sense to talk of the impotence, residualisation and/or rolling back of nation-states, but perhaps more usefully the 're-tooling' of the state (see Jones and Novak, 1999).

Finally, in connection with Mishra's seventh proposition, Bob Deacon notes that increasingly national social policies and social development itself are being decided and shaped by international institutions (Deacon, et al., 1997, Deacon, 2000). In this 'globalisation of social policy' the IMF, World Bank, OECD, the WTO (the International Financial Institutions – IFIs) and the 'supra-states' like the European Union and the North American Free Trade Agreement countries are particularly important organisations. In raising social policy issues to a supranational level, it is claimed, a global discourse emerges 'on the best way to regulate capitalism in the interests of social welfare' (Deacon et al., 1997: 195). For Deacon (1997) the only hope is for a series of globally accepted social clauses enshrined in the policy and practice of the IFIs, and which will provide a global regulatory system to control the worst excesses of global capitalism. The possibility of this approach is the subject of the next two sections. We start with a review of the impact of the IFIs – and their pro-globalisation agenda – on Third World countries before looking at the potential of 'global reformism' to establish treaties promoting the health and well being of people across the globe.

Structural adjustment programmes – promoting the global neo-liberal agenda

There is one area where the neo-liberal globalisation orthodoxy has had a major impact – in the proscriptive and proactive policies determined by the IFIs and implemented across much of the Third World by govern-ments following 'stabilisation and structural adjustment programmes' (SAPs) (now rather bizarrely called Poverty Reduction Programmes).

SAPs have been promoted within the IFIs to solve the problem of indebtedness. Debt was a direct consequence of the of the dominant developmentalist project of the post-War era. During the post-War boom underdeveloped and newly industrialising countries were encouraged to industrialise to share the benefits of the growth being experienced in the advanced economies. Years of imperialist rivalry and conquest had already detrimentally shaped these countries – their economies, their political regimes and their social structures more widely – and it was from this already subordinate position within the world system that they were encouraged to engage with the world market and compete within the world system. As O'Brien and Hanlon note:

> The effect of colonialism was to drain wealth in the form of raw materials, mineral wealth and human labour, so at a very early stage the less developed countries became locked into a situation from which they found it difficult to escape and in which the majority of their populations suffered terrible poverty and exploitation. (1999: 15)

To industrialise required vast resources, so countries had to borrow and, at the same time, to go for export-led growth (the dominant strategy) of, especially, raw materials and natural resources. The economies tended to become over-reliant on the export performance of a small number of commodities and hence the economies became particularly vulnerable to fluctuations in world prices. In this situation, short-term borrowing was common. In 1970 the poor countries of the world owed $70 billion but interest rates were low. Banks were chasing after poor countries to borrow money to finance a range of economic and military schemes, as well as various projects that aimed to flatter and aggrandise the already power-ful and wealthy within the developing countries themselves.

With the end of the post-War boom and the crisis of the mid-1970s things started to change dramatically. First, the crisis was a global one. In the newly industrialising countries export markets declined and the economies went into recession. Second, and making the problem much worse, interest rates started to rise. From 1977 to 1981 interest rates rose 10 per cent and countries started to struggle to pay the interest on their loans – never mind the loans themselves. The countries had to take new loans to pay the old loans with the consequence that the debt spiral moved out of control.

Third World debt has been growing at a phenomenal rate in recent years. In 1955 it was running at an estimate US$9 billion; this increased to US$572 billion in 1980 and to a staggering US$2,200 billion in 1998 – servicing this level of debt (paying the interest and some of the capital) costs developing countries US$200 billion a year (Madeley, 2000). According to Susan George, between 1982 and 1990 indebted Third World countries paid US$1,345,300,000,000 ($1.34 trillion) to the banks and governments of the first world (1992: xiv).

Neo-liberal ideas have dominated the governments of the advanced economies for the last 25 years and, over the same period, have been the dominant orthodoxy within the IMF, the World Bank, the OECD and the IFI newcomer, the WTO. Since the mid-1970s these institutions have imposed the neo-liberal globalisation agenda on various poor (debtor) nations applying for loans to overcome their economic problems. In order to obtain a loan from the IMF or World Bank, debtor governments have had to agree to implement SAPs. According to the United Nations Research Institute for Social Development (UNRISD, 1995: 38) SAPs generally required debtor nations to:

- lower trade barriers – opening national economies to global levels of 'efficiency';
- cut subsidies and price controls – on basic food staples, for example;
- restructure their financial systems – removing controls on capital movements and tying their currency to the dollar;
- denationalise/privatise state owned enterprises – allowing for 'rationalisation' and 'restructuring' (and mass unemployment);
- remove controls 'to encourage' private foreign investment – the largest and most profitable areas of national economies thus becoming vulnerable to take-over by MNC; and
- reduce state intervention to a minimum – not only in the economy, but also in the provision of social services.

SAPs promote the neo-liberal globalisation agenda. Their aim is to open economies up to the global market, to privatise nationalise industries, to cut public spending – or at least social welfare spending – to slash subsidies on food and other essential items and to create the conditions for multinational and local capital to increase their profits by attacking trade unions and forcing down wages. For the neo-liberal globalisers the consequence of following these policies would be to create self-regulating economies through open competition between firms, with a 'passive' public sector. But as UNRISD note, 'this picture ... corresponds to no known place on earth' (1995: 38).

The aim of SAPs is to make the working class in the cities and the rural poor pay for the crisis of the Third World countries. The consequences have been traumatic. Madeley notes many of the social consequences: 'reduce[d] spending on social programmes such as health care and education, [and the] elimination of food subsidies ... Many health-care services ... have been starved of funds in recent years, largely because of government spending cutbacks to meet the demands of structural adjustment programmes' (2000: 58, 40).

One of the first countries to go down this road was Jamaica. Between 1983 and 1985 unemployment increased by 30 per cent; there was a 30 per cent fall in public investment and a fall of 48 per cent in real incomes. By 1984 the World Bank proclaimed Jamaica one of its success stories because its trade balance had shifted into surplus. But it was a 'success' in which 29 per cent of children under three were malnourished, 43 per cent of mothers were anaemic, and polio deaths appeared for the first time in 30 years (McAfee, 1994; O'Brien and Hanlon, 1999).

Brazil was another country where the SAP experiment was carried out in the early 1980s. Here, as a result of 'debt control', the vast majority of its population went through extreme suffering, but the debt increased.

From 1980 to 1989, Brazil paid a total of $148 billion as service on its debt – $90 billion in interest and the rest in principal. In 1980, the debt was $64 billion. Ten years later, having paid $148 billion on that debt, Brazil ... owe[d] $121 billion. (Arruda, 1994: 45)

In Africa SAPs have had even more devastating consequences. According to a UN Economic Commission for Africa, SAPs 'undermine the human condition ... and the future potential for development' (in Madeley, 2000: 58). Ex-IMF economist Davison Budhoo (1994: 21) notes that in the 1980s in Africa, as a result of SAPs, expenditure on health declined by 50 per cent and on education by 25 per cent. While the UN Human Development Report in 1997 argued that if Africa was relieved of its annual debt repayments it would have enough money to invest in services that would save the lives of 7 million children a year and, at the same time, allow 90 million women and children access to basic education.

In Tanzania, where 40 per cent of people die before the age of 35, debt repayments are six times greater than health spending. While in Senegal:

Despite implementing policy reforms designed to reduce the country's debt ... its foreign debt has sharply increased from 44 percent of GNP in 1980 to close to 80 percent in 1989 ... Cuts in health services and education, rising unemployment in the public sector and a decrease in purchasing power have all [been the result]. (Ndiaye, 1994: 87)

The effects of SAPs have, as Danaher and Yunus note, 'been devastating to the poor ... The most vulnerable population groups, in particular women, youth, the disabled and the aged, have been severely and adversely affected' (1994: 3). While as Susan George caustically notes:

> If the goals of official debt managers were to squeeze the debtors dry, to transfer enormous resources from the South to North and to wage undeclared war on the poor ... then their policies have been an unqualified success. (1992: xiii)

Of course SAPs have benefited some people. Local and multi-national corporations have increased their profits on the back of low taxation rates and low wages and the banks themselves made record profits in the early 1980s on the backs of debt repayments. Susan George again:

> Third world elites ... weathered the 'lost decade of the 1980s' with relative ease and have sometimes profited handsomely from it. They too benefit from plummeting wages and their money is often in safe havens outside their own countries ... And although public services may deteriorate or close down, rich people can afford private ones. (1992: xvii)

Furthermore, many loans to Third World countries were handed over to corrupt regimes and dictators – with large sums taken to boost the personal wealth of the local rulers. Around $500 billion – a quarter of all loans – went to Third World dictators in 25 different countries (including Duvalier in Haiti, Mobutu in Zaire, Marcos in the Philippines and Suharto in Indonesia). The foreign holdings of Third World rulers at the end of the twentieth century stood at $400 billion (O'Brien and Hanlon, 1999). Taking one example (Indonesia), Pilger notes that according to 'an internal World bank report ... "at least 20–30%" of the banks loans "are diverted through informal payments to GOI [Government of Indonesia] staff and politicians"' (2001: 22). While, as Hanlon and O'Brien (1999) notes, many of the loans were 'Cold War' loans, used to prop up corrupt regimes as part of the larger geo-political struggle between the empires of the East and West, with much of the money used to buy weapons of mass destruction for use at home and abroad.

Finally, although SAPs were formally committed to reducing state intervention, they were often pushed through on the back of high levels of local repression by the military and police. The local state, and its repressive arm in particular, was an essential tool to implement SAPs.

SAPs represent the clearest experiment in neo-liberal economic and social policy. Along with GATS – general agreements on trade and services – whose aim is the progressive liberalisation of *all* service industries (Coates, 2001). Their implementation brings deliberate poverty, destitution and brutality for the vast majority but increases the vast wealth of the corrupt, the powerful and the already wealthy. For the vast majority it is an experiment that has failed, but given this, how can it be stopped before it destroys even more lives?

2000 – 'a fork in the road'

Until the end of 1999, critiques of the globalisation thesis of the sort outlined above took place largely within the publications of the left or, less frequently, in the pages of little-read academic journals. In November of that year, however, the critique of globalisation moved from the seminar room onto the streets. The mass protests in Seattle which succeeded in closing down the proceedings of the WTO also put the fight against the effects of neo-liberal policies onto the agenda of the world's press. Seattle, as US Green Party presidential candidate Ralph Nader noted, 'was a fork in the road' (in Charlton, 2000b) – it marked the turning point for the growth of a new mass social movement against globalisation and neo-liberalism.

What distinguished the Seattle protest from previous protests which had focused on specific issues or grievances can be summed up in an idea to which we have made repeated reference throughout this book: the notion of *totality*, that it is the system itself that is at fault and is the main source of so many of the world's ills. That sense of totality was brought out clearly in a report in the *Washington Post* on the protests against George W. Bush's inauguration on 20 January 2001:

> The activists sometimes confound onlookers with the diversity of their concerns, from the environment and civil rights to Third World Debt and corporate power ... The international finance and trade bodies seek to make the world profitable for the same corporations that are running the show in US politics, the demonstrators say ... Framing the issues in this way has allowed disparate causes to unite against common enemies. Save the rainforest and anti-sweatshop activists, for example, stand against the same trade and development policies that might boost corporate investment in a poor country engaged in selling off its natural resources (cited in Rees, 2001: 4–5).

Exactly the same comments could be made about any of the several mobilisations against international capitalism which took place in the months after Seattle: at Washington, Millau, Melbourne, Prague, Seoul, Davos, Nice, Barcelona, Gothenburg and Genoa. On the one hand, these mobilisations represented the biggest outpouring of activist energy since the 1970s; on the other, all were characterised by an anti-capitalist mood, reflected in the most popular slogans such as 'The world is not for sale' and 'People before profit'.

The academic and anti-capitalist activist Walden Bello is justified in suggesting that the year 2000 'will probably go down as one of the defining moments in the history of the world economy, like 1929' (2001: 70).

What is less clear, however, is how that movement will develop in the coming years. One of the central debates is likely to be over the extent to which the institutions of global capital – the IMF, the World Bank, the WTO – are capable of reform. Even prior to Seattle, some critics of globalisation, such as Bob Deacon, were explicitly calling for a 'global social reformist project' (Deacon et al., 1997: 25–6). This would involve fairer taxation regimes and the 'social regulation' of the world economy. His demand was for greater global governance comprising the management of global competition; reforming the United Nations; strengthening global political, social and legal rights; 'empowering international civil society' and making global institutions such as the WTO and World Bank more accountable (Deacon, et al., 1997: 203). Such arguments have not diminished since Seattle. At the World Social Forum at Porto Alegre in January 2001, for example, broadly similar views were expressed by a range of different groupings including representatives of the CONGOS – Co-opted Non-Governmental Organisations – supporters of the radical French news-paper *Le Monde Diplomatique* and those associated with the French organisation ATTAC whose central demand is for a tax – the 'Tobin Tax' – on financial transactions across national boundaries.

In turn, the leaders of the world global institutions, sensing that the legitimacy of their system is increasingly being called into question, have responded by showing a willingness to engage in dialogue – and even accept the validity of some of the protestors' criticisms – while still maintaining that there is no alternative to neoliberal economic policies. This apparent willingness on the part of the leaders of world capitalism to accept the need for reform that has led critics such as Deacon to suggest that the IMF, OECD, WTO and so on can play a key role in the 'new politics of global social responsibility'. He claims that these organisations now:

> appear to be more concerned than they used to be about the negative social impact of globalisation, and are revising their remedies accordingly ... Fundamentalist economic liberalism and inhumane structural adjustment appear to be giving way ... to a global politics of social concern. (Deacon, 2000: 254–5)

At Porto Alegre and at the other international mobilisations during 2000, those who rejected arguments like Deacon's and argued instead that the world economic system was incapable of reform and needed to be completely replaced were denounced as 'utopian'. Yet while demands such as the Tobin Tax and other measures that have been put forward to limit the power of global capital (see, for example, Danaher, 2001) should be fully supported, it may be that the charge of 'utopian' is more accurately levelled at those who believe that the leaders of global capital will willingly place the needs of the environment and the world's people above the drive for profit. For as Waldon Bello has pointed out, despite the fact that the Davos Forum, the annual think-tank for the world elite, has placed reform of the global economic system at the top of its agenda, since Seattle there has been precious little in the way of concrete action. In fact, as he notes, the most prominent reform initiative, the G8's plans to lessen the servicing of the external debt of the 41 Highly Indebted Poor Countries (HIPC) has delivered a reduction of only $1 billion since it began in 1996 – or a reduction of their debt servicing of only 3 per cent in four and a half years! (Bello, 2001: 74).

Similarly, the decision of the newly-elected president George W. Bush in March 2001 to place the interest of US capitalism above the health of the planet by ripping up the Kyoto protocol on global warming within weeks of taking up office (and, in a less publicised decision, to forge ahead with plans for oil exploration in the Arctic National Wildlife Refuge), hardly provides good evidence of the 'global politics of social concern' to which Deacon refers and in which he and others place their hopes for the future of the planet (Vulliamy, 2001a). Nor, given that the US is also by far the main player within all of the major institutions of global capital, are there many grounds for believing that these bodies will behave in a radically different manner. Indeed Noam Chomsky (2000) has argued that the US is a prime example of a 'Rogue State' – a state which refuses to act according to international regulations and laws. He argues that the US and some of its more powerful allies operate across the globe violating all types of international agreements and laws that it claims to uphold – a prognosis which questions the usefulness of international reform strategies. As Bello notes:

> One year after the Seattle collapse, talk about reforming the decision-making process at the WTO has vanished, with director-general Mike Moore saying that the non-transparent, undemocratic 'consensus/green room' system that the developing country revolt in Seattle is non-negotiable ... At the World Bank strong resistance to innovations that would put the priority on social reforms led to the resignation of two reformers – Joseph Stiglitz, the chief economist and Ravi Kanbur, the head of the World Development Task Force. (Bello, 2001: 74–75)

And that was before the election of George W. Bush!

9 'A system designed not for yesterday, but for today': New Labour and Welfare

In May 1997, New Labour were elected to government on the back of a wave of popular resentment against 18 years of Conservative rule. 'Things,' they told us, 'could only get better,' and with a relatively strong economy and a huge majority of 179 expectations were high. The sense of euphoria accompanying that election victory is well captured in a sympathetic evaluation of New Labour's first term of office:

> Strangers embraced: 'Where were you when Portillo lost?' A seventy-year-old woman brought a red rose for Tony Blair – 'If I live to be a hundred there'll never be another day like it!' ... In their wild euphoria they even talked of the night the Berlin Wall fell, of Nelson Mandela's release. It was the day the country exulted – even the sneering editorial writers at Wapping. (Toynbee and Walker, 2001: 1)

Labour, the party of reform and the party most clearly identified with the welfare state, had never been in such a position before – surely May 1997 would mark the start of a process that would reverse the cuts in state welfare that had been such a feature of the previous 20 years of government policy?

Four years later, however, as the country prepared for a new General Election, much of the early optimism had evaporated. As Toynbee and Walker note, one commitment overrode all others and shaped much of that first term of office: the freeze on public spending for two years at the level set by the last Conservative chancellor, Keneth Clarke (a level which, as Toynbee and Walker (2001) note, he later admitted he would have breached if the Conservatives had been re-elected), coupled with a pledge not to increase public spending at all. At the end of that two-year period, the Comprehensive Spending Review promised that billions were now available to spend on health, education and housing as a result of the fiscal prudence exercised by the government. In fact, despite enormous hype and over-claiming of the amounts actually being spent, when the balance-sheet was finally drawn up at the end of four years, it became clear that spending on public services by New Labour was actually *less* than it had been under the previous Conservative government: 'Under Tony Blair, the public sector actually shrank' (Toynbee and Walker, 2001: 2).

In stark contrast to this miserly attitude to the public sector was the government's unwavering commitment, both ideological and financial, for the private sector and big business generally. As George Monbiot has noted:

> Even before the Labour government came to power, corporation tax in Britain was the lowest of any major industrialized country. The Conservatives had reduced it from 52 per cent to 33 per cent. In 1997, the Labour Government cut it by a further 2 per cent. In 1999, it cut the tax again, to 30 per cent. The Chancellor, Gordon Brown, boasted that this was 'now the lowest rate in the history of British corporation tax, the lowest rate of any major country in Europe and the lowest rate of any major industrialised country anywhere, including Japan and the United States'. (2000: 350)

That commitment to business also included a huge increase in the number of leading businessmen in key government, or government-related, posts (helpfully detailed by Monbiot in his *Captive State* in a chapter entitled 'The Fat Cats Directory') and plans for an extension of privatisation (in the form of the Public–Private Partnership) into areas where previous Conservative governments would not have dared to tread, including air traffic control, the London Underground and – astonishingly, given the frequency of food crises in Britain during the 1990s – meat safety inspectors.

As well as continuing the economic policies of previous administrations, the thrust of much of the new government's social policy also mirrored the tone, language and punitive approach of earlier Tory governments. Thus single parents, the 'work-shy', 'inadequate parents', teenage delinquents, 'beggars', welfare dependents, 'teen-mums', 'dysfunctional' families (and their communities), asylum seekers and all those deemed to have excluded themselves from accepting their civic responsibilities have been subject to vociferous denouncement by Labour leaders or their representatives since the 1997 election.

Perhaps unsurprisingly, the commitment to the market and big business on the part of the New Labour leadership has been accompanied by an explicit rejection of key elements of the Beveridgean welfare reforms introduced in the aftermath of the Second World War. Dismissed as 'statist' or 'old Labour', the Beveridgean–Keynesian welfare state is an anathema to New Labour. Leading Labour politicians, notably Tony Blair himself, have been at pains to emphasise that 'the world of 1997 is not that of 1947'. Stressing instead that the 'new' conditions of 'globalisation' render the necessity of welfare state restructuring, New Labour has also dismissed as a failure many of the welfare reforms introduced in the immediate post-War period by Labour (and Conservative) governments, a dismissal which is often couched in language not dissimilar to that employed by the Thatcherite New Right.

In the face of such attacks on state welfare in the final quarter of the twentieth century, it is not surprising that increasing numbers of people have seen the kinds of policies developed during the post-War period – a period often identified as being the 'Golden Age' of 'Old' Labour – as offering the only sane alternative to the market madness of the Tories and New Labour. The experience of having to rely on privatised public services over the past decade has convinced many of the benefits of public ownership. One major opinion survey conducted in early 2001, for example, found that more than 66 per cent of those polled (and more than 50 per cent of Conservative voters!) favoured the re-nationalisation of the railway network (The *Herald*, 15 January). Similarly the election of Ken Livingstone as mayor of London in 2000, despite the vicious campaign waged against him by the New Labour leadership, owed much to his opposition to privatisation of the London Underground network.

The calls for a return to public ownership, as well as the growing demands for the retention and extension of universal benefits for older people following the publication of the Sutherland Committee Report in Scotland, are very welcome and clearly demonstrate the widespread nature of the disillusionment with market-based policies.

There is a danger, however, that disillusionment with New Labour can also lead to a romanticisation of 'Old Labour', to the creation of a myth of a socialist past which bears very little resemblance to the real history of Labour in government. In the discussion of welfare and the family in the previous chapter, for example, we argued that the Beveridgean welfare state was premised upon certain understandings of the organisation of domestic life and accepted without question the notion of a male bread-winner/female dependent and the idea that women were primarily domestic workers. In addition the welfare system was based upon a racialised understanding of the nature of the post-War population that effectively discriminated against 'immigrants' and the 'non-British' (Lewis, 2000). Rightly then, the Beveridgean welfare settlement has been criticised for its oppressive and exclusionary practices. In this chapter, therefore, before critically assessing New Labour's welfare policies, it is necessary to revisit the experience of welfare under previous Labour regimes, as well as (briefly) considering the major shifts in welfare provision that took place under the four Conservative regimes between 1979 and 1997.

The political economy of welfare: from Beveridge to Thatcher

The various initiatives and policies that combined to create a 'welfare state' in post-War Britain can only be fully grasped if we remind ourselves of the immense suffering experienced by millions of working-class families during the inter-War period (see Lavalette and Penketh, 2002). The growth in long-term mass unemployment was accompanied by widespread hunger, malnutrition and disease, often compounded by the dreadful housing conditions in which a large proportion of the population lived. In these conditions the 1920s and 1930s were characterised by widespread demands for the expansion of state welfare from the organised working class. This represented a significant change from the suspicion of state provision embodied in many working class self-help organisations at the end of the nineteenth century (Yeo, 1980; Jones and Novak, 1999).

The election of the Labour Government of Clement Atlee in 1945 was on the back of such struggles and on the promise that there would be 'no return to the 1930s' and the widespread unemployment, hunger, poverty and high levels of mortality at this period. Ian Birchall (1986) has argued that Atlee's government had two main aims: to direct the expectations and demands for reforms which were being made by the working class into parliamentary channels and to restructure and improve the efficiency of the British economy by nationalising those sectors that were classed as unproductive or inefficient. Under Labour these two goals would be reconciled in very particular ways and this was reflected in the proposals adopted for the construction of the welfare state.

Social Democracy involves a commitment to the interests of both the working class and to the nation state and 'national interests' – it tries to balance the interests of 'nation' and 'class', essentially by channelling working-class aspirations through the institutions of the nation state (Cliff and Gluckstein, 1988). History attests to the fact that when the interests of these two clash, Labour defends and pursues national interests over those of their working-class constituency (see Miliband, 1972; Lavalette and Penketh, 2002). In the immediate post-War period, however, the economic conditions allowed Labour to oversee the restructuring of capital while meeting *some* of the demands from the working class for employment, better housing, education and health provision. This meant that the system could deliver real benefits and improvements in living standards for much of the population, thanks primarily to the sustained period of economic growth that lasted up until the late 1960s, and to the very low levels of unemployment that exceeded 3 per cent nationally on only three occasions between 1945 and 1975.

The post-War boom represented the greatest period of sustained economic growth in human history – growth that was to characterise the entire global economy, both West and East. The basis of this boom – which was generally characterised by an increasing role for the state in the management and regulation of key areas of the economy – is to be found in the massive and unprecedented increase in military expenditure in the aftermath of 1945, itself a direct consequence of the military competition between the two great rival imperialist blocks of the Cold War Era (Kidron, 1968). The increase in arms expenditure was most notable in the US. In 1939 the US state spent just 1.5 per cent of gross national product on arms, a figure which rose to 4.3 per cent in 1948 and 13.6 per cent in

1953, at the end of the Korean War, and although it declined after this it remained high by comparison with pre-War (and immediate post-War levels) – 10.2 per cent in 1957, 8.8 per cent in 1963 and 9.1 per cent in 1967 (Harman, 1984: 80). Likewise in Britain throughout the 1950s and 1960s arms expenditure far surpassed that which had featured in any previous peacetime period, thanks in part to the costs of nuclear weapons. Arms expenditure 'accounted for 10 per cent of national output in the early 1950s, from which it slowly slid down to about 6 per cent in the late 1960s' (Harman, 1984: 80).

The creation of this 'permanent arms economy' fuelled the post-War boom. The high level of arms spending meant that the state took control of a substantial portion of surplus value, which would otherwise have looked to other sources of profitable investment, and directed it into 'wasted' munitions investments. Such expenditure represented a 'leak' of surplus value from the assumed closed cycle of production/investment/ production and offset (for a period) the tendency of the rate of profit to fall. The consequence was a period characterised by a low level of sustained economic growth. As Harman notes:

> Comparing the post-war and the pre-war economy was like comparing the hare and the tortoise of Aesop's fable. The pre-war economy bounded forward at great speed – and then stopped short … The post-war economy, 'burdened' by the waste of huge arms expenditure, moved forward far more slowly, but did not stop short in the same abrupt way. Its rate of profit was not forced down, and so it could continue going forward year after year, decade after decade. Its long-term growth rate was greater than anything the system had ever known before. (1984: 82)

But the conditions of the post-War boom could not be sustained forever. The disparity between those regimes which were spending vast amounts of their GNP on arms – notably Britain, the US and the former Soviet Union – and those which, following their defeat in the Second World War, were expressly forbidden from spending on arms – notably, West Germany and Japan – eventually became intolerable, with economic competition from the latter two regimes forcing the big arms spenders to cut back on military expenditure, leading to a marked slowing-down of the economic boom in the late 1960s and the return of economic crisis in the early 1970s – given its final expression as a result of the Middle East Oil Crisis of 1973.

The period of the post-War boom was to provide the growth necessary to finance the expansion of state welfarism in Britain. The proposals for the post-1945 welfare system are generally attributed to William Beveridge, civil servant and later Liberal MP – although the Atlee admini- stration built upon some pre-War elements of social and welfare policy established by the Liberals in the 1906–1911 period, such as the system of contributory insurance based upon weekly payments from employees, employers and the state. The *Social Insurance and Allied Services* report of 1942 (hereafter the Beveridge Report) is largely credited with providing the 'blueprint' upon which the welfare state was constructed.

Beveridge provided the incoming Labour government with a ready-made plan from which it could begin to respond to the demands for reform from the organised working class, whilst at the same time meeting the requirements of a restructured capitalist economy. The report was widely welcomed and much sought after when it was first published in 1942. It was promoted as a boost to flagging wartime morale at a time when the war had been going badly, with increasing hardship for many working-class families. As Conservative MP and future Law Lord Quinton Hogg (Lord Hailsham) said of the report:

> It was not that it was a bible or a panacea, but it was a flag to nail to the mast, a symbol, a rallying point for men of good will. (quoted in Calder, 1969: 530)

While at the same time Beveridge claimed:

> The purpose of victory … is to live in a better world than the old world. … Each individual citizen is more likely to concentrate upon his war effort if he feels that his government will be ready in time with plans for that better world. (quoted in Calder, 1969: 530)

The report was endorsed not only by the Labour Party and the TUC, but also the Liberals, Winston Churchill and other sections of the Conservatives. However, as Jones and Novak argue, it was the rhetoric of 'the five giants' rather than the reality of change within the welfare system that characterised the Report (Jones and Novak, 1999: 131). Tackling these five giants: want (poverty), ignorance (education), squalor (housing), idleness (unemployment) and disease (ill-health) was the major thrust of the proposals but in essence it was the issue of 'want' that dominated the report itself.

Despite generally welcoming the report – on a tide of popular acclaim for its proposals – some sections of the Conservative party (along with elements in the higher ranks of the civil service) attacked it as being excessively expensive. In the face of this minority opposition, Beveridge was persuaded to make several concessions so that the cost of the system amounted to only one-fifth of what he had initially envisaged. His other response to such criticism betrays the implicit conservatism that underpinned his thinking. For a start contributions would pay for all benefits, with benefits set at a level that did not undermine a willingness to work. Opponents of state welfare had expressed such a fear since the nineteenth century poor laws at least and Beveridge, in emphasising the importance of individual responsibility, echoes the language and sentiments of organisations such as the Charity Organisation Society in the late nineteenth century:

To give compulsory insurance more than is needed for subsistence is an unnecessary interference with individual responsibilities. (Beveridge, 1942: 294)

The state should organise security for service and contribution, but the state in organising security should not stifle incentive, opportunity and responsibility. (Beveridge, 1942: 92)

Further, the welfare system envisaged by Beveridge contained little commitment to greater equality of outcome and ruled out any redistribution of wealth from rich to poor. Indeed any redistribution that would take place would be between workers through their insurance contributions, for example, from workers without children to workers with children. To emphasise this point, between 1936/38 and 1960 the share of the wealthiest 5 per cent of the population declined by only 4 per cent from 79 per cent to 75 per cent (Wedderburn, 1965: 134). However, unlike the period from the mid-1970s on, there was a slight relative decline in inequality over this period.

For both Beveridge and the Atlee government the development of a welfare state in the post-War period was an important precondition for economic growth. Beveridge repeatedly stressed the economic benefits to be gained through increased social expenditure while he also argued that much of this expenditure, for instance on schools or on the health service, could be classed as 'productive' in that it would serve the needs of the economy. He further claimed that employers would be willing to make payments towards the new system as they would be assured not only of a healthier, better educated and hence more productive labour force, but also of the political stability that was essential for investment and economic growth. Therefore for Beveridge, the achievement of greater equality came second to the emphasis placed upon the creation of a more secure society.

The post-War welfare state, together with the political commitment to full employment and to Keynesian-inspired state administered capitalism, was essentially about managing and regulating the 'disorderliness' of markets and the labour force as a means of restructuring British capitalism to operate more efficiently, thereby competing in the new global economic context emerging in the aftermath of the Second World War. In this respect support for the new welfare system across much of the political spectrum reflected the post-War settlement or 'consensus', a series of shared understandings that capitalism could deliver. Under both the Labour government of 1945–51 and the Conservative government that replaced it in 1951, there was expressed support for the general principles of the post-War social democratic consensus which can be summarised as involving support for a mixed economy, a commitment to full employment and to a comprehensive welfare system, the active conciliation of trade unions and support for the United States in the new era of cold-war politics.

The defeat of Labour in 1951 did not mark the end of the post-War settlement, as the incoming Conservative government was largely committed to similar policies. So much so in fact that *The Economist* magazine coined the label 'Butskellism' in 1954 to illustrate the convergence between Conservative and Labour policies, the term an amalgam of the names of the relevant party Chancellors leaders, the Conservative Rab Butler and Hugh Gaitskell for Labour. In the context of Britain's declining world role, the 1950s were to be characterised by a climate of rising living standards and virtually full employment and this was reflected in major debates within the Labour Party, in particular about the nature of post-War British capitalism. One of the central themes to emerge here centred on the idea that capitalism had been largely reformed and was now able to deliver prosperity for all and that only piecemeal reforms were now required to maintain social progress. As we noted in Chapter 3, this was accompanied by the notion that the working class of post-War Britain had changed significantly and its members were adopting middle-class values and lifestyles. Within the Labour Party in the late 1950s such arguments helped fuel a heated debate over (the old) Clause 4 and the Party's commitment to the common ownership of the means of production. The leading advocate of the idea that British capitalism had evolved into a new and more benign form of society was Anthony Crosland. In his most notable work, *The Future of Socialism*, he claimed that:

> Today the capitalist business class has lost … [its] commanding position. The change in the balance of economic power is reflected in, and may be inferred from, three developments. First, certain decisive sources and lever of economic power have been transferred from private business to other hands; and new levers have emerged, again concentrated in other hands than theirs. Secondly, the outcome of clashes of group or class economic interests is markedly less favourable to private employers than it used to be. Thirdly, the social attitudes and behaviour of the business class have undergone a significant change, which appears to reflect a pronounced loss of strength and self-confidence.
>
> Of course we still have strikes, hostilities, and periodic outbursts of emotion – perhaps even to a surprising extent. But they no longer take the same prolonged, dogged and embittered form. The disputes are conducted within more moderate limits; compromises are more quickly reached; and the militant language of class war, the terminology of revolt and counter-revolt, is itself passing out of usage. (Crosland, 1956: 26, 65–6)

While Crosland's views may have been out of touch with those of a substantial number of ordinary Labour Party members, on its return to Government in 1964 Labour once again committed itself to 'modernising' the British economy amidst the rapid slow-down of the post-War boom. In part this was to be achieved by addressing the issue of working class militancy, through pay freezes and incomes policies, culminating in 1969 with the publication of *In Place of Strife* (DSEP, 1969), and proposed legislation to limit the rights of Trade Unions. In particular Labour was concerned to increasingly regulate and control the power of rank and file organisations on the shop floor, organisations that had widely developed amidst the conditions of full employment and economic growth. In return for wage 'restraint' the Labour government of Harold Wilson promised increased expenditure on housing, health, education and welfare but again this was to prove limited. Between 1964 and 1968, expenditure on education increased from 4.8 per cent to 5.9 per cent of GNP, on health from 3.9 per cent to 4.6 per cent and on housing from 2.8 per cent to 3 per cent (quoted in Birchall, 1986: 110). This was also accompanied by higher welfare benefits and the replacement of National Assistance by Supplementary Benefits. But Wilson ruled out a major upgrading of universal benefits on the basis of cost and, in opposition both to Labour Party policy and to Beveridge's proposals for universal benefits, extended means testing. By 1975 there were no fewer than 45 major means-tested benefits in operation.

If the post-War boom was beginning to slow-down by the mid-1960s, by the mid 1970s, following the world oil crisis of 1973, it was becoming a distant memory. Fittingly enough, the official pronouncement that 'The party's over' and that spending on health and social services would need to be cut back came from none other than Anthony Crosland, by then a minister in the 1974–76 Wilson Government. In Britain, which had in any case been experiencing considerably slower growth rates throughout the period of the post-War era than most of its major economic competitors, the end of the boom was to have dramatic effects. Foremost among these was a significant rise in industrial conflict amidst rising unemployment, that reached over 1 million in 1975, cuts in the social wage and attacks on trade union rights. Under the 1974 government of Wilson and then (from 1976) James Callaghan, Labour sought to address the growing economic crisis by attacking working class standards of living. In an oft-quoted speech to the Labour Party Conference in 1976, Labour leader Jim Callaghan commented:

> We used to think that you could just spend your way out of a recession and increase employment by cutting taxes and boosting government spending. I tell you in all candour, that option no longer exists, and that in so far as it ever did exist, it worked by injecting inflation into the economy. And each time that happened the average level of unemployment has risen. Higher inflation was followed by higher unemployment. That is the history of the last twenty years. (Labour Party, 1976)

Faced with the choice of protecting workers from the ravages of economic recession or sacrificing workers in an attempt to re-invigorate the economy on terms favourable to business and the market, Labour's message was only too clear: as the crisis developed it was workers who were going to have to pay the costs of economic decline through reduced wages, unemployment and cuts in social provision. At the same time as crucial areas of social policy expenditure were being cut back, the police benefited from more resources and there was more aid to the private sector through, for instance, the National Enterprise Board. As with the Tories in the 1980s and 1990s, there was not so much a *total cut* in state spending during this period, more a restructuring and re-ordering of priorities (Gough, 1979: 131). As the government itself expressed it in 1976:

> Within total public expenditure, a higher priority is being given to expenditure which is designed to maintain or improve our industrial capability. (quoted in Gough, 1979: 131)

Few things better illustrate the nature, role and priorities of a Labour government than its period in office between 1975 and 1979. If little in the way of a significant redistribution of income and substantial progress towards equality had taken place during the period from 1949 to 1974, the period from 1975 to 1977 was to signify a major turning point in post-War trends in income inequality. This was also a period marked by redistribution, but under the Wilson and Callaghan government it was redistribution *from* the working class to those who were already affluent and privileged. A key element of this was the so-called 'Social Contract' that Wilson arranged with Trade Union leaders, in which it was agreed that wages would not increase faster than prices. The outcome was that for the first time in several decades real wages actually declined in the period following 1974. In the period from 1970 to 1974, capital expenditure on personal social services had risen by an average of 11.95 per cent per year and overall expenditure on the personal social services by 15.8 per cent. But between 1975 and 1979, capital expenditure fell on average by 9.2 per cent per year with only a modest rise of 1.9 per cent per annum in total expenditure (NALGO, 1989: 9).

The 1974–79 Labour Government was only too willing to ditch the substantial gains made by millions of working-class people in the two decades that followed the end of the Second World War. 'National economic interests', that is ensuring profitability for British capital, was given much greater priority than meeting the needs of the rapidly increasing numbers of people requiring welfare benefits and other forms of state support. Between 1976 and 1978 there was a 9.5 per cent decline in public spending in real terms. Labour's cuts in welfare benefits and other social expenditure paved the way for even more far-reaching cuts in the welfare system under the Conservative governments between 1979 and 1997: Labour provided Thatcher with an argument that she was to use on many an occasion – that she was only continuing what Labour had started. Thus the reality of Labour's period in power during the 1970s is far removed from the 'tax and spend' image conjured up by Blairite spin-doctors in the late 1990s.

The welfare state under the Tories: 1979–97

It would be wrong to suggest that all Conservative governments in the post-War era were ideologically committed to cutting welfare. The post-War 'consensus' represented a broad agreement between the main political parties about the legitimacy of state direction of the economy and support for state welfare provision. In terms of housing provision, for example, the Conservatives made much of the fact that they built more council houses in the four-year period between 1952 and 1956 than did any other government during a period of similar length. More surprisingly, later Conservative governments were able to boast that:

... the largest number of comprehensive schools was opened while Margaret Thatcher was Education Secretary. (Lowe, 1993: 247)

Nevertheless, when we cast our minds back to the period of Conservative rule in the 1980s and 1990s, among the most enduring memories will be of lengthening queues for NHS treatment, school and hospital closures, long lines of the unemployed and other claimants at social security and benefits offices and continual reports of others in need being refused benefits or being forced to live on the most meagre state incomes. Lying behind these stark images is a story of increasing attacks on working class living standards and the degradation and casualisation of work – at a time when the rich saw their incomes rise dramatically.

One of the grandest claims made by both Margaret Thatcher and her successor John Major was that everyone would reap the benefits of their policies, which they continually reminded us had led to a more prosperous Britain. As Thatcher herself put it in 1988: 'Everyone in the nation has benefited from increased prosperity – everyone' (House of Commons, *Hansard*, 17 May, Col. 796). The reality was markedly different from the political rhetoric. As we have discussed in previous chapters, there was increasing prosperity for the rich, but there were few signs that this had, in the terms used by the Conservatives, 'trickled down' to the more disadvantaged sections of British society (Cox, 1995: 59–64).

The Tories' goal was to re-assert the profitability of British capital by cutting wages, emasculating the trade unions, and increasing 'incentives' for those already wealthy by cutting taxation and de-regulating the 'business world' (Lavalette and Mooney, 2000b). 'Greed was good' was the message conveyed to the wealthy and privileged by successive Conservative policies.

One of the most useful ways of illustrating this is to focus on changes in the taxation system introduced by the Conservatives. The Child Poverty Action Group has estimated that if the tax regime in place during the final year of the last Labour government in 1978/79 were in place in the final years of Conservative rule in the mid-1990s, the Blair government would have had an additional £31.8 billion to fund new hospitals and schools, and to improve the welfare system. Of the £31 billion given away in tax cuts by the Tories, the poorest 50 per cent of the population received 14 per cent, while the richest 1 per cent received one-third of the total (Oppenheim and Harker, 1996). In particular this was a direct result of changes to direct personal taxation (income tax) and Value Added Tax (VAT) (Lavalette et al., 2001). When the Tories were elected in 1979 personal direct taxation was levied at a basic rate of 33 per cent with earnings-related increases to a maximum top rate of 98 per cent (on unearned income) and 83 per cent (on earnings), by 2000 the basic rate was down to 22 per cent (with a low-start 10 per cent tax rate on the first £1,520 of taxable income), while the top rate had been reduced to a mere 40 per cent. Over the same period the standard rate of VAT increased from 8 per cent to 17.5 per cent (Chennells et al., 2001).

But the growth of poverty and inequality was not only a result of changes to the taxation system. The British economy underwent a rapid period of restructuring that brought large-scale factory closures, increasing unemployment and a growth in part-time and temporary forms of employment (see Chapter 4). There were attacks on wages (although unlike the Labour government of 1974–79, the Conservative party failed to reduce wages in real terms), reductions in benefit levels and the increasing regulation of benefit entitlement in ways that were discriminatory and punitive. There were drastic reductions in council housing expenditure and the NHS and educational systems were subjected to major organisational changes in ways what contributed to a deteriorating service (Lavalette and Penketh, 2002). Finally, policies like the poll tax represented an attack on local government welfare provision as well as a further attempt to redistribute wealth from the poor to the rich (Lavalette and Mooney, 1989; 2000a).

While direct use of privately provided social welfare services remains limited and beyond the reach of the overwhelming majority of people in Britain, the end of the twentieth century witnessed a gradual – though uneven and contradictory – shift away from state welfare provision towards a greater role for the market. This took a number of diverse forms: a shift in the welfare 'mix' in which public sector provision was diminished or steadily replaced by both voluntary and for-profit agencies. That this was uneven across the public sector does not detract from the major inroads that were made in the marketisation of the public sector. For the Conservatives the 'Right to Buy' legislation introduced under the Housing Act (1980), the Assisted Places Scheme brought in under the Education Act (1980) and tax relief for private pensions and private health care insurance, would reduce welfare dependency while opportunities for the exercise of individual choice would be maximised. The reality was increased differentiation in service provision, increasing stigmatisation of public welfare provision and – in the case of housing in particular – a number of deep-seated problems which can be directly attributable to underfunding and marketisation (see Philo and Miller, 2000).

An important aspect of Conservative social policy was to transform those state agencies that remained significant providers (such as social work/services) into more 'business-like organisations'. Through this it was argued that more efficient forms of delivery could be developed, offering more 'value for money'. Contracting-out services and Compulsory Competitive Tendering (CCT) opened up important sectors of local government to the market, while in many areas driving down the costs of labour and eroding conditions of employment. Key to this was the claim that 'more and better' management was the route to a more cost-effective welfare system. The growth of managerialism in the public sector during the 1980s and 1990s has been well documented (see Clarke et al., 1994; Clarke and Newman, 1997; Clarke et al., 2000). Public services in both Britain and the US were, in the language of New Right critics, lacking 'real' management and 'managerialism' as an ideology became established as the means through which public sector agencies would become more effective service providers. In turn 'more could be had for less'.

The period of Conservative rule was characterised by lengthening queues for hospital treatment, a decaying public sector housing stock and in general by a gradual undermining of central aspects of the post-War welfare system.

Taken together these changes have, as has been noted, led to pronounced shifts in welfare delivery and in the prevailing view about the role of the welfare state. There is a continuing debate as to whether these changes led to the 'end of the welfare state' or represented the restructuring of an otherwise 'resilient' welfare system. While it is important to recognise the vast changes in the welfare system and in social policy in general that characterised the Conservative years, and not least the massive increases in inequality that ensued, it would be wrong to over-state the 'success' that they enjoyed with regard to the restructuring of the welfare state. One of the most notable features of the first two Conservative governments was their failure (in their terms) to cut social spending significantly. In part this was a legacy of the cuts previously made by Labour between 1976 and 1979. But it also reflected spiralling levels of unemployment and poverty and the increasing demands for state support that this produced. However, in addition, this failure to dramatically cut the 'costs of welfare' was also a result of Thatcher's *caution* – her belief that the welfare state was immensely popular (as repeated attitude surveys and opinion polls testified) and that the privatisation of welfare could prove politically costly. As Nicholas Ridley commented:

> She (Thatcher) was adamant that she would not start down this sort of road … (that is, privatising the welfare state). There was enough to do sorting out industry, the economy, taxation and the trade unions. The supply side must come first she said. (quoted in Timmins, 1996: 372)

Despite the cuts and privatisations which marked the Conservative period in general, in particular following their third successive general election success in 1987, the conclusion of one welfare commentators' assessment provides a fairly accurate summation of the consequences of Conservative social policy:

> The welfare state has not yet been dismantled. The major services, much changed and with inadequate resources, are still in place. (Johnson, 1990: 225)

There are two main points to draw from this account. First, the degree of continuity in state social policy from 1976 onwards, reflected in an attempt to break from the post-War 'consensus' and to restructure the economy in part by attacking the social wage. The Social Contract of Wilson and Callaghan, with its goals of reducing wages and reducing social policy expenditure, was part and parcel or a wider attempt to rein- vigorate the British economy. The main aims of the Tories, to increase inequality, curtail and reduce the collective provision of services and to generally 'reform' the welfare state, was part of an agenda to redistribute resources from the working class to the privileged and wealthy. Behind New Labour's reform agenda, then, and its talk of a modern politics for a modern Britain – the so-called *third way* – lay many of the same themes that have shaped government social policy for at least two decades and more: the need to 'regulate' or control (that is reduce) social spending as part of the project of ensuring that British capital is fit to compete in the conditions of late twentieth-century global capitalism.

New Labour and welfare reform

Reform is a vital part of rediscovering a true national purpose, part of a bigger picture in which our country is a model of a 21st century developed nation: with sound, stable economic management; dynamism and enterprise in business; the best educated and creative nation in the world; and a welfare state that pro- motes our aims and achievements. But we should not forget why reform is right, and why, whatever the concerns over individual benefits, most people know it is right. Above all, the system must change because the world has changed, beyond the recognition of Beveridge's generation ... We need a system designed not for yesterday, but for today. (Blair, quoted in IPPR, 1998: iii–iv)

Labour has presented the 'modernisation' of the welfare state as one of its key political objectives and has proved to be as enthusiastic about welfare 'reform' as had the Tories. Central to the Conservative approach was an attack on 'welfarism', the argument that state provision creates a depen- dent 'underclass'. This was linked to a generalised attack on state welfare as unproductive, inefficient and primarily serving the interests of the professional groups employed in its delivery. This anti-public sectorism paved the way for the opening-up of welfare provision to competition from a range of statutory, voluntary and corporate agencies. By the mid-1990s these changes in the organisation of welfare provision had con- tributed to a diminishing of the scale and significance of direct public sector provision while enhancing the role of the private sector. Together with increasing emphasis on individual and family 'responsibility', the landscape of welfare provision was significantly altered – though not totally transformed – under the Conservatives. The Conservative legacy was to exert considerable influence on Labour. As leading New Labour architect Peter Mandelson once famously commented: 'New Labour's mission is to move forward from where Margaret Thatcher left off, rather than dismantle every single thing she did' (quoted in Mandelson and Liddle, 1996: 1).

Mandelson betrays the true nature of much of the New Labour project here. In turn the Labour Government of Blair has shown itself willing to adopt many of the understandings of neo-Liberalism, together with the language of the market: choice, competition and performance-related pay (see Fairclough, 2000). Further, as we noted at the beginning of this chapter, Labour is committed to further privatise important areas of the public sector, including the London Underground and, despite widespread opposition and concerns about safety, the National Air Traffic Control Service.

The Conservatives were able to introduce major changes in relation to health and welfare, albeit ones that were partial, uneven, ambiguous and, at times, contradictory. However, they did succeed to a significant extent in securing legitimation for the role of the market in the delivery of heartland social and welfare services, and in the role of management in securing cost effectiveness. More significantly perhaps, they also created a new culture around welfare that New Labour were quick to embrace. One of the key themes that have emerged in the on-going debates about the basis of the New Labour ideology is the extent to which it is founded upon ground already secured by the New Right. Speaking in 1992 New Labour's leading welfare thinker highlights once more Labour's gradual convergence to the taxation policies of the Tories:

> ... an expanding welfare system is a failing welfare system – not because of any deep faith in the philosophies of the minimal state, but because it means people are being dragged down and snared in the safety net ... An increasing proportion of the electorate see Labour as a backward looking party, intent on holding them down ... the aim must be to illustrate the potential for redistribution in our society and how the main forms of redistribution to be enacted by a future Labour government does not involve more taxes. (Frank Field in The Daily Mail, 21 December 1992)

There are several threads that emerge in the debate about New Labour's project. These include its apparent pragmatism and emphasis on presentation; its reassertion of the social and communal over the rampant individualism of neo-liberalism; the support for European notions of 'social exclusion' and its close relationship with the Clinton administration in the US. In addition to this there is New Labour's own story about its political trajectory and how it seeks to transcend the 'old differences' between left and right in constructing a 'Third Way' in British politics. Blair contrasts the political commitments of Old Labour/the left, as pro-state and anti-market, with the pro-market and anti-state position of the Right (Blair, 1998). For Blair these represent two 'failed pasts', based upon the state or the market or, to borrow the language of the 1998 Green Paper on Health, *Our Healthier Nation*, 'nanny state engineering' on the one hand and 'individual victim blaming' on the other (Secretary of State for Health, 1998). Between these two sharply polarised positions, it is claimed, a new pragmatic and modern approach to politics can be developed that embraces both public and private sectors:

> New Labour will be wise spenders, not long spenders. We will work in partnership with the private sector to achieve our goals. We will ask about public spending the first question that a manager in any company would ask – can existing resources be used more effectively to meet our priorities? And because efficiency and value for money are central, ministers will be required to save before they spend. Save to invest is our approach, not tax and spend. (Labour Party, 1997: 12)

This approach is underpinned by the rhetoric of the 'Third Way', which represents a conscious attempt to provide New Labour with an intellectual basis. For Giddens the Third Way provides a:

> ... framework of thinking and policy making that seeks to adapt social democracy to a world that has changed fundamentally over the past two or three decades ... No one has any alternatives to capitalism – the arguments that remain concern how far, and in what ways, capitalism should be governed and regulated. (1998b: 26, 43–4)

What links the Third Way and the approach outlined in the 1997 Manifesto is a shared view of a changing world, a world in which the death of socialism is proclaimed. To quote Blair again, 'the policies of 1997 cannot be those of 1947 or 1967'. So what has changed then? New Labour shared with the Democrat Administration in the US in the late 1990s a view of the world shaped by globalisation: where the inexorable forces of the global market render the nation-state unable to moderate its effects expect in the most limited of ways. As Richard Heffernan has observed:

> As leader, Blair made clear his commitment to the enterprise society fashioned in the 1980s and made no secret of his determination to both win the endorsement of businessmen and to forge a partnership with business: 'The deal is this: we leave intact the main changes of the 1908s in industrial relations, and enterprise. And now, together we address a new agenda for the twenty-first century: education, welfare reform, infrastructure and leadership in Europe'. In pursuing this 'accord' with business, Labour's unwillingness to closely associate with trade union rights was almost worn as a badge of courage. In a piece written for the *Daily Mail* in March 1997, Blair argued: 'Even after the changes the Labour Party is proposing in this area, Britain will remain with the most restrictive trade union laws anywhere in the western world'. Blair made clear that Labour would encourage rather than limit flexible labour markets: 'Our proposals for change, including the minimum wage, would amount to less labour market regulation than in the US'. (2000: 23)

For Blair, then, 'Modernisation' is, therefore, central to the overall goal of economic competitiveness and in this respect welfare plays an important role. Welfare strategies that enhance competitiveness, such as Welfare to Work, are to be welcomed. In his speech to the Trade Union Congress in 1997, Blair claimed that there were two crucial elements in the process of modernisation:

> The first is to create an economy fully attuned to a new global market; one that combines enterprise and flexibility with harnessing the creative potential of all our people. The second is to fashion a modern welfare state, where we maintain high levels of social inclusion based on values of community and social justice, but where the role of government changes so it is not necessary to provide all social provision, and fund all social provision but to organise and regulate it most efficiently and fairly. (1997)

Only through the Third Way for social and welfare policy could Britain build a 'twenty-first century' welfare system. Against critics who have attacked his plans as bringing about the end of the welfare state he claimed that New Labour:

> ... is not dismantling welfare, leaving it simply as a low-grade safety net for the destitute; nor keeping it unreformed and under performing; but reforming it on the basis of a new contract between citizen and state, where we keep a welfare state from which we all benefit, but on terms that are fair and clear. (Blair, 1998: v)

These arguments suggest a radical re-thinking of the role of the state in general, and in relation to welfare provision in particular. The Third Way questions the degree to which services should be provided by the state and emphasises instead the role of non-state agencies, albeit in 'partnership' with the state. Thus the state takes on an enabling function, rather than the mass provider that characterised the social democratic state. As Giddens again claims:

> Investment in human capital wherever possible, rather than direct provision of economic maintenance. In place of the welfare state we should put the social investment state, operating in the context of a positive welfare society. (1998b: 117)

In this regard Blair and other architects of the Third Way project have much in common with both Thatcher and Major. Thus the state is to be harnessed in the drive for global competitiveness. In place of a role as large-scale provider, a myriad of partners and providers will be steered from the centre through regular audits, inspections and appraisal systems conducted by a range of elected agencies, 'task forces' and assorted quangos. For Blair:

Governments ... now need to learn new skills: working in partnership with the private and voluntary sector; sharing responsibility and devolving power ... answering to a much more demanding public ...

In the key public services, the third way is about money for modernisation – new investment of £40 billion over the next three years driving reform and higher standards ... In all areas, monitoring and inspection are playing a key role, as an incentive to higher standards and as a means of determining appropriate levels of intervention. (Blair, 1998: 7, 16)

The further managerialisation of welfare, and local government in particular, with the introduction of competitive practices and the stress on partnerships, undermines the traditional role of local state agencies in service delivery. For New Labour, however, these methods will ensure, in the discourses employed previously by the Conservatives, value for money, efficiency and flexibility and responsiveness among service providers.

While New Labour is committed to reducing the role of the state in particular areas of social and economic life, in significant other ways the power of the state has been extended through, for example, the 1998 Crime and Disorder Act. The Government has extended processes of criminalisation through curfews, the first introduced at Hamilton in Lanarkshire in 1998, parenting orders and the forced removal of the homeless from the streets of some towns and cities. In his speech to the 2000 Labour Party Conference, Blair talked of a 'zero tolerance of the yob culture' using language that would have enthralled the audience at a similar Conservative event (quoted in the *Scotsman*, 9 October). In its many pronouncements about 'social exclusion', the government has not been slow to link this to issues of crime, truancy and various forms of 'anti-social' behaviour. The emphasis on fighting crime and 'disorder' reflects the moral authoritarianism at the heart of New Labour and signifies the greater disciplinary role of the state.

A number of New Labour politicians and ideologues have made public pronouncements that stress their view that the family has a central role to play within society, one that is expected to operate as a moralising and socialising influence on family members and, conversely, one whose breakdown is depicted as being the cause of many – if not most – of society's social problems. Thus it is not uncommon to hear that family 'breakdown', or 'dysfunctional' families, produce educational failure, crime, violence and other forms of anti-social behaviour. Blair has drawn a direct link between family formation and crime:

I have no doubt that the breakdown of law and order is intimately linked to the break up of a strong sense of community. And the break up of community in turn is, to a crucial degree, consequent on the breakdown of family life. If we want anything more than a superficial discussion on crime and its consequences we cannot ignore the importance of the family. (cited in Callinicos, 1996: 16)

Home Secretary Jack Straw has followed suit in arguing that 'parenting classes' should become more commonplace and has overseen the introduction of these classes for parents of 'anti-social' or 'delinquent' children (*Guardian*, 24 July 1998). The message of all this moralising is clear; for New Labour the family, and family policy, have become central elements in their attempts to forge a politics of the Third Way, a politics which mobilises some very conservative notions that reinforce family hierarchies and women's oppression within society (Lavalette and Mooney, 1999).

The idea of a Third Way as employed by New Labour has been widely criticised (see, for example, Jones and Novak, 1999; Rose, 1999; Callinicos, 2001). However, there is little that is new about the idea of a 'Third Way' itself: Labour has always sought to tread a path between the state on the one hand and the market on the other (Lavalette and Mooney, 1999). However, in its current formulation, the Third Way represents an acceptance that the market is the most effective way of organising economic life, albeit with some marginal role for the state as regulator. Through this there is an attempt to marry for profit services with a never to be defined elusive 'public interest'. For Jones and Novak:

> In the third way capitalism is not challenged: rather it is embraced. New Labour's acceptance of the market differs little from that of the new right, echoing its predecessor's claim that 'there is no alternative'. ... The global market is seen as the final and unchallengeable, arbiter in economic – and ultimately in social – life. But the market is not only accepted as setting the agenda and imposing constraints which national governments are powerless to resist. It is also embraced as the main provider. (1999: 181)

This is reflected in Labour's enthusiasm for another Conservative policy – the Private Finance Initiative (PFI), now renamed Public Private Partnerships (PPPs). For Sir Alastair Morton, Co-Chair of Eurotunnel and a member of the Government's Private Finance Panel, PFI is:

> ... the Heineken of privatisation – taking the private sector to the parts of the Government machine not reached by previous privatisations. (quoted in Monbiot, 2000: 86)

Labour had opposed PFI under the Conservatives but by 1997 support for PFI had become a central element of New Labour policy and was nevertheless being adopted by a growing number of financially hard-pressed Labour councils. In early 2000, over £16 billion of PFI projects had been agreed by the Government who have enthusiastically embraced PFI as a means of delivering its promises of improved public services, new hospitals, better transport links and a wide range of schemes across the range of public services, without resorting to increased taxation. The Treasury Financial Statement and Budget Report in July 1997 stated that:

The Government sees productive public/private partnerships as being key to delivering high quality public services that offer the taxpayer value for money ... Effort will be focused where it will achieve results, cutting costs for the public and private sectors alike ... The Government is committed to make PFI work where appropriate. (Treasury Taskforce on Private Finance, 1997)

By the time of the 1997 General Election there were already widespread concerns about PFI following well-publicised cases where it was shown to be a very costly way of providing public services and infrastructure. One of the most notorious examples of this was the Skye road bridge project (see Monbiot, 2000). This was a PFI scheme that permitted the firm involved to charge users, thereby securing a return on investment – and a healthy profit for the financers and operators, The Bank of America. Originally costing at £10.5 million, the final estimated price tag to the public purse of this one bridge (with the highest tolls in Western Europe) is around £128 million. However, it is in relation to the NHS where some of strongest criticisms of PFI have been voiced. For Health Services Trade Unions and organisations such as the British Medical Association, PFI effectively means little more than '*Profits from Illness*' and has meant that the number of beds and staff employed in hospitals built with PFI have frequently been slashed. For Labour this is a major political headache. It has historically portrayed itself as 'the Party of the NHS' and argued in opposition that it would rescue the NHS from the years of Conservative under-funding. It has increasingly looked to PFI to build new hospitals and to finance other health projects. Since the early 1990s most major capital projects in the NHS have been through PFI schemes of one kind or another. The private sector is not only involved in building but in a range of activities ranging from the designing of new hospitals through to running them, which are then leased back to the NHS for periods of up to 60 years. A whole industry of advisers, consultants, banks, brokers and managers have sprung up around PFI in the NHS – at great cost – and at a time when services are deteriorating and where lengthening queues for treatment and scandals about people being denied health care have become increasingly commonplace.

However, it is not only in relation to the NHS can we see Labour's commitment to the market in operation. Labour inherited a housing environment that was markedly different from when it was last in power in 1979. In 1981 council housing accounted for 30 per cent of all housing in Britain, but by 1996 this had declined to 19 per cent. Over the same period owner-occupation increased from 56 per cent to 67 per cent. From its opposition to the Right to Buy legislation brought in by the Tories in the early 1980s, it now appears to accept many of the policies of the Conservatives in relation to council housing (Kemp, 1999: 172). To quote Housing Minister Hilary Armstrong:

Our over-riding aim is to make the housing market work for all the people. If the housing market worked perfectly there would be no need or rationale for government intervention but the free market cannot accommodate the needs and aspirations of all. Government must intervene – but that intervention must be limited and strategic, empowering and enabling, not centralising and controlling. (New Labour) will make no preference between public or private sectors … I have no ideological objection with the transfer of local authority housing. If it works, and it is what tenants want, transfer maybe an appropriate option. What matters is what works. (Armstrong, 1998: 3–4)

The limited role provided here for the state is very much in line with both Conservative policies and the politics of the Third Way. While Armstrong has sought to emphasise that she is in line with New Labour's pragmatism by repeating the 'what matters is what works' mantra, Labour has gone further than the Conservatives in favouring the demunicipalisation of housing stock and its transfer to an assortment of partnerships, cooperatives and housing associations. Once more this transfer has been couched in terms of promoting choice, self-reliance and responsibility. According to the National Campaign to Defend Council Housing, between 1997 and 2000 over 140,000 homes were removed from the public sector housing stock through transfer schemes, more than the Conservatives achieved during their last decade in office (Campaign to Defend Council Housing, 2000). On 24 January, 2000, the *Guardian* ran with the headline 'Prescott plans to abolish council housing' as the Housing Green Paper was published announcing proposals to transfer up to 200,000 more council houses each year until 2010.

New Labour has placed considerable importance on 'modernising' Britain's education sector. It has closely linked education and employment/employability in its eagerness to increase Britain's capacity to compete in the global marketplace. In the enthusiasm to promote the 'knowledge economy', education plays a significant role. The relationship between education and the economy extends to adopting business practices in the provision of education and in the management of schools. Labour's distrust of local education authorities is evidenced by the commitment of Education Minister (for England) David Blunkett to 'making PPPs (in education) attractive to the private sector (Blunkett, 1997), through the Education Action Zones (EAZs) programme. For Blunkett, EAZs represent:

… the beginning of an entirely new way of delivering the education service. It is about partnership based on success rather than outdated dogman on either side. (quoted in Gewirtz, 1999)

For New Labour EAZs would address problems of under-funding (though few additional resources are available) while tackling social exclusion in the localities concerned, through strategies such as those to reduce truancy rates (see Davies, 2000). Parental choice remains as do league tables detailing each school's performance and there may also be some academic selection and marketisation (Gewirtz, 1999: 148). For Sharon Gewirtz, through the EAZs the way is open for a full privatisation of school education. In what Whitfield refers to as the 'commodification and marketisation of education', the opportunities for business are immense (Whitfield, 1999). A good example of this is the Glasgow's Secondary School PPP, one of the largest PFI/PPP schemes in Britain and the largest in the education sector. According to Glasgow City Council this PPP will create:

> ... a stimulating and supportive learning environment in all of the City's secondary schools by August 2002. (Glasgow City Council, 2000)

Through a new education 'consortium', '3Ed Glasgow Ltd.', which includes the Miller Construction Group, Hewlett Packard, Amey and Mitel, the local education authority plans to refurbish all existing secondary schools as well as building 12 new ones. Some 8000 computers will be provided and each of the schools electronically networked. In turn '3Ed' will be paid £40.5 million in 2003 rising each year to £58.4 million in the final year, 2032. The total cost is estimated at £1.2 billion. In addition to concerns about the high price tag that comes with this package, which is estimated to cost over £34 million more than by the public sector route, teaching and other unions have complained that the proposals will lead to a reduction in capacity, the loss of important sports facilities and fewer classrooms and staff rooms. The plan also involves transferring cleaning and janitorial staff to the private sector-led consortium. As with the stock transfer of houses, much valuable publicly-owned land would now become available to private developers.

Labour's commitment to Conservative spending plans for the first three years in office resulted in further cuts in public expenditure, estimated by the *Guardian* to be at its lowest for 40 years at 39.4 per cent of GDP (see also Callinicos, 2000: 104), leading the paper to comment that: 'Thatcher was more lavish than Labour' (*Guardian*, 25 August 1999).

Where there is opportunity, then, it would appear that Labour is committed to providing the private sector with all the necessary support to participate in delivering public services. In July 1999 speaking to the British Venture Capital Association, Blair stated that:

> One of the things I would like to do, as well as stimulating more entrepreneurship in the private sector, is to get a bit of it into the public sector as well. (*Guardian*, July 7 1999)

In the same speech he also attacked Britain's public sector workers for being deeply resistant to change. Identified by Blair as one of the key 'forces of conservatism' in the country, leading Labour politicians have not been slow in criticising public sector workers for failing to embrace 'reform', notably teachers and others who are 'not forward looking'. For 'Old Labour' the key objective was to control the market and free the people. Under New Labour it is a story of controlling and regulating the working class – and freeing the market.

As we argued above, at the heart of the New Labour philosophy is to be found a pervasive culture of moral disapproval. Labour's moral authoritarianism permeates almost every aspect of the Government's political strategy, whether it is attacking – in the language of Home Secretary Jack Shaw – 'squeegee merchants', asylum seekers, or social security 'fraudsters' (Blunkett, 2001). As Secretary of State for Social Security Alastair Darling commented during yet another attack on those in receipt of welfare:

> We're toughening up the penalties for those who persistently steal from the taxpayer. So from now on, if people commit fraud more than once, there will be no second chances. Two strikes and they're out. (*Herald*, 28 November, 2000)

Blair and other leading Labour politicians increasingly compete with the Conservatives over the use of the 'tough' and hostile language so long the preserve of the right. They share with them a *Daily Mail* view of the world that sees the population of Britain as conservative, reactionary, xenophobic and racist: that tells them not to give to beggars, that asylum seekers are criminally motivated 'welfare refugees', that the poor largely contribute to their own 'misfortune' and that teachers are at the heart of the 'crisis of education'. Yet successive opinion polls and attitude surveys show that while there certainly is substantial reaction, racism and prejudice, there is also significant anti-racism, widespread support for state welfare and against the gulf between rich and poor (National Centre for Social Research, 2000), for the re-nationalisation of key sectors of the economy such as the railways, and for massive investment in the NHS and education sectors.

In defence of state welfare

> [Labour's] new programme accepts the basic parameters of the Thatcher settlement, in much the same way that the Conservative government of the fifties accepted the parameters of the Atlee settlement. It does not seek to extend the public sector or reverse privatisation to any significant degree. It does not propose to raise the overall level of taxation, but promises to adjust its incidence in a mildly more egalitarian direction. It does not substantially depart from the

laws that now regulate industrial action, while rendering them a little more favourable to trade unions. It does not abandon the British nuclear deterrent. All these changes of the Thatcher years are uncontested. (Perry Anderson, quoted in Hay, 1999: 42)

Writing in 1992, Perry Anderson could be forgiven for underestimating just how far New Labour would not only accept Conservative policies but would seek to extend them in new directions. In office, the language of 'reform' and 'modernisation' has meant the privatisation of large swathes of the public sector through PPP (Public Private Partnerships), leading to declining services and poorer conditions of employment for public sector workers who remain among some of the poorest paid groups in the country.

The world of New Labour is a world of declining services and public squalor, deepening health inequalities and a growing income gap between the richest and poorest sections of society, a world far removed not only from the gains of the post-War settlement, but also from New Labour's rhetoric of social inclusion, social justice and equality of opportunity. In key respects, Britain under New Labour is no less a land of extremes than it was under the Conservatives.

That said, it would be wrong to ignore the important elements of continuity between the policies of the Blair administrations and those of previous Labour governments. From Ramsay MacDonald's commitment to orthodox economic policies and benefit 'restraint' in the early 1930s through to Callaghan's devastating attacks on state welfare in the 1970s, *every* Labour government has engaged in the pursuit of a 'third way' in which the market and the needs of capital have always eventually been given priority. While New Labour has gone further than previous Labour governments in abandoning some of the key principles of the post-War welfare state, arguably Labour had began to desert the 1945 settlement in the mid-1960s. In this respect there is a clear link between New Labour and some of its predecessors. As John Rees has pointed out, Blair:

> ... has yet to split his party, as did a previous generation of Labour leaders ... when they formed the Social Democrats. Nor has he split his party and joined a Tory government, as Ramsay MacDonald did in the 1930s. It all seems premature, therefore, to conclude that Blair is more right wing than all his political ancestors. Neither are the policies of the Labour government more right wing than those of Jim Callaghan's government in the 1970s. That Labour government still holds the distinction of being the only government in post-war British history which, through the Social Contract, forced down the real wages of employed workers. Its policy on immigration, including the introduction of virginity tests, was a match for New Labour's. (Rees, 2001: 13)

New Labour *does*, however, represent a shift from the policies of previous Labour governments in terms of the extent to which it has explicitly embraced the market. In this context it is necessary and legitimate to defend the 'Old Labour' agenda of state intervention and state-provided services as a means of protecting the working class from the untrammelled operation of market forces. With all their limitations, state services, properly funded via progressive taxation policies, can begin to meet the basic human needs of the vast majority within society. Universal state welfare provides services to all as a right – regardless of class, gender, 'race', disability, sexual orientation and so on. It stresses a politics of commonality – as opposed to a politics of exclusion, privilege or particularism – that entails:

> ... [a] fight for the attainment of the immediate aims, for the enforcement of the momentary interests of the working class. (Marx and Engels, 1848/1973: 97)

A *National Health Service*, providing a range of health services free at the point of delivery – including prescriptions and dental, eye and hearing tests – offers the minimum requirement to protect and enhance the quality of life of all within society. Access to these services should not be based on ability to pay (why should someone get access to life-enhancing treatment, drugs – or even eye tests – simply because they are rich?), nor should they be reduced to the provision of profitable commodities – making vast profits for the already wealthy like the major shareholders of British multinational pharmaceutical company GlaxoSmith-Kline. *Housing* is one of the most basic human needs. Cheap, well-built, state-funded council rented-housing could provide homes for vast numbers of people living in poor or inadequate housing. *Education* should be a right for all – properly funded, with small classes, properly stocked libraries and appropriate IT provision. Furthermore, education should be a life-long service, with state provided grants and maintenance fees to allow people to expand their knowledge in a high quality, state provided service. *Universal benefits*, free from stigma, paid at income replacement levels allow those in poverty to gain access to society. Adequate *state pensions* – linked to earnings – would allow those who have worked all their lives to retire without the threat of poverty and destitution. *Nurseries* provide an excellent environment for young pre-school children; they free parents from some of the burdens of child care, while allowing parents to return to employment. While *social services* departments that are properly staffed and have access to resources for clients can start to address the problems of those at the very bottom of the social pile.

This list is not exclusive but it stresses the key point. Market-provided services make profit for profit-seeking companies and reduce access to those with the ability to pay. Universal state services provide services for all – paid for by progressive income tax – so that the rich give a small proportion of their surplus wealth (obtained as a direct result of their privileged position within the class structure) for social and welfare services for their fellow citizens. There is no doubt that the world could afford such levels of welfare spending – the vast riches of the fabulously wealthy we discussed in Chapter 1 provide one source of funding, as does the vast amounts spent on arms and munitions each year (according to the United Nations Development Programme this amounted to $780 billion in 1999 alone, Health Matters, 2000). Of course state welfare still remains embedded within capitalist social relations and however generous it may be it does not undermine those basic relationships. It is clear that state welfare continues to repress and regulate people – and as we have argued, Marxism is at the forefront of the critique of such oppressions. In defending *properly resourced* state welfare, council housing, comprehensive education and the NHS, in promoting universal benefits and state support for refugees *today* and in opposing marketisation, PFI/PPP, and cuts in public sector provision – we do not blind ourselves to the oppressive and exploitative nature of much of this form of provision, reflecting as it does the dominant social relations of capitalism. But it does offer a basic material benefit – as Brecht would have it 'a bed for the night' – which is vital to those reliant on such welfare services.

10 '... Waiting for something else': Welfare Futures

The widespread acceptance on much of the Left that the market has triumphed, that there is no alternative to neo-liberalism, has meant that until very recently there has been very little consideration of welfare futures, of what form 'the good society' might take. In part, this is because, for some commentators like Fukuyama (1992), we already live in the best of all possible worlds – the good society has arrived in the shape of neo-liberalism and Western-style democracy. For others, discussion of welfare futures is regarded as frankly naïve, since the two projects which have dominated thinking about welfare and social change for most of the twentieth century – social democracy in the West, 'actually existing socialism' (in reality, as we have argued, state capitalism) in much of the rest of the world – lay in tatters at the end of that century.

As we noted in Chapter 1, one effect of the collapse of these projects, in the short-term at least, was to reinforce the growing 'postmodern turn' in social thought, which represented notions of progress of any sort as at best illusory, at worst dangerous.

> The idea of progress as possible, probable or necessary was rooted in the certainty that the development of the arts, technology, knowledge and liberty would be profitable to mankind as a whole. After two centuries, we are more sensitive to signs that signify the contrary. Neither economic nor political liberalism, nor the various Marxisms, emerge from the sanguinary last two centuries free from the suspicion of crimes against mankind ... What kind of thought is able to sublate (*Aufheben*) Auschwitz in a general (either empirical or speculative) process towards a universal emancipation? (Lyotard, cited in Callinicos, 1989: 10)

Such a despairing perspective clearly provides few grounds for developing alternatives to neo-liberalism. At best, it might permit small-scale, localised change, 'piecemeal social engineering' of the type envisaged by the Cold War intellectual Karl Popper. More often, however, it has encouraged a stance of 'ironic detachment', an apathy or nihilism in the face of oppression and exploitation which provides no basis for an emancipatory welfare.

But in Chapter 1 we also noted that, in recent years, there have been a number of factors – including the evidence of growing social and economic inequality, the growth of resistance to the ravages of global capitalism, and an increasing awareness of the extreme relativism and fragmentation of postmodern perspectives – which have given rise to tentative attempts to begin once again to 'imagine welfare futures' (Hughes, 1998b). The most common starting point for such attempts is the evident failure of market-based policies to meet the most basic needs of millions of people. Jones and Novak capture this shifting mood well when, in concluding their biting critique of social policy towards the poor under both the Tories and New Labour, they express the hope that:

> If it leads to one thing we hope it leads to a greater rage against a system that debases people for private profit. Too many seem to have lost their sense of anger at what is happening in our midst. Yet without anger the possibilities of fundamental social and political change will always be elusive. (1999: 202)

A similar point is made by Leonard when he argues that a reinvigorated emancipatory project needs to be based both on a politics of hope and on a feeling of *anger*:

> ... of rage at the degrading conditions of existence – material, social, cultural – which are experienced by millions of people in the Third World and in 'advanced' capitalist countries ... Not intellectual *detachment* but anger is the human attribute which has the most possibility of generating the kind of individual and collective resistance which is a necessary precondition of emancipation. (1997: 162)

While the postmodernism which Leonard celebrates has been an important factor in encouraging this intellectual detachment, such calls to arms are nevertheless welcome and refreshing. They contain echoes of Sartre's argument for the *intellectuel éngagé* who uses his or her intellectual and moral authority to engage with, and intervene of behalf of, the exploited and oppressed. Such a model is best exemplified in our own time by figures such as the American linguist Noam Chomsky, the writer and environmental activist Susan George and the leading French sociologist Pierre Bordieu. Bordieu in particular has played an active role in most of the key struggles in France over the past decade, making speeches to rallies of striking railway workers in 1995, throwing himself into the struggles of the unemployed and establishing himself as a key theorist in the developing anti-capitalist movement (Bordieu, 1998).

While, however, anger is an essential prerequisite of any attempt to generate resistance to the policies of neoliberalism, by itself it is not enough. Theoretical clarity is also important if the hope to which Leonard refers is not to turn to despair and if that anger is not to be dissipated in the face of setbacks and defeats at the hands of a global ruling class whose only imperative is the accumulation of profit.

To that end, in this final chapter, we shall focus on two areas of current debate where it seems to us that the need for theoretical clarity is greatest in terms of the discussion of welfare futures: firstly, in connection with the ongoing debate within social policy between universalism and particularism, and the need to develop what one writer has called 'a politics of commonality' (Gitlin, cited in Johnson, 2000); secondly, the question of *agency* – how is the kind of welfare settlement to which Jones and Novak, Leonard and others refer to be achieved?

Identity, difference and common human needs

> If a new, emancipatory project of welfare is to be developed it must be based upon a moral critique of modernity *from within*. This internal criticism directs its attention to the side of the Enlightenment implicated in domination and contrasts this with the emancipatory potential remaining in those critical discourses of modernity expressed in the revolutionary ideals of liberty, justice and equality. (Leonard, 1997: 162)

For much of the past 20 years notions of identity and difference have dominated social theory. We have already explored the roots of this dominance in Chapter 6 where we argued that it stemmed, at least in part, from the view that the 'grand narratives' of the Enlightenment, including Marxism, were committed to a view of universal emancipation which in practice involved the subordination and silencing of minorities. The emancipatory claim of poststructuralism on the one hand and identity politics on the other was to give a voice to those hitherto silenced minorities by deconstructing dominant ideologies and exposing their phoney universalism.

It is increasingly evident, however, that a politics based primarily on identity and difference, be it cultural identity or ethnicity, is far from being the cuddly alternative to class politics that its adherents have often implied.

Firstly, such a politics can lead to a neglect of issues of material inequality within groups which supposedly share a common identity. As Williams notes, for example, in a paper concerned with outlining the principles of recognition and respect which need to underpin any new welfare settlement:

> If groups simply pursue the politics of recognition without addressing socio-economic inequalities, then they will win social justice for some in their group, but not for others. On the other hand, the singular pursuit of issues of economic inequality can make invisible cultural injustices which render some groups more vulnerable to economic exploitation. (Williams, 2000: 350)

The growing acknowledgement of the inadequacies of identity politics stems in large part from the failure of such a politics to challenge the poverty and inequality experienced by the members of many oppressed groups over the past twenty years (Smith, 1994). Consequently, both Fraser (1995, 2000) and Williams (2000) have argued the need to combine what they call a 'politics of recognition' with an emphasis on issues of material redistribution.

A second criticism of identity politics is that it can contribute to a process of fragmentation within and between oppressed groups, developing antagonisms that may in turn become the basis for new oppressions. In terms of welfare this can lead to what one observer of the American political scene has described as 'the Balkanization of urban America' where women are pitted against other 'minority' or 'minority ethnic' groups in the areas of jobs, housing, educational opportunities and health benefits (Benhabib, cited in Johnson, 2000). As Alan Johnson has forcefully argued in a discussion of welfare struggles in Britain, such antagonisms are not an accidental by-product of identity politics but rather flow directly from its basic premises:

> ... particularistic social policy is inescapably divisive not because it accepts the reality of diverse needs but because in essentializing each group or identity and positioning each in a unilateral relationship to the state as a client it detaches social policy from any ethic of solidarity and therefore from any possibility of systemic social change and so risks replicating rather than rupturing the ugly and unequal textures of capitalist society. (2000: 112)

On a global scale, Johnson's point is borne out by the extreme breakdown of human solidarity which became a feature of the 1990s and which vividly highlighted the dark side of identity politics. As Fraser comments:

> In the seventies and eighties, struggles for the 'recognition of difference' seemed charged with emancipatory promise. Many who rallied to the banners of sexuality, gender, ethnicity and 'race' aspired not only to assert hitherto denied identities but to bring a richer, lateral distribution to battles over the redistribution of wealth and power as well. With the turn of the century, issues of recognition have become even more central, yet many now bear a different charge: from Rwanda to the Balkans, questions of 'identity' have fuelled campaigns for ethnic cleansing and even genocide – as well as movements that have mobilized to resist them. (2000: 107)

Not surprisingly, then, an increasingly common feature of recent critical welfare writing is the plea for a return to a notion of common human needs as a basis for a critical welfare policy. Leonard, for example, describes the idea of common needs as 'an invaluable moral premise on which to build solidarity amongst diversity' (1997: 166). In his study of the Poplar Councillors' revolt in the 1920s referred to above, Johnson suggests that a fight for universalistic social reforms which remains sensitive to the diverse needs of the poor, such as that led by George Lansbury and his comrades in Poplar,

> ... has the potential to be the social ground upon which unity can be constructed and difference mediated, particularism embraced but located within a wider coalition of interest. (2000: 112)

The point is an important one and one that we would fully endorse. Moreover, as we have argued in Chapter 5, given that the overwhelming majority of the world's population can live only by selling their skills and talents – in other words, their labour-power – shared class interests and common human needs will often coincide. In the past both social democratic governments and Stalinist regimes have often used the cloak of 'class interests' as a cover for the denial of the needs of minorities. Within the revolutionary socialist tradition, by contrast, class unity is seen as only achievable when all sections of the working class respect and fight for the rights of minorities. Furthermore, as Rosa Luxemburg argued early in the twentieth century, there is no Chinese Wall between industrial or welfare struggles on the one hand and political struggles or struggles against oppression on the other (Luxemburg, 1906/1986). They flow into and reinforce each other. The dynamic of this process is well-illustrated by the journalist Mike Marqusee in his study of Muhammad Ali and the struggles of the 1960s:

> Ali's evolution in the sixties paralleled a broader evolution in black (and white) opinion. His assertion of his personal prerogatives led him to embrace a universal cause. Like Malcolm, he emerged from the cocoon of nationalism to spread his wings as an internationalist. But he did so under the pressure of circumstances – the war, the draft, the heavyweight championship, the pull of alternative constituencies. It was Ali's capacity to embody so many of the underlying trends of the time – especially the interaction between personal self-definition and global politics – that made him a representative figure, a hero to the insurgents and a criminal in the eyes of the state. (1999: 192)

The key point here is that in the maelstrom of the 1960s when capitalism was being challenged on every front – by students, workers, women, gays, blacks – in a manner not seen since the great revolutionary wave that followed the First World War, the struggles of each group became the common property of all, lent inspiration and sustenance to every other struggle. It was only when that struggle subsided in the mid to late 1970s that each group began to see each other, rather than the capitalist system itself, as 'the enemy', leading to the fragmentation and antagonism discussed above.

It is against the background of this fragmentation that the emergence of the new anti-capitalist movement in Seattle in 1999 is potentially so significant. That movement is characterised by its enormous diversity on the one hand and on the other its universalism, reflected in its opposition to a common enemy, usually characterised as 'corporate capitalism'. According to one Seattle participant, Doug Henwood:

> Togetherness was the theme of the labour rally – not only solidarity among workers of the world, but of organised labour with everyone else. There were incredible sights of Teamster president James Hoffa sharing a stage with student anti-sweatshop activists, of Earth Firsters marching with Sierra Clubbers, and a

chain of bare-breasted BGH-free Lesbian Avengers weaving through a crowd of machinists. (cited in Charlton, 2000b: 8)

Subsequent large demonstrations in Washington, Millau in France, Prague, Nice, and Genoa – Europe's Seattle – have shared much of that diversity and that same identification of a common enemy – neo-liberal-ism – reflected in slogans such as 'Capitalism is costing the earth' and 'The world is not for sale'.

It seems clear that the globalisation which we discussed in Chapter 8 is producing a global resistance, which is redefining our notions of common human needs in two important ways: first, the definition of 'common human needs' is being extended to include environmental needs; second, the movement is striving to achieve a balance between universality and diversity in new and imaginative ways. The nature of this latter process is neatly summarised in a recent newspaper article exploring the politics of one of the movement spokespersons, Naomi Klein:

> In the 60s and 70s, activists concentrated their anti-racism and feminism on maters of equality – equal rights and equal pay. In Klein's 80s and 90s, they cam-paigned instead on issues of culture and identity: portrayal in the media, who gets to the board. But the new generation of activists is taking the best bits of both; developing a radical critique of the global economy, while incorporating identity politics as a matter of course ... This is a far more inclusive movement than those that have gone before. (Viner, 2000: 21)

As has so often been the case in the past, once again it is popular strug-gles and protests rather than the musings of academics or policy-makers which are giving rise to new demands, new forms of thinking and organi-sing, new notions of welfare. That said, both the protestors on the streets and those seeking to sketch out visions of a new welfare future share a common dilemma: how do we get from where we are just now to where we want to be, or, as it is more commonly referred to in academic dis-course, the question of *agency*.

Transforming society – the question of agency

As Draper has argued in a classic pamphlet, within the socialist tradition the question of agency has historically been addressed in two very different ways:

> There have always been different 'kinds of socialism' and they have customarily been divided into reformist or revolutionary, peaceful or violent, democratic or authoritarian, etc. These divisions exist but the underlying division is something else. Throughout the history of socialist movements and ideas, the fundamental divide is between *socialism-from-above* and *socialism-from-below*. (1966/96: 4).

The divide is not, of course, an equal one. For most of the last one hundred years, the dominant tradition amongst those seeking to change society has been to look to the election of reformist governments of various hues to bring about change *from above*. Even where the potential of popular movements is acknowledged and celebrated, the vehicle for translating their demands into policy is usually seen as being a labour or social-democratic government of some sort. Thus, for example, writing shortly before the British General Election in 1997, Rogers and Pilgrim, two of the leading commentators on the mental health users' movement in Britain, argued that:

> If user campaigning has had an influence on Labour policy, it raises some inte-resting conceptual questions about making a neat separation between old and new social movements …. With the collapse of Leninism in much of the East and the political diversification of the aims of Western social democratic parties beyond the demands of labour it may be that old and new social movements are being brought together rather than being separated. What is currently missing in regard to the influence of the mental health service users' movement is the opportunity of a Labour government to be tested in its commitment to a new pluralistic health and welfare agenda. (1996: 171)

Leaving aside their mistaken equation of Stalinism with Leninism, this willingness to give New Labour a chance, widely shared and perhaps understandable after almost 20 years of Conservative governments, now seems over-generous. As we have attempted to demonstrate in the pre-vious chapter, on issue after issue – lone parents, disability benefits, pensions – the current New Labour government has demonstrated that its commitment to fiscal prudence and economic 'rigour' far outweighs the desire to combat poverty and inequality.

That said, the roots of this tendency to seek change from above are not hard to find. Faced with the seemingly overwhelming power of dominant ideologies and of the state on the one hand and the limited resources of oppressed groups on the other, it is hardly surprising that the leaderships of social movements often adapt and settle for much less than their origi-nal demands, leaving large sections of their adherents feeling betrayed and demoralised. This pattern of oppressed groups and social movements looking to Labour governments to bring about change and then experi-encing disillusionment is a depressingly familiar one (for a specific and related example with regard to 'imposed' anti-racism within social work, see Penketh, 2001). Unless, however, alternative bases of agency are identified, means through which the demands of oppressed and exploited groups can be achieved, then there is a danger that even the very best critiques of reformism generally and New Labour specifically may inad-vertently contribute to a sense of pessimism and despair.

It is here that the classical Marxist view of the working class as not simply a suffering class but as the gravedigger of corporate capitalism, the *subject* rather than simply the *object* of history, is central. For if real social change from below is to become a reality, then it requires that there is a force that is capable of challenging both the economic and the political power of capital.

To assert the central role of the working class in bringing about radical social change is not to minimise the significance of the struggles of oppressed groups, nor does it require us to ignore the fact that sections of workers are often influenced by racist, sexist or homophobic ideas. Rather it is based on the recognition that in a society whose driving force is profit, the most effective countervailing force to the power of capital is the power of those whose labour produces that profit – that where, as Luxemburg argued almost a century ago, the chains of capital are forged, there must they be broken. It is, moreover, in the course of these struggles that many of the divisions can be overcome. We have attempted elsewhere to high-light some of the key moments in this 'hidden history' of working-class struggles for welfare (Lavalette and Mooney, 2000a). Here we shall men-tion only two.

In 1987 the newly-elected Conservative administration launched its flagship – the 'community charge' or, as it soon became known, the poll tax. As we have argued elsewhere (Lavalette and Mooney, 1989; Lavalette and Mooney, 2000b), this was a blatantly class-based piece of legislation aimed at shifting a bigger burden of taxation onto the poor which, through the mechanism of 'capping', also forced local (mainly Labour) councils to reduce their spending on services to remain within government-decreed spending limits.

The tax was introduced following the Tories' defeat of the miners two years previously and at a time when the conventional wisdom on most of the left (articulated mainly through the Communist Party journal *Marxism Today*) was that structural changes in British society on the one hand (the 'end of the working class' thesis) and profound ideological shifts on the other (reflected in, and providing a base for, the alleged hegemony of 'Thatcherism' or 'authoritarian populism') meant that Thatcher could only be removed and a Labour government re-elected – if at all – through alliances with non-working-class parties (principally the Liberal Democrats) and a shift in Labour's policies to appeal to 'Middle England'. Space does not permit a discussion of the assump-tions underpinning this profoundly pessimistic – and profoundly false – analysis which nevertheless provided the main ideological fuel for the rightward shift of the Labour Party in the 1980s and early 1990s, culmi-nating in the emergence of the New Labour project (for critique, see Callinicos, 1985; Sivanandan, 1990). Suffice it to say that less than three years after the launch of the poll tax, the supposedly invincible Margaret Thatcher had been removed as Tory party leader and the poll tax consigned to the dustbin of history, a consequence not of the timid and ineffectual 'Stop It' campaign organised by the Labour Party but of a massive popular campaign of non-payment, involving up to 17 million people in non-payment and culminating in two huge demonstrations – 50,000 people in Glasgow, 200,000 in London – with the London demonstration ending in pitched battles between police and demonstrators in Trafalgar Square.

While the lack of confidence engendered by the defeat of the miners' strike in 1985 meant that the level of industrial action in support of the poll tax struggle was less than it was during some earlier welfare struggles, such as the Glasgow Rent Strike of 1915 which we discussed in a previous chapter, in terms of composition and support it was nevertheless a solidly working-class struggle and an important example of the way in which struggles from below can successfully challenge ruling-class attacks to reduce welfare provision and shift an even greater burden of taxation onto the shoulders of the poor.

Our second example of a successful class struggle which profoundly shaped both the nature and extent of welfare provision – and much more besides – is more recent. In France in 1995, Jacques Chirac, the newly-elected right-wing President, appointed as his Prime Minster Alain Juppé to head a Conservative government elected the previous year with an overwhelming majority in the National Assembly. The prospects for the French working class, the left in general and the strategy of socialism from above had seldom seemed more dismal. Not only had the Socialist Party won only a miserable 14 per cent of the vote in the 1994 election – a damning verdict on the performance of the Socialist Party in government – but the rise of the far-right National Front under Jean-Marie Le Pen seemed unassailable. Within months of Chirac's election, however, France was in the grip of the biggest General Strike since May 1968.The trigger was the launch of the Juppé Plan, the aim of which was to bring about swinging cuts in the social security budget. Initially, resistance to the plan came from public sector workers concerned both about their jobs and the effects on the living standards of those dependent on benefits. Soon, however, it turned into something much bigger. As Woolfries notes in his account of this struggle:

> What began as a public sector strike against the Juppé government's plans to reform the social security system sparked a sea-change in French politics, creating a new mood characterised by a backlash against free market economics, a belief that strikes work and widespread rejection of the scapegoating of immigrants and the stigmatising of the unemployed. (1999: 36)

The public sector workers' strike connected with a mood of bitterness and alienation within the French working class as a whole, the result of a decade and a half of austerity policies, and in the years after 1995 unleashed a tidal wave of struggles too numerous to mention but including: a high-profile campaign by immigrants seeking residence papers (*sans-papiers*), which culminated in the occupation of a Paris church in the summer of 1996; a militant strike by lorry drivers in autumn the same year; the occupation of a major bank by 2,000 employees protesting its closure in January 1997; a massive demonstration against plans to strengthen anti-immigrant legislation the following months and a 50,000-strong march on the National Front's annual congress in Strasbourg; a second lorry drivers' strike later that year; and many more struggles, including dozens of occupations and protests by organisations representing the unemployed. Even the defeat of Juppé's government and the election of a left coalition government under Lionel Jospin on a neo-Keynesian platform in June 1997 did little to curb the wave of struggle with teachers, medical staff, pilots and the unemployed continuing to protest against the new government. Joining the struggle in late 1998 were school students protesting at the lack of teachers and resources and the state of school buildings, with over a million of them demonstrating in over 350 towns in a single week (Woolfries, 1999: 32).

The effect of this 'social movement' has been profound. On the one hand, it has fractured and demoralised the fascists of the far right, as well as the Gaullist RPR; on the other, it has revived the left and the working class movement on a scale not seen for decades. Above all, however, it has led to a massive shift in the confidence and political consciousness of millions of people and has led to a questioning both of capitalism as a system and to a breaking down of the individualism and sectionalism (or 'particularism') which capitalism creates (with the main slogan of the strikes, for example, being '*Tous ensemble*'). For one Paris Metro worker cited by Woolfries:

> Strikes completely change a man. People live in their own little corner. They come first, never mind their neighbour ... During the strikes individualism was completely broken up. Completely! The chains were broken. Spontaneously. Because we were discussing things all the time, we learned to get to know each other. We were at the firm 24 hours a day. In our job we're very isolated and we only see each other during the ten minute breaks. Here we learned to live together. (1999: 36)

One nurse, who has previously been involved in political activity, felt that:

> If I felt concerned again it's because it was about essential demands, political ... It was the rejection of a capitalist society, the rejection of money. People were mobilised more against that than against the Juppé social security plan ... At the end of the demos, people stayed where they were, as if they were waiting for something else. (Woolfries, 1999: 36–7).

Conclusion: Basta! Enough!

What all of these struggles discussed above – the campaign against the poll tax in Britain in the late 1980s, the class struggles in France of the mid to late

1990s, and the 1915 Glasgow rent strike discussed in Chapter 9 – have in common is that they illustrate the validity and the relevance of the central assertion of classical Marxism – that it is in collectively struggling to change and improve the world they live in that people change themselves: that, in the words of the young Marx, 'the coincidence of the changing of circumstances and of human activity or self-changing can be conceived and rationally understood only as *revolutionary practice*' (1845/1975: 422) . For it is in the course of such struggles that people begin to see through and reject what Marx elsewhere called 'all the old shit' – the sexist, racist and homophobic ideas which perpetuate the existing system of exploitation and prevent men and women joining together in defence of their common interests. In our view, in a world increasingly dominated and laid waste by global capitalism, it is that common struggle which continues to offer the best hope for the creation of a society – a 'welfare future' – based on the recognition of both universal *and* particular needs. Nor is this is a utopian perspective, in the pejorative sense in which that term has often been used by those who believe that a stance of cynical or ironic detachment is the only viable intellectual position at this point in history. As we have noted earlier in this chapter, the final years of the twentieth century and the opening years of the twenty-first have seen a return to commitment on a mass scale, a re-awakening of the realisation that human action *can* challenge and change the structures and policies which condemn millions to lives of drudgery. The mobilisation to stop the World Trade Conference at Seattle in November 1999 was, of course, the key moment in this re-awakening. We end this book, however, not with Seattle but with the words of those involved in another struggle of the late 1990s, a welfare struggle in every sense, which similarly caught the imagination of the world and showed that, even in the most adverse circumstances, resistance is possible. We refer to the Zapatista-led uprising in the Chiapas region of Mexico in 1994, sparked by the attempts of the governments of North America and Mexico to extend neo-liberal trade policies to the poorest areas of rural Mexico. Recognising that such policies could only increase the poverty and degradation of those inhabiting what was already one of the most impoverished parts of the globe, the insurgents responded with a statement which, like the Zapatista struggle itself, could easily stand as a summary of the sentiments and aspirations of so many around the world who are both suffering under, and struggling against, global capitalism:

We have been denied the most elemental instruction, in order thus to use us as cannon fodder and loot the wealth of our country without any care for the fact that we are dying of hunger and curable diseases; without any care for the fact that we have nothing, absolutely nothing; no roof worthy of the name, nor land, nor work, not health, nor food, nor education; without the right to elect our authorities freely and democratically; without independence from foreigners, without peace or justice for ourselves or our children.

Today we say Basta! Enough! (cited in Gonzalez, 2000: 63)

Bibliography

Abberley, P. (1996). 'Work, Utopia and Impairment', in L. Barton (ed.), *Disability and Society: Emerging Issues and Insights*. London: Longman.

Abel-Smith, B. and Townsend, P. (1965). *The Poor and the Poorest*. Occasional Paper on Social Administration. London: Bell.

Acheson, D. (1998). *Independent Inquiry into Inequalities in Health*. London: The Stationery Office.

Adonis, A. and Pollard, S. (1998). *A Class Act*. Harmondsworth: Penguin.

American Prospect Online, The (1995). http://www.prospect.org/

Anderson, P. (1976). *Considerations on Western Marxism*. London: New Left Books.

Anderson, P. (2000). 'Renewals', *New Left Review*, (ns) **1**.

Armstrong, H. (1998). *Speech to the Annual Conference of the Chartered Institute of Housing*. Harrogate: June.

Aronowitz, S. (1992). *The Politics of Identity: Class, Culture, Social Movements*. London: Routledge.

Arruda, M. (1994). 'Brazil: Drowning in Debt', in K. Danaher and M. Yunus (eds), *50 Years is Enough: The Case Against the World Bank and the International Monetary Fund*. Boston, MA: South End Press.

Atkinson, A.B., Rainwater, L. and Smeeding, T.M. (1995). *Income Distribution in OECD Countries*. Paris: OECD Social Policy Studies, no. 18.

Bailey, R and Brake, M. (1975). *Radical Social Work*. London: Edward Arnold.

Balloch, S., Andrew, T., Ginn, J., McLean, J., Pahl, J. and Williams, J. (1995). *Working in the Social Services*. London: NISW.

Balloch, S., McLean, J. and Fisher, M. (eds) (1999). *Social Services: Working Under Pressure*. Bristol: Policy Press/National Institute for Social Work.

Barber, B. (1996). *McWorld*. New York: Ballantine.

Barrett, M. (2000). 'Post-feminism' in G. Browning, A. Halcli and F. Webster (eds) *Understanding Contemporary Society*, London: Sage.

Barrett, M. and McIntosh, M. (1985). *The Anti-Social Family*. London: Verso.

Barrett, M. and Phillips, A. (eds) (1992). *Destablilizing Theory: Contemporary Feminist Debates*. Cambridge: Polity Press.

Becker, S. (1997). *Responding to Poverty*. London: Longman.

Bell, D. (1973). *The Coming of the Post-Industrial Society*. New York: Basic Books.

Bello, W. (2001). '2001: the Year of Global Protest', *International Socialism*, 90.

Bensaid, D. (1996). 'Neo-Liberal Reform and Popular Rebellion', *New Left Review*, (05) 215.

Berman, M. (1982). *All That is Solid Melts into Air*. London: Verso.

Berman, M. (1999). *Adventures in Marxism*. London: Verso.

Beveridge, W. (1942). *Social Insurance and Allied Services* (The Beveridge Report). Cmnd. 6404. London: HMSO.

Birchall, I. (1986). *Bailing Out the System*. London: Bookmarks.

Blair, T. (1996). *New Britain: My Vision of a Young Country*. London: Fourth Estate.

Blair, T. (1997). *The Modernisation of Britain*. Speech to the 1997 Trade Union Congress.

Blair, T. (1998). *The Third Way*. London: The Fabian Society.

Blair, T. (1999). Speech to Institute of Public Policy Research, London: January 14, 1999.

Blunkett, D. (1997). *PPPs Key to Tackling Crumbling Schools*. London: Department for Education and Employment: Press Release 152.97, 23 June.

Blunkett, D. (2001). 'No Hiding Place for Fraudsters', *Observer*, 14 January.

Borger, J. (2000). 'The Texan Way of Death' *The Guardian* 13 December.

Bourdieu, P. (1998). *Acts of Resistance*. Cambridge: Polity Press.

Bowles, S. and Gintis, H. (1976). *Schooling in Capitalist America*. London: Routledge.

Bradbury, R. (1988). 'What is Post-Structuralism?', *International Socialism*, **41**.

Bradley, H. (2000). 'Social Inequalities: Coming to Terms with Complexity', in G. Browning, A. Halcli and F. Webster (eds) *Understanding Contemporary Society*. London: Sage.

Braverman, H. (1974). *Labour and Monopoly Capital*. New York: Monthly Review Press.

Brecher, J. (1997). *Strike!* (revised edition) Boston, MA: South End Press.

Brenner, J. and Ramas, M. (1986). 'Rethinking Women's Oppression', *New Left Review*, **144**.

Brown, P. and Scase, R. (eds) (1991). *Poor Work*. Buckingham: Open University Press.

Brownmiller, S. (1976). *Against Our Will*. Harmondsworth: Penguin.

Bryson, L. (1992). *Welfare and the State*. London: MacMillan.

Budhoo, D. (1994). 'IMF/World Bank Wreak Havoc on Third World', in K. Danaher and M. Yunus (eds), *50 Years is Enough: The Case Against the World Bank and the International Monetary Fund*. Boston, MA.: South End Press.

Bukharin, N. (1973). *Imperialism and the World Economy*. New York: Monthly Review Press.

Burchardt, T. and Hills, J. (1999). 'Public Expenditure and the Public/Private Mix', in M. Powell (ed.), *New Labour, New Welfare State?* Bristol: The Policy Press.

Burr, V. (1995). *An Introduction to Social Constructionism*. London: Routledge.

Burr, V. (1998). 'Realism, relativism, social constructionism and discourse', in I. Parker (ed.) *Social Constructionism, Discourse and Realism*, London: Sage.

Burrows, R. and Loader, B. (eds) (1994). *Towards a Post-Fordist Welfare State*. London: Routledge.

Bytheway, B. (1995). *Ageism*, Milton Keynes: Open University Press.

Bywaters, P. and MacLeod, E. (2000). *Social Work, Health and Equality*. London: Routledge.

Calder, A. (1969). *The People's War: Britain 1939–1945*. London: Pimlico.

Callinicos, A. (1983). *The Revolutionary Ideas of Karl Marx*. London: Bookmarks.

Callinicos, A. (1985). 'The Politics of Marxism Today', *International Socialism*, **29**.

Callinicos, A. (1987). *Making History*. Cambridge: Polity Press.

Callinicos, A. (1989). *Against Postmodernism: A Marxist Critique*. Cambridge: Polity Press.

Callinicos, A. (1990). *Trostskyism*, Buckingham: Open University Press.

Callinicos, A. (1992). *Race and Class*. London: Bookmarks.

Callinicos, A. (1996). 'Betrayal and Discontent: Labour under Blair', *International Socialism*, **72**.

Callinicos, A. (2000). *Equality*. Cambridge: Polity Press.

Callinicos, A. (2001). *Against The Third Way*. Cambridge: Polity Press.
Callinicos, A. and Harman, C. (1987). *The Changing Working Class*. London: Bookmarks.
Campaign to Defend Council Housing (2000). *Defend Council Housing*. www.defendcouncilhousing.org.uk/
Campbell, J. and Oliver, M. (1996). *Disability Politics*. London: Routledge.
Cannadine, D. (1998). *Class in Britain*. Harmondsworth: Penguin.
Carr, E.H. (1966). *The Bolshevik Revolution*, 1917–1923 Volume 3 London: Penguin.
Carver, T. (2000). 'Post-Marxism', in G. Browning, A. Halcli and F. Webster (eds), *Understanding Contemporary Society*. London: Sage.
Castells, M. (1996). *The Rise of the Network Society*. Oxford: Blackwell.
Castells, M. (1997). *The Power of Identity*. Oxford: Blackwell.
Castells, M. (1998). *End of Millennium*. Oxford: Blackwell.
Castells, M. (2000). 'Information Technology and Global Capitalism', in W. Hutton and A. Giddens (eds), *On the Edge*. London: Jonathan Cape.
Charlton, J. (2000a). 'Class Struggle and the Origins of State Welfare Reform', in M. Lavalette and G. Mooney (eds), *Class Struggle and Social Welfare*. London: Routeldge.
Charlton, J. (2000b). 'Talking Seattle', *International Socialism*, **86**.
Chennells, L., Dilnot, A and Roback, N. (2001). A Survey of the UK Tax System, Institute of Fiscal Studies, Briefing Paper 9 *http://www.ifs.org.uk/consume/taxsurvey.pdf*.
Chomsky, N. (2000). *Rogue States*. London: Pluto.
Clarke, J. (ed.) (1993). *A Crisis in Care*. London: Sage.
Clarke, J. (1996). 'After Social Work', in N. Parton (ed.), *Social Theory, Social Change and Social Work*. London: Routledge.
Clarke, J. (2000). 'A World of Difference? Globalisation and the Study of Social Polity', in G. Lewis, S. Gewirtz and J. Clarke (eds), *Rethinking Social Policy*. London: Sage.
Clarke, J. and Cochrane, A. (1998). 'The Social Construction of Social Problems', in E. Saraga (ed.), *Embodying the Social*. London: Routledge.
Clarke, J., Cochrane, A. and McLaughlin, E. (1994). *Managing Social Policy*. London: Sage.
Clarke, J., Gewirtz, S. and McLaughlin, E. (2000). 'Reinventing the Welfare State', in J. Clarke, S. Gewirtz and E. McLaughlin, (eds), *New Managerialism: New Welfare?* London: Sage.
Clarke, J. and Newman, J. (1997). *The Managerial State*. London: Sage.
Clegg, S. and Gough, R. (2000). 'The Struggle for Abortion Rights', in M. Lavalette and G. Mooney (eds), *Class Struggle and Social Welfare*. London: Routledge.
Cliff, T. (1948/1974). *State Capitalism in Russia*, London: Pluto.
Cliff, T. (1974). *State Capitalism in Russia*. London: Pluto.
Cliff, T. and Gluckstein, D. (1988). *The Labour Party: A Marxist History*, London: Bookmarks.
Coates, B. (2001) 'GATS' in E. Bircham and J. Charlton (eds) *Anti-Capitalism: a Guide to the Movement*, London: Bookmarks.
Cohen, N. (2001). 'At the Global Alter', *Observer*, 4 March.
Collini, S. (1994). 'Escape from DWEMSville', *Times Literary Supplement*, 27 May.
Cook, D. (1998). 'Racism, Immigration Polity and Welfare Policing: The Case of the Asylum and Immigration Act', in M. Lavalette, M. Penketh and C. Jones (eds), *Anti-Racism and Social Welfare*. Aldershot: Ashgate.

Corby, B. (2000). *Child Abuse: Towards a Knowledge Base* (2nd edn). Buckingham: Open University Press.

Corrigan, P. and Leonard, P. (1978). *Social Work Practice Under Capitalism*. London: MacMillan.

Cox, J. (1995). 'Wealth, Poverty and Class in Britain Today', *International Socialism*, **69**.

Creighton, C. (1985). 'The Family and Capitalism in Marxist Theory', in M. Shaw (ed.), *Marxist Sociology Revisited*. London: MacMillan.

Croix, G.E.M. de Ste, (1981). *The Class Struggle in the Ancient Greek World*. London: Duckworth.

Crompton, R. (1998). *Class and Stratification (Second Edition)*, Cambridge: Polity.

Crosland, A. (1956). *The Future of Socialism*. London: Cape.

Damer, S. (1980). 'Housing, Class and the State', in J. Melling (ed.), *Housing, State and Social Policy*. London: Croom Helm.

Damer, S. (2000). '"The Clyde Rent War!": The Clydebank Rent Strike of the 1920s', in M. Lavalette and G. Mooney (eds), *Class Struggle and Social Welfare*. London: Routledge.

Danaher, K. (ed.) (2001). *Democratising the Global Economy*, Philadelphia: Common Courage Press.

Danaher, K. and Burbach, R. (eds) (2000). *Globalise This!* Maine: Common Courage Press.

Danaher, K. and Yunus, M. (eds) (1994). *50 Years is Enough: The Case Against the World Bank and the International Monetary Fund*. Boston, MA: South End Press.

Danos, J. and Gibelin, M. (1986). *June '36: Class Struggle and the Popular Front in France*. London: Bookmarks.

Davidson, N. (2000). *The Origins of Scottish Nationhood*. London: Pluto.

Davies, L. and Shragge, E. (1990). *Bureaucracy and Community*. Toronto: Black Rose Books.

Davies, N. (1998). *Dark Heart*. London: Vintage.

Davies, N. (2000). *The School Report*. London: Vintage.

Davin, A. (1982). 'Child Labour, the Working Class Family and Domestic Ideology in Nineteenth Century Britain', *Development and Change*, **13**.

Deacon, B. (1983). *Social Policy and Socialism*. London: Pluto.

Deacon, B. (2000). 'Globalisation: a Threat to Equitable Social Provision?', in H. Dean, R. Sykes and R. Woods (eds), *Social Policy Review 12*. Newcastle Upon Tyne: Social Policy Association.

Deacon, B. with Hulse, M. and Stubbs, P. (1997). *Global Social Policy*. London: Sage.

Delphy, C. (1977). *The Main Enemy: A Materialist Analysis of Women's Oppression*. London: WRRCP.

Department of Social Security (1998). *Households Below Average Income: A Statistical Analysis, 1979–1995/96*. London: The Stationery Office.

Departments of State for Employment and Productivity (1969). *In Place of Strife: A Policy for Industrial Relations*, London: Cmnd. 3888.

Derrida, J. (1994). *Spectres of Marx*. London: Routledge.

Devine, F. (1997). *Social Class in America and Britain*. Edinburgh: Edinburgh University Press.

Dollar, D. and Kraay, A. (2000). *Growth is Good for the Poor*. Washington, DC: The World Bank.

Draper, H. (1966/96). *The Two Souls of Socialism*. London: Bookmarks.

Draper, H. (1978). *Karl Marx's Theory of Revolution, Volume 2*. New York, Monthly Review Press.

Driver, S. and Martell, L. (1998). *New Labour: Politics After Thatcherism*. Cambridge: Polity Press.

Easlea, B. (1987). *Fathering the Unthinkable: Masculinity, Scientists and the Nuclear Arms Race*, Pantheon Books.

Edgell, S. (1993). *Class*. London: Routledge.

Ellison, N. and Pierson, C. (eds) (1998). *Developments in British Social Policy*. London: MacMillan.

Ellwood, W. (2000). 'Questioning the Oligarchs', *New Internationalist*, **320**.

Engels, F. (1845/1973). *The Condition of the Working Class in England*. London: Lawrence and Wishart.

Engels, F. (1884/1978). *The Origins of the Family, Private Property and the State*. Beijing: Foreign Languages Press.

Esping-Andersen, G. (1990). *The Three Worlds of Welfare Capitalism*. Cambridge: Polity Press.

Esping-Andersen, G. (1993). *Changing Classes: Stratification and Mobility in Post-Industrial Societies*, London: Sage.

Esping-Andersen, G. (1996). *Welfare States in Transition: National Adaptations in Global Economies*. London: Sage.

Fairclough, N. (2000). *New Labour: New Language?* London: Routledge.

Faludi, S. (1992). *Backlash: The Undeclared War Against American Women*. London: Anchor Books.

Faludi, S. (2000). *Stiffed: The Betrayal of Modern Man*, London: Vintage.

Fantasia, R. (1988). *Cultures of Solidarity*. California: The University of California Press.

Federal Bureau of Investigation (1991). *Uniform Crime Reports*. (Accessed at Safetynet, Domestic Violence: The Facts. http://www.cybergrrl.com/dv/book/tqc.html)

Ferguson, I. (1994). 'Containing the Crisis: Crime and the Tories', *International Socialism*, **62**.

Ferguson, I. (2000). 'Identity Politics or Class Struggle? The Case of the Mental Health Users' Movement', in M. Lavalette and G. Mooney (eds), *Class Struggle and Social Welfare*. London: Routledge.

Ferguson, I. and Lavalette, M. (1999). 'Social Work, Postmodernism and Marxism', *European Journal of Social Work*, **2** (1).

Ferguson, I. and Lavalette, M. (2000). 'Marxism and Social Work Research' paper presented to BASW/NISW conference *Researching Social Work*, Dec 2000, Manchester.

Field, N. (1995). *Over the Rainbow: Money, Class and Homophobia*. London: Pluto.

Fimister, G. (ed.) (2001). *An End in Sight? Tackling Child Poverty in the UK*. London: Child Poverty Action Group.

Firestone, S. (1979). *The Dialectic of Sex*. London: The Women's Press.

Forgacs, D. (ed.) (1999). *The Antonio Gramsci Reader*. London: Lawrence and Wishart.

Fraser, N. (1995). 'From Recognition to Redistribution? Dilemmas of Justice in a Post-Socialist Age', *New Left Review*, **212**

Fraser, N. (2000). 'Rethinking Recognition', *New Left Review*, (ns) **3**.

Frölich, P. (1972). *Rosa Luxemburg*. London: Pluto.

Fromm, E. (1989). *Beyond the Chains of Illusion*. London: Abacus.

Fryer, P. (1984). *Staying Power*. London: Pluto.

Fukuyama, F. (1992). *The End of History and the Last Man*. Harmondsworth: Penguin.

Furniss, N. and Tilton, T. (1979). *The Case for the Welfare State*. London: St. Martin's Press.

Fysh, P. and Woolfries, J. (1998). *The Politics of Racism in France*. London: St. Martin's Press.

George, S. (1992). *The Debt Boomerang*. London: Pluto.

George, S. (1999). *The Lugano Report*. London: Pluto.

German, L. (1988). 'The Rise and Fall of the Women's Movement', *International Socialism*, **37**.

German, L. (1989). *Sex, Class and Socialism*. London: Bookmarks.

German, L. (1990). *A Question of Class*, London: Bookmarks.

Gewirtz, S. (1999). 'Education Action Zones', in H. Dean and R. Woods (eds), *Social Policy Review 11*. Luton: University of Luton/Social Policy Association.

Giddens, A. (1981). *The Class Structure of the Advanced Societies*. London: Hutchinson.

Giddens, A. (1998a). 'After the Left's Paralysis', *New Statesman*, 1 May.

Giddens, A. (1998b). *The Third Way*. Cambridge: Polity Press.

Giddens, A. (2000). *The Third Way and Its Critics*. Cambridge: Polity Press.

Ginsborg, P. (1990). *A History of Contemporary Italy*. Harmondsworth: Penguin.

Ginsburg, N. (1979). *Class, Capital and Social Policy*. London: MacMillan.

Ginsburg, N. (1992). *Divisions of Welfare*. London: Sage.

Glasgow City Council (2000). *Project 2002: Glasgow's Secondary School Public/Private Partnership*.

Glennerster, H. (1999). 'A Third Way?', in H. Dean and R. Woods (eds), *Social Policy Review 11*. Luton: University of Luton/Social Policy Association.

Glenny, M. (2000). 'Peace won't come to Serbia if we keep baying for blood' *The Sunday Times* 8 October.

Goldson, B. (ed.) (2000). *The New Youth Justice*. Lyme Regis: Russell House Publishing.

Goldthorpe, J.H. (1987). *Social Mobility and Class Structure in Modern Britain*. Oxford: Oxford University Press.

Goldthorpe, J.H., Lockwood, D., Bechofer, F. and Platt, J. (1969). *The Affluent Worker in the Class Structure*. Cambridge: Cambridge University Press.

Gonzalez, M. (2000). 'The Zapatistas: the challenges of revolution in a new millenium', *International Socialism*, 2: 89.

Goodman, A., Johnson, P. and Webb, S. (1997). *Inequality in the UK*. Oxford: Oxford University Press.

Gordon, D. (2000). 'Inequalities in Income, Wealth and Standard of living in Britain', in C. Pantazis and D. Gordon (eds), *Tackling Inequalities*. Bristol: The Policy Press.

Gordon, D. and Townsend, P. (2001). *Breadline Europe*. Bristol: The Policy Press.

Gorz, A. (1968). *The Socialist Register 1968*. London: Merlin.

Gorz, A. (1982). *Farewell to the Working Class*. London: Pluto.

Gough, I. (1979). *The Political Economy of the Welfare State*. London: MacMillan.

Gould, A. (1993). *Capitalist Welfare Systems*. London: Longman.

Gramsci, A. (1971). *Selections from the Prison Notebooks*. London: Lawrence and Wishart.

Gray, J. (1998). *False Dawn: The Delusions of Global Capitalism*. London: Granta.

Gubbay, J. (1997). 'A Marxist Critique of Weberian Class Analysis', *Sociology*, **31** (1).

Halliday, F. (1975). *A Political History of Japanese Capitalism*. London: Monthly Review Press.

Harman, C. (1983). 'Philosophy and Revolution', *International Socialism*, **21**: 58–87.

Harman, C. (1984). *Explaining the Crisis*. London: Bookmarks.

Harman, C. (1988). *The Fire Last Time*. London: Bookmarks.

Harman, C. (1991). 'State and Capital', *International Socialism*, **51**.

Harman, C. (1996). 'Globalisation: a Critique of a New Orthodoxy', *International Socialism*, **73**.

Harman, C. (1999). *A People's History of the World*. London: Bookmarks.

Harrington, M. (1963). *The Other America: Poverty in the United States*. New Jersey: Penguin.

Harris, J. (1998). 'Scientific Management, Bureau-Professionalism, New Managerialism: The Labour Process of State Social Work', *British Journal of Social Work*, **28**.

Harris, N. (1986). *The End of the Third World*. Harmondsworth: Penguin.

Hartmann, H. (1979). 'The unhappy marriage of Marxism and Feminism: Towards a more progressive union', *Capital and Class*, **11**.

Harvey, D. (1999). *The Limits to Capital*. London: Verso.

Harvey, D. (2000). *Spaces of Hope*. Edinburgh: Edinburgh University Press.

Hay, C. (1999). *The Political Economy of New Labour*. Manchester: Manchester University Press.

Health Matters, (2000). *Globalisation and Health*. http://www.healthmatters.org.uk

Heffernan, R. (2000). *New Labour and Thatcherism*. London: MacMillan.

Held, D., McGrew, A.G., Goldblatt, D. and Perraton, D. (1999). *Global Transformations*. Cambridge: Polity Press.

Herrnstein, R.J. and Murray, C. (1994). *The Bell Curve*. New York: Free Press.

Hills, J. (1995). *Inquiry into Income and Wealth (Two Volumes)*. York: Joseph Rowntree Foundation.

Hills, J. (1998). *Income and Wealth: The Latest Evidence*. York: Joseph Rowntree Foundation.

Hirst, P. and Thompson, G. (1999). *Globalisation in Question* (2nd edn). Cambridge: Polity Press.

Hobsbawm, E. (1994). *Age of Extremes*. Harmondsworth: Penguin.

Hobsbawm, E. (1998). *Introduction to the 1998 Edition of the Communist Manifesto*. London: Verso.

Hoggart, R. (1995). *The Way We Live Now*. London: Pimlico.

Holman, R. (1998). *Faith in the Poor*. Oxford: Lion.

Howarth, C., Kenway, P., Palmer, G. and Miorelli, R. (1999). *Monitoring Poverty and Social Exclusion*. York: Joseph Rowntree Foundation.

Hudson, R. (1988). 'Labour Market Changes and New Forms of Work in "Old" Industrial Regions', in D. Massey and J.Allen (eds), *Uneven Redevelopment: Cities and Regions in Transition*. London: Sage.

Hughes, G. (1998a). 'A Suitable Case for Treatment? Constructions of Disability', in E. Saraga (ed.), *Embodying the Social*. London: Routledge.

Hughes, G. (ed.) (1998b). *Imagining Welfare Futures*. London: Routledge.

Hughes, G. and Lewis, G. (eds) (1998). *Unsettling Welfare: The Reconstruction of Social Policy*. London: Routledge.

Humphries, J. (1977a). 'Class Struggle and the Persistence of the Working Class Family', *Cambridge Journal of Economics*, **1** (3).

Humphries, J. (1977b). 'The Working Class Family, Women's Liberation and Class Struggle: the Case of Nineteenth Century British History', *Review of Radical Political Economy*, **9**.

Hutton, W. (1995). *The State We're In*. London: Verso.

Hutton, W. and Giddens, A. (eds) (2000). *On the Edge*. London: Jonathan Cape.

International Socialism (2000). 'Special Edition – Talking Seattle', *International Socialism*, **86**.

IPPR (1998). *Leading the Way: A New Vision for Local Government*. London: Institute for Public Policy Research.

James, J. (ed.) (2000). *States of Confinement: Policing, Detention and Prisons*, New York: St Martin's Press.

Jessop, B. (1994). 'The Transition to Post-Fordism and the Schumpetarian Welfare State', in R. Burrows and B. Loader (eds), *Towards a Post-Fordist Welfare State*. London: Routledge.

Johnson, A. (2000). 'The Making of a Poor People's Movement: a Study of the Political Leadership of Poplarism, 1919–1925', in M. Lavalette and G. Mooney (eds), *Class Struggle and Social Welfare*. London: Routledge.

Johnson, N. (1990). *Reconstructing the Welfare State*. London: Harvester Wheatsheaf.

Jones, C. (1998). 'Setting the Context: Race, Class and Social Violence' in Lavalette, M, Penketh, L and Jones, C (eds), *Antiracism and Social Welfare*. Aldershot: Ashgate.

Jones, C. (1983). *State Social Work and the Working Class*. London: MacMillan.

Jones, C. (1999). 'Social Work: Regulation and Managerialism', in M. Exworthy and S. Halford (eds), *Professionals and the New Managerialism in the Public Sector*. Buckingham: Open University Press.

Jones, C. (2001). 'Voices from the Front Line: State Social Workers and New Labour', *British Journal of Social Work*, **31** (4).

Jones, C. and Novak, T. (1980). 'The State and Social Policy', in P. Corrigan (ed.), *Capitalism, State Formation and Marxist Theory*. London: Quartet.

Jones, C. and Novak, T. (1985). 'Welfare against the workers: Benefits as a political weapon' in H. Benyon (ed.), *Digging Deeper: Issues in the Miners Strike*. London: Verso.

Jones, C. and Novak, T. (1999). *Poverty, Welfare and the Disciplinary State*. London: Routledge.

Jones, C. and Novak, T. (2000). 'Class Struggle, Self-Help and Popular Welfare', in M. Lavalette and G. Mooney (eds), *Class Struggle and Social Welfare*. London: Routledge.

Jones, H. (ed.) (1997). *Towards A Classless Society?* London: Routledge.

Jordan, B.(1998). *The New Politics of Welfare*. London: Sage.

Joyce, P. (ed.) (1995). *Class*. Oxford: Oxford University Press.

Kemp. P.A. (1999). 'Making the Market Work? New Labour and the Housing Question', in H. Dean and R. Woods (eds), *Social Policy Review 11*. Luton: University of Luton/Social Policy Association.

Kemp, P.A. (2000). 'Housing Benefit and Welfare Retrenchment in Britain', *Journal of Social Policy*, **29** (2).

Kidron, M. (1968). *Western Capitalism Since the War*. Harmondsworth: Penguin.

Klein, N. (2000). *No Logo*. London: Flamingo.

Korsch, K. (1937/1971). *Three Essays on Marxism*. London: Pluto.

Labour Party (1976). *Report of the 75th Conference of The Labour Party*. London: The Labour Party.

Labour Party (1997). *New Labour: Because Britain Deserves Better*. London: The Labour Party.

Labour Research (2000). 'A Tale of Two Centuries', *Labour Research*, January.

Laclau, E. and Mouffe, C. (1985). *Hegemony and Socialist Strategy: Towards a Radical Democratic Politics*. London: Verso.

Laclau, E. and Mouffe, C. (1997). 'Post-Marxism Without the Apologies', *New Left Review*, **166**.

Langan, M. and Clarke, J. (ed.) (1994). 'Managing the Mixed Economy of Care', in J. Clarke, A. Cochrane and E. McLaughlin (eds), *Managing Social Policy*. London: Sage.

Lash, S. and Urry, J. (1987). *The End of Organised Capitalism*. Cambridge: Polity Press.

Lash, S. and Urry, J. (1994). *Economies of Signs and Space*. London: Sage.

Lavalette, M. (ed.) (1999). *A Thing of the Past?: Child Labour in Britain in the Nineteenth and Twentieth Centuries*. Liverpool: Liverpool University Press.

Lavalette, M. and Cunnigham, S. (2001). 'Globalisation and Child Labour: Protection, Liberation or Anti-Capitalism?', in R. Munk (ed.), *Labour and Globalisation: Results and Prospects*. Liverpool: Liverpool University Press.

Lavalette, M. and Flanagan, N. (2001). 'Defending the Sefton 2: Contested Leadership in a Trade Union Dispute', in C. Barker, A. Johnson and M. Lavalette (eds), *Leadership and Social Movements*. Manchester: Manchester University Press.

Lavalette, M. and Kennedy, J. (1996). *Solidarity on the Waterfront: The Liverpool Lock Out of 1995/96*. Liverpool: Liver Press.

Lavalette, M. and Mooney, G. (1989). 'The Struggle Against the Poll Tax in Scotland', *Critical Social Policy*, **26**.

Lavalette, M. and Mooney, G. (1999). 'New Labour: New Moralism: The Welfare Politics and Ideology of New Labour Under Blair', *International Socialism*, **85**.

Lavalette, M. and Mooney, G. (eds) (2000a). *Class Struggle and Social Welfare*. London: Routledge.

Lavalette, M. and Mooney. G. (2000b). '"No Poll Tax Here": the Tories, Social Policy and the Great Poll Tax Rebellion, 1987–1991', in M. Lavalette and G. Mooney (eds), *Class Struggle and Social Welfare*. London: Routledge.

Lavalette, M., Mooney, G., Mynott, E., Evans, K. and Richardson, B. (2001). 'The Woeful Record of the House of Blair', *International Socialism*, **90**.

Lavalette, M. and Penketh, L. (2002). 'The British Welfare State from Beveridge to Blair' in C. Aspalter (ed.) *The Welfare State: East-West Comparisons*. New York: Nova Science.

Le Grand, J. (1998). *Quasi-Markets and Social Policy*. Bristol: Policy Press.

Leacock, E. (1981). *Myths of Male Dominance*. New York: Monthly Review Press.

Leadbetter, C. (1987). 'In the Land of the Dispossessed', *Marxism Today*, April.

Lee, D. and Turner, B.S. (1996). *Conflicts About Class*. London: Longman.

Lee, P. and Raban, C. (1988). *Welfare Theory and Social Policy: Reform or Revolution*. London: Sage.

Lenin, V.I. (1912). Resolutions of the Conference (of the RSDLP) 'The Party's attitude to the Workers State Insurance Bill' in *V.I. Lenin Collected Works* Volume 17. London: Lawrence and Wishart.

Leonard, P. (1997). *Postmodern Welfare*. London: Sage.

Lewis, J. (1993). *Women and Social Policies in Europe: Work, Family and the State*. London: Edward Elgar.

Lewis, G. (2000). 'Discursive Histories: the Pursuit of Multiculturalism and Social Policy', in G. Lewis, S. Gewirtz and J. Clarke (eds), *Rethinking Social Policy*. London: Sage.

Lewis, G., Gewirtz, S. and Clarke, J. (eds) (2000). *Rethinking Social Policy*. London: Sage.

Leys, C. and Panitch, L. (1998). 'The political legacy of the Manifesto', in L. Panitch and C. Leys (eds), *Socialist Register 1998*. London: Merlin.

Linebaugh, P. (1991). *The London Hanged*. Harmondsworth: Penguin.

Lowe, R. (1993). *The Welfare State in Britain Since 1945*. London: MacMillan.

Lowe, S. (2000). 'Here We Go Again', *Guardian*, 14 December.

Lukács, G. (1970). *History and Class Consciousness*. London: Merlin.

Lukács, G. (1971). *Lenin: A Study in the Unity of his Thought*. London: Verso.

Luttwark, E. (1999). *Turbo-Capitalism*. London: Texere Publishing.

Luxemburg, R. (1900/1970). *Reform or Revolution* London: Pathfinder.

Luxemburg, R. (1906/1986). *The Mass Strike*. London: Bookmarks.

MacGregor, S. (1999). 'Welfare, Neo-Liberalism and New Paternalism: Three Ways for Social Policy in Late Capitalist Societies', *Capital and Class*, **67**.

MacKenzie, D. and Wacjman, J. (eds) (1985). *The Social Shaping of Technology*. Milton Keynes: Open University Press.

McAfee, K. (1994). 'Jamaica: The Showpiece that Didn't Stand Up', in K. Danaher and M. Yunus (eds), *50 Years is Enough: The Case Against the World Bank and the International Monetary Fund*. Boston, MA: South End Press.

McGarr, P. (2000). 'Why Green is Red: Marxism and the threat to the environment', *International Socialism*, 88.

McKibbon, R. (1998). *Classes and Cultures: England 1918–1951*. Oxford: Oxford University Press.

McShane, H. and Smith, J. (1978). *No Mean Fighter*. London: Pluto.

Madely, J. (2000). *Hungry for Trade*. London: Zed Books.

Maidment, R. and Dawson, M. (eds) (1999). *The US in the Twentieth Century: Key Documents* (2nd edn). London: Hodder Staughton/OUP.

Mandelson, P. and Liddle, R. (1996). *The Blair Revolution*. London: Faber and Faber.

Marqusee, M. (1999). *Redemption Song: Muhammed Ali and the Spirit of the Sixties*. London: Verso.

Marx, K. (1844/1975). 'Economic and Philosophical manuscripts', in K. Marx, *Early Writings*. Harmondsworth: Penguin.

Marx, K. (1845/1978). 'The German Ideology', in R.C. Tucker (ed.), *The Marx-Engels Reader* (2nd edn). New York: Norton.

Marx, K. (1845/1975). 'Theses on Feuerbach', in K. Marx, *Early Writings*. Harmondsworth: Penguin.

Marx, K. (1867/1976). *Capital*, Volume 1. Harmondsworth: Penguin.

Marx, K. (1894/1974). *Capital*, Volume 3. Harmondsworth: Penguin.

Marx, K. (1865/1996). *Wages, Prices and Profits* London: Bookmarks.

Marx, K. and Engels, F. (1848/1973). *The Communist Manifesto*. in K. Marx, *The Revolutions of 1848*. Harmondsworth: Penguin.

Massey, D., Allen, J. and Pile, S. (eds) (1999). *City Worlds*. London: Routledge.

Merrick, D. (1996). *Social Work and Child Abuse*. London: Routledge.

Meszaros, I. (1970/1986). *Marx's Theory of Alienation*. London: Merlin.

Miliband, R. (1972). *Parliamentary Socialism*. London: Merlin.

Miliband, R. (1989). *Divided Societies*. Oxford: Oxford University Press.

Milner, A. (1999). *Class*. London: Sage.

Mishra, R. (1984). *The Welfare State in Crisis*. Brighton: Wheatsheaf.

Mishra, R. (1993). 'Social Policy in a Post-Modern World', in C. Jones (ed.), *New Perspectives on the Welfare State in Europe*. London: Routledge.

Mishra, R. (1999). *Globalisation and the Welfare State*. Cheltenham: Edward Elgar.

Mitchell, J. (1971). *Women's Estate*. Harmondsworth: Penguin.

Mitchell, J. (1975). *Psychoanalysis and Feminism*. Hamondsworth: Penguin.

Molyneux, J. (1983). 'What is the Real Marxist Tradition?', *International Socialism*, **20**.

Monbiot, G. (2000). *Captive State*. London: MacMillan.

Moody, K. (1997). *Workers in a Lean World*. London: Verso.

Mooney. G. (1997). 'Quasi-Markets and the Mixed Economy of Welfare', in M. Lavalette and A. Pratt (eds), *Social Policy: A Conceptual and Theoretical Introduction* (1st edn). London: Sage.

Mooney, G. (1998). '"Remoralizing" the Poor?: Gender, Class and Philanthropy in Victorian Britain', in G. Lewis (ed.), *Forming Nation: Framing Welfare*. London: Routledge.

Mooney, G. and Johnstone, C. (2000). 'Scotland Divided: Poverty, Inequality and the Scottish Parliament', *Critical Social Policy*, **63**.

Moore, Jnr, Barrington (1973). *Lord and Peasant in the Making of the Modern World*, Hemel Hempstead: Harvester.

Mosely, W. (2000). *Workin' on the Chain Gang: Shaking off the Dead Hand of History*. Trinidad: Ballantyne Books.

Mullard, M. and Spicker, P. (1998). *Social Policy in a Changing Society*. London: Routledge.

Mullender, A. (1996). *Rethinking Domestic Violence: The Social Work and Probation Response*. London: Routledge.

Muncie, J. and Wetherall, M. (1997). 'Family Policy and Political Discourse', in J. Muncie, M. Wetherall, M. Langan, R. Dallos and A. Cochrane (eds), *Understanding the Family* (2nd edn). London: Sage.

Municipal Services Project (2000). *Progressive Urban Futures*. Johannesburg: University of Witwatersrand.

Murray, C. (1990). *The Emerging British Underclass*. London: IEA.

Murray, R. (1988). 'Life After Henry (Ford)', *Marxism Today*, October.

Mynott, E. (2000). 'Analysing the Creation of Apartheid for Asylum Seekers in the UK', *Community, Work and Family*, **3** (3).

National Centre for Social Research (2000). *British Social Attitudes: Focusing on Diversity. The 17th Report*. London: Sage.

NALGO (1989). *Social Work in Crisis: A Study of Conditions in Six Local Authorities*, London: NALGO.

Navarro, V. (1989). 'Why some countries have national health insurance, others have national health services, and the US has neither', *Social Science and Medicine*, **28** (9).

Ndiaye, A. (1994). 'Food for thought: Senegal's Struggle with Structural Adjustment', in K. Danaher and M. Yunus, (eds), *50 Years is Enough: The Case Against the World Bank and the International Monetary Fund*. Boston, MA: South End Press.

Neale, J. (2000). *The American War: Vietnam 1960–1975*. London: Bookmarks.

Netten, A. and Beecham, J. (1993). *Costing Community Care: Theory and Practice*. Aldershot: Ashgate.

New Internationalist (2000). Special Edition on the Global Economy. *New Internationalist*, **320**.

Nicolaus, M. (1972). 'The Unknown Marx', in R. Blackburn (ed.), *Ideology in Social Science*. Glasgow: Fontana/Collins.

Novak, T. (1988). *Poverty and the State*. Milton Keynes: Open University Press.

O'Brien, M. and Penna, S. (1998). *Theorising Welfare*. London: Sage.

O'Brien, R. (1992). *Global Financial Integration: The End of Geography*. London: Royal Institute for International Affairs.

O'Brien, M. and Hanlon, D. (1999). 'Debt crisis: who pays?', *Socialist Review*, September.

Office for National Statistics (2000). *Social Inequalities 2000*. London: The Stationery Office.

Ohmae, K. (1990). *The Borderless World: Power and Strategy in the Interlinked Economy*. London: Collins.

Oliver, M. (1996). *Understanding Disability: From Theory to Practice*. London: Macmillan.

Oliver, M. and Barnes, C. (1998). *Disabled People and Social Policy*. London: Longman.

Ollman, B. (1976). *Alienation*. Cambridge: Cambridge University Press.

Oppenheim, C. and Harker, L. (1996). *Poverty: The Facts* (3rd edn). London: Child Poverty Action Group.

Park, A., Jowell, R. and Curtice, J. (eds) (1996). *British Social Attitudes: 13th Report*. Aldershot: Dartmouth Publishing.

Pakulski, J. and Waters, M. (1996). *The Death of Class*. London: Sage.

Pantazis, C. and Gordon, D. (eds) (2000). *Tackling Inequalities*. Bristol: The Policy Press.

Pascall, G. (1986). *Social Policy: A Feminist Analysis*. London: Tavistock.

Pearson, G. (1988). 'Men and Women Without Work' in C. Rojek, G. Peacock and S. Collins (eds) *The Haunt of Misery: Critical Essays in Social Work and Helping*. London: Routledge.

Penketh, L. (2001). 'Racism and Social Policy' in M. Lavalette & A. Pratt (eds) *Social Policy: A conceptual and theoretical introduction* (2nd Edition). London: Sage.

Penketh, L. (2001). *Tackling Institutional Racism*. Bristol: Policy Press.

Philo, G. (ed.) (1996). *Media and Mental Distress*. London: Longman.

Philo, G. and Miller, D. (eds) (2000). *Market Killing*. London: Longman.

Pierson, C. (1991). *Beyond the Welfare State*. Cambridge: Polity Press.

Pierson, P. (1996). 'The New Politics of the Welfare State', *World Politics*, **48**: 147–79.

Pile, S., Brook, C. and Mooney. G. (eds) (1999). *Unruly Cities?* London: Routledge.

Pilger, J. (2001). 'Spoils of a Massacre' *Guardian Weekend*, 14 July.

Pollert, A. (1988). 'The Flexible Firm: Fixation or Fact?', *Work, Employment and Society*, **2** (3): 281–316.

Powell, M. (ed.) (1999). *New Labour, New Welfare State?* Bristol: The Policy Press.

Pugh, R. and Gould, N. (2000). 'Globalisation, Social Work and Social Welfare', *European Journal of Social Work*, **3** (2).

Rahman, M., Palmer, G., Kenway, P. and Howarth, K. (2000). *Monitoring Poverty and Social Exclusion 2000*. York: Joseph Rowntree Foundation.

Reed, E. (1975). *Women's Evolution*. New York: Pathfinder.

Rees, J. (1998a). *The Algebra of Revolution*. London: Routledge.

Rees, J. (1998b). 'The Return of Marx?', *International Socialism*, **79**.

Rees, J. (1998c). 'Revolutionary Marxism and Academic Marxism', in J. Rees (ed.), *Essays on Historical Materialism*. London: Bookmarks.

Rees, J. (2001). 'Anticapitalism, reformism and socialism' *International Socialism*, **90**.

Reisman, D. (1959/1969). *The Lonely Crowd: A Study of the Changing American Character*. Yale: Yale University Press.

Rhodes, M. (1996). 'Globalisation and West EuropeanWelfare States: A Critical Review of Recent Debates', *Journal of European Social Policy*, **6** (4).

Rogers, A. and Pilgrim, D. (1996). *Mental Health Policy in Britain: A Critical Introduction*. London: MacMillan.

Rojek, C., Peacock, G. and Collins, S. (1988). *Social Work and Received Ideas*. London: Routledge.

Rorty, R. (1999). *Philosophy and Social Hope*. Harmondsworth: Penguin.

Rosdolsky, R. (1977). *The Making of Marx's 'Capital'*. London: Pluto.

Rose, N. (1999). 'Inventiveness in Politics', *Economy and Society*, **28** (3).

Rose, S., Lewontin, R. and Kamin, L. (1984). *Not in Our Genes*. Harmondsworth: Penguin.

Rosenberg, C. (1987). *1919: Britain on the Brink of Revolution*. London: Bookmarks.

Rowbotham, S. (1999). *Threads Through Time*. Harmondsworth: Penguin.

Ruigrok, W. and van Tulder, R. (1995). *The Logic of International Restructuring*. London: Routledge.

Savage, M. (2000). *Class Analysis and Social Transformation*. Buckingham: Open University Press.

Saville, J. (1983). 'The Origins of the Welfare State', in M. Loney, D. Boswell and J. Clarke (eds), *Social Policy and Social Welfare*. Buckingham: Open University Press.

Scrambler, G. and Higgs, P. (1999). 'Stratification, Class and Health: Class Relations and Health Inequalities in High Modernity', *Sociology*, **33** (2).

Seal, B. (1970). *Seize the Time: The Story of the Black Panther Party*. London: Arrow Books.

Seccombe, W. (1986). 'Patriarchy Stablized: the Construction of the Male Breadwinner Norm in the Nineteenth Century', *Social History*, **11**.

Secretary of State for Health (1998). *Our Healthier Nation: A Contract for Health*. Cm. 3852. London: HMSO.

Shaw, M., Dorling, D., Gordon, D. and Smith, G.D. (1999). *The Widening Gap*. Bristol: The Policy Press.

Sheridan, T. and McCombes, A. (2000). *Imagine: A Socialist Vision for the 21st Century*. Edinburgh: Rebel Inc.

Simpkin, M. (1979). *Trapped Within Welfare*. London: Macmillan Press.

Sivananden, A. (1990). 'All that is solid melts into air: The hokum of New Times', in A. Sivananden (ed.), *Communities of Resistance*. London: Verso.

Smelser, M.J. (1974). 'Sociological history – The Industrial Revolution and the British Working Class Family' in M.W. Flinn and T.C. Smout (eds), *Essays in Social History*. Oxford: Clarendon.

Smith, S. (1994). 'Mistaken Identity – or can Identity Politics Liberate the Oppressed?', *International Socialism*, **62**: 3–50.

Smith, S. (1999). 'The Trickle Up Effect', *Socialist Review*, November, 15.

Solomon, S.G. and Hutchinson, J.F. (eds) (1990). *Health and Society in Revolutionary Russia*. Bloomington: Indiana University Press.

Soros, G. (1995). *Soros On Soros*. New York: John Wiley.

Sparks, C.(1998). 'The Eye of the Storm', *International Socialism*, **78**.

St.Clair, J. (1999). 'Seattle Diary: It's a Gas, Gas, Gas', *New Left Review*, **238**.

Stack, P. (1995). 'Equal Access', *Socialist Review*, **183**.

Standing, G. (1991). 'State Policy and Child Labour: Accumulation versus Legitimation', *Journal of European Social Policy*, Vol, 1.

Steele, J. (2000). 'An outrage too far – Milosevic on trial', *The Observer*, 8 October.

Stephens, J. (1979). *The Transition from Capitalism to Socialism*. London: MacMillan.

Stites, R. (1989). *Revolutionary Dreams*. New York: Oxford University Press.

Stites, R. (1990). *The Women's Liberation Movement in Revolutionary Russia*. New Jersey: Princeton University Press.

Sykes, R., Palier, B. and Prior, P. (2001). *Globalisation and European Welfare States*. Basingtoke: Palgrave.

Tarrow, S. (1994). *Power in Movement*. Cambridge: Cambridge University Press.

Taylor-Gooby, P. (1997). 'In Defence of Second-Best Theory: State, Class and Capital in Social Policy', *Journal of Social Policy*, **26** (2).

Thompson, E.P. (1968). *The Making of the English Working Class*. Harmondsworth: Penguin.

Thompson, E.P. (1978). *The Poverty of Theory and Other Essays*. London: Merlin.

Thompson, E.P. (1991). *Customs in Common* Harmondsworth: Penguin.

Thompson, N. (1993). *Anti-Discriminatory Practice*. London: MacMillan.

Thompson, N. (1998). *Promoting Equality*. London: MacMillan.

Thompson, N. (2000). *Understanding Social Work: Preparing for Practice*. London: MacMillan.

Thornhill, R. and Palmer, C. (2000). *A Natural History of Rape: Biological Bases of Sexual Coercion*. Cambridge, MA: MIT Press.

Tilly, L.A. & Scott, J.W. (1987). *Women, Work and Family* London: Methuen.

Timmins, N. (1996). *The Five Giants: A Biography of the Welfare State*. London: Fontana.

Toynbee, P. and Walker, D. (2001). *Did Things Get Better?* Harmondsworth: Penguin.

Treasury Taskforce on Private Finance (1997). *Partnerships for Prosperity: The Private Finance Initiative*. London: H.M. Treasury.

Trotsky, L. (1934/1972). *The Revolution Betrayed*. New York: Pathfinder.

Trotsky, L. (1972). *Permanent Revolution and Results and Prospects*. New York: Pathfinder.

Trotsky, L. (1975). *The History of the Russian Revolution*. London: Pluto.

Tucker, R.C. (1978). *The Marx–Engels Reader* (2nd edn). New York: Norton.

UNICEF (2000). *The State of the World's Children 2000*. http://www.unicef.org/

Union of Concerned Scientists (2000). 'World scientists call for action' http://www.ucsusa.org/about/callforaction.html.

United Nations (1998). *Human Development Report 1998*. Oxford: Oxford University Press.

United Nations (1999). *Human Development Report 1999*. http://www.undp.org.

UNRISD (1995). *States of Disarray: The Social Effects of Globalization* London: United Nations Research Institute for Social Development.

United States Department of Justice (1983). *Report to the Nation on Crime and Justice: The Data*. Washington, DC: Office of Justice Program, US Department of Justice (Accessed at Safetynet, Domestic Violence: The Facts. http://www.cybergrrl.com/dv/book/tqc.html).

United States Department of Justice (2000). *Bureau of Justice Statistics*. http://www.oip.usdoj.gov/bjs/cvict-c.ht.

University of Paisley (2000). *Draft HE2000 contract* (the contract was subsequently amended following pressure from the trade union).

Viner, K. (2000). 'Hand-to-Brand Combat', *Guardian*, 23 September.

Vleminckx, K. and Smeeding, T.M. (2001). *Child Well-Being, Child Poverty and Child Policy in Modern Nations*. Bristol: The Policy Press.

Vulliamy, E. (2001a). 'The President who Bought Power and Sold the World', *Observer*, 1 April.

Vulliamy, E. (2001b). 'Bush's Hard Men Sweep Away the Clinton Legacy', *Observer*, 21 January.

Walker, A. and Walker, C. (eds) (1997). *Britain Divided*. London: Child Poverty Action Group.

Walter, N. (1998). *The New Feminism*, London: Little Brown.

Walton, P. and Gamble, A. (1972). *From Alienation to Surplus Value*. London: Sheed and Ward.

Wedderburn, D. (1965). 'Facts and Theories of the Welfare State', in R. Miliband and J. Saville (eds), *The Socialist Register*. London: Merlin Press.

Weeks, J. (1977). *Coming Out: Homosexual Politics in Britain from the Nineteenth Century to the Present*. London: Quartet.

Westergaard, J. (1995). *Who Get's What?* Cambridge: Polity Press.

Wheen, F. (1999). *Karl Marx*. London: Fourth Estate.

Whitfield, D. (1999). 'Private Finance Initiative: The Commodification and Marketisation of Education', *Education and Social Justice*, **1** (2).

Widgery, D. (1988). *The National Health: A Radical Perspective*. London: Hogarth Press.

Wilding, P. (1997). 'Globalisation, Regionalism and Social Policy', *Social Policy and Administration*, **31** (3).

Williams, F. (1996). 'Postmodernism, Feminism and Difference', in N. Parton (ed.), *Social Theory, Social Change and Social Work*. London: Routledge.

Williams, F. (2000). 'Principles of Recognition and Respect in Welfare', in G. Lewis., S. Gewirtz and J. Clarke (eds), *Rethinking Social Policy*. London: Sage.

Wilson, R. (1999). 'Definitions Fuel Debate', *The Guardian*, January 15.

Wilson, A. (2001). 'Social Policy and Homosexuality', in M. Lavalette and A. Pratt (eds), *Social Policy: A Conceptual and Theoretical Introduction* (2nd edn). London: Sage.

Wiseman, J. (1998). *Global Nation? Australia and the Politics of Globalisation*. Cambridge: Cambridge University Press.

Woodroffe, J. and Ellis-Jones, M. (2000). *States of unrest: resistance to IMF policies in poor countries*, http://www/udm/org.uk/camriefs/Debt/unrest.pdf.

Woods, E.M. (1986). *The Retreat From Class: A New 'True' Socialism*. London: Verso.

Woodward, K. (ed.) (1997). *Identity and Difference*. London: Sage.

Woodward, K. (2001). 'Feminist Critiques of Social Policy', in M. Lavalette and A. Pratt (eds) *Social Policy: A Conceptual and Theoretical Introduction* (2nd edn). London: Sage.

Woolfries, J. (1999). 'Class Struggles in France', *International Socialism*, **84**.

Woolfries, J. (2000). 'In Defence of Marxism', *International Socialism*, **86**.

World Bank (1997). *Development Report 1997: The State in a Changing World*. Oxford: Oxford University Press.

Wright, E.O. (1979). *Class, Crisis and the State*. London: Verso.

Yeo, S. (1980). 'State and Anti-State: Reflections on Social Forms and Struggles from 1850', in P. Corrigan (ed.), *Capitalism, State Formation and Marxist Theory*. London: Quartet.

Young. J. (1999). *The Exclusive Society*. London: Sage.

Zweig, F. (1961). *The Worker in an Affluent Society*. London: Heinemann.

Subject Index

Name Index